WOMEN EMPOWERMENT AND TWELFTH FIVE-YEAR PLAN

Approach Towards Twelfth Plan

WOMEN EMPOWERMENT AND TWELFTH FIVE-YEAR PLAN

Approach Towards Twelfth Plan

By

Arpita Sharma

Doctoral Research Scholar

UGC-JRF Fellowship

Dept. of Agricultural Communication

College of Agriculture

G.B. Pant University of Agriculture & Technology

Pantnagar – 263 145 (Uttarakhand)

(India)

DISCOVERY PUBLISHING HOUSE PVT. LTD.

NEW DELHI-110 002

Published by:
Tilak Wasan

DISCOVERY PUBLISHING HOUSE PVT. LTD.
4383/4B, Ansari Road, Darya Ganj
New Delhi-110 002 (India)
Phone : +91-11-23279245, 43596064-65
Fax : +91-11-23253475
E-mail : discoverypublishinghouse@gmail.com
sales@discoverypublishinggroup.com
parul.wasan@gmail.com
web : www.discoverypublishinggroup.com

***First Edition:* 2013**

ISBN: 978-93-5056-351-9

Women Empowerment and Twelfth Five-Year Plan
Approach Towards Twelfth Plan

Printed at:
Dynamic Printers
Delhi

DEDICATED
TO
OM SRI SAI RAM

Preface

Women empowerment is an age old concept. In the past centuries women are empowered in society. In the pace of time, in the changing scenario, in the changing economy and increasing population, government formulated certain plans, policies and schemes to make the women healthier, wealthier. There are special acts articulated for them and seminars, conferences organized to analyze, task forces organized to trace the activities, utilizations and improvements held. The women empowerment is a concept to improvise the socio-economic status of women especially in less developed centuries and in every part of globe in whole. Empowerment is multi-faceted, multi-dimensional and multi-layered concept. Women empowerment is the process in which we gain greater share of control over resources-material, human and intellectual like knowledge, information, ideas and financial recourses like money and access to money and control over decision making in the home, community, society and nation and to gain power. Empowerment of women is one of the central issues in the process of development of countries all over the world. India has a glorious tradition of recognizing the importance of empowering women over several centuries now.

Empowerment in the literature refers to the act of bestowing power and authority on some one. Thus, women empowerment refers to the conferring of leverage to women who are otherwise deprived. This includes granting to women effectual decision-making power/authority and the power to influence others decisions along with economic, social and civil freedom. Empowerment, by its very definition, implies an increase in the ability to exercise power. In India, as in most developing countries, women are believed to be and treated as inferior to men. Moreover, as the lives of women and men are embedded in a matrix of unequal gender relations, a decrease in the gender inequality is necessary for an outcome of 'empowerment' for women. In other words, changes such as increased income, skills and self-confidence, may be better understood as enablers that promote women's empowerment. However, the women, in order to be significantly empowered to achieve their perceived goal, firstly need authority at home, which in most cases they do not have. The process should, therefore, be carried out concurrently at home and outside. Within the family they must have equal say as men and so should be the case at work. The most extensive element of women empowerment is providing them with social rank, status and justice. Major attributes that contribute to women empowerment are education, social equity and status, improved health, economic or financial stability and political participation. In India, a whopping 56 per cent of the women are illiterate as against a considerably 24 per cent in case of men, evincing the striking inequality. This has to be significantly enhanced in a five year time-frame. Educating the girl child is now an integral part of the Right to Education Act in force which should, therefore, significantly enhance the women literacy level at par with men in a five year time-frame. This apart adult literacy programs should be initiated in villages to contribute to the education in female literacy.

Present book demonstrates the current status of Indian women and powerful strategies which will help women to overcome discrimination achieve full equality, well-being and participation in the decision that determine their lives and the future of their communities. It will be a highly valuable references tool for policy makers, planners, developmental leader, academicians and women empowerment agencies. I hope that this book will further stimulate and inspire our inner being and contribute to promote women empowerment policies in India.

—Author

Acknowledgement

First of all, I bow my head with immense veneration to him "THE CREATOR" who is omnipresent, omnipotent and omniscient and who causes behind every effect and without whose blessings and grace it would have been impossible for me to go ahead with my endeavor for this piece of work.

I would like to express my regards to my parents and family members for their encouragement for writing and preparation of the book completed. They also encouraged me for writing research topics.

I would be grateful to readers and users of the book if they could provide their valuable suggestions leading to better strategies for women.

I would like to place on record my thanks to Discovery Publishing House Pvt. Ltd. for their all round support in bringing out this volume suggestions to improve the outlook of this book shall be welcome.

Contents

Approaches Towards Twelfth Five-Year Plan *Need for Focused Attention*

Mahatma Gandhiji had a vision that India after its independence should achieve self-sufficiency of villages in which every one would have adequate food, shelter, clothing, proper hygienic and sanitation facilities and every person willing to work is provided gainful employment. Let not history of India record that Mahatma Gandhiji brought political independence for India but the Government could not bring economic emancipation for rural poor. In this context, this paper highlights following alarming state of poverty, hunger, child nutrition and food security in the country and suggests that Twelfth Plan [2012-17] should give focused attention to significantly ameliorate the deteriorating situation.

Poverty: According to NSS round [2004-05], 41.8 per cent rural population had monthly per capita expenditure of Rs. 447 as against 25.7 per cent urban population having monthly per capita expenditure of Rs. 578.8. According to Multi-dimensional Poverty Index [MPI] worked out by UNDP & Oxford University, July 2010, about 645 million people [55%] in India are poor. As against 410 million MPI poor in 26 of the poorest African countries, eight Indian States [Bihar,

Chhattisgarh, Jharkhand, Madhya Pradesh, Orissa, Rajasthan, Uttar Pradesh and West Bengal] have 421 million MPI poor. The MPI reveals a vivid spectrum of challenges facing the poorest households. MPI considers 10 sharp indicators, namely Education [child enrolment and years of schooling]; Health [child mortality and nutrition] and Standard of living [electricity, drinking water, sanitation, cooking fuel, flooring and assets]. A global report on poverty eradication of the U.N. Secretary-General shows that economic growth is evident for the progress in China in reducing extreme poverty and raising living standards, whereas India is expected to be home to more than 300 million in poverty out of 900 million predicted to be in extreme poverty in 2015.

Hunger: In India, the right to food campaign launched in 2001 focused its demand to address the structural roots of hunger since India's commitments to tackle the problem of hunger and malnutrition are among the worst. India currently has world's largest food insecure population with more than 260 million people facing hunger and deprivation. According to the Global Hunger Index [2008], India ranks 66 among 88 countries surveyed by the Washington-based International Food Policy Research Institute. India comes below Sudan, Nigeria and Cameroon. Under the United Nation's Millennium Development Goal No.1, for Sustainable Human Security and Peace India is committed to reduce hunger and poverty by half by 2015

Child Nutrition: Despite Integrated Child Development Scheme has been under implementation since early 1970s, according to the National Family Health Survey, 2006, in India [i] the child under-nutrition rate is 46 per cent, which is almost double that of sub-Saharan Africa. India has 40 per cent of the world's underweight children and ranks 126 out of 177 countries in the UNDP Human Development Index and [ii] 20 per cent of children under five-years-old are wasted [too thin for their age] due to acute under-nutrition and 48 per cent were stunted [too short for their age] due to chronic under-nutrition and 70 per cent of children between six months and 59 months were anaemic. The percentage of children below five years of age who are underweight is 42.5 per cent as compared with 4 per cent in Brazil and 6 per cent in China. More than a third of all deaths in children aged five years or younger can be attributable to under-nutrition. Infancy deaths were 53 per 1000 live births in 2008.The Global Hunger Index [2010] identified child under-nutrition as a major contributory factor behind *'persistent hunger'*. According to Washington-based International Food Policy Research Institute India is among 29 countries that face *'alarming'* situation of hunger. Malnutrition among children under two years of age is one of the serious challenges to reduce hunger, which if not timely attended can cause lifelong harm to child's health, productivity and earning potential. Our Prime Minister Dr. Manmohan Singh had once referred to under-nutrition as a *'matter of national shame'*.

Experiences of successes in China, Brazil, Thailand, Viet Nam and other countries suggest:

1. according top priority to child nutrition with adequate investments in nutrition interventions and related critical areas impacting multiple deprivations;
2. targeting nutrition interventions to prevent and moderate under-nutrition and treat severe under-nutrition as a part of continuum of care for children, particularly among the most vulnerable children, the youngest, the poorest and the socially-excluded;
3. strengthening community-based primary health care to facilitate wider and deeper coverage through community-based frontline workers;
4. strong supervision, monitoring and evaluation of the effectiveness of policy, programmes and budgetary allocations to yield expected outcomes and provide timely documented feedback to re-look policy, programmes and budgetary action;
5. reducing malnutrition calls for serious concern for poor, strong political will to commit, good governance and accountability;

6. Cash Transfer Scheme to be effective need to be supported by adequate staff and infrastructure for public sector health facilities.

With serious concern and commitment China reduced child under-nutrition from 25 per cent to 8 per cent between 1990 and 2002, Brazil from 18 per cent in 1975 to 7 per cent in 1989, Thailand from 50 per cent in 1982 to 25 per cent in 1986 and Viet Nam from 45 per cent to 27 per cent between 1990 and 2006. India has the financial & human resources as well as administration and managerial capabilities to address, once and for all, the challenge of child under-nutrition. Let the prevention and treatment of child under-nutrition in the first two years of life be a national development priority and let National Nutrition Week be celebrated in September every year to create mass awareness about the programmes and exercise right to hold implementers accountable.

Food Security: Per capita availability of food grains and other essential food products in India is below the world average and significantly lower than in developed countries. Food is unaffordable for a large number of the poor in India. Under the proposed legislation for food security to India's teeming millions, the Expert Committee has estimated procurement & distribution of food not less than 63.98 million tons, rising to 73.98 million tons by 2016-17 against the likely procurement of 57.61 million tons in 2013-14.As about 800 million persons are sought to be covered under Food Security Act, it is necessary to substantially increase food productivity & output to facilitate the estimated level of procurement, create additional facilities for transport, processing, storage and evolve transparent distribution mechanism. A large amount of the subsidized food grains targeted at BPL households, some APL households and other vulnerable groups find its way to the open market. Scientific studies revealed that in 2001-02, 18.2 per cent of PDS rice and 67 per cent PDS wheat were diverted. In other words, over 40 per cent of all grain targeted at the poor did not reach the poor. Using the NSS expenditure survey of 2004-05, overall diversion was of 55 per cent of the grain meant for the poor. The same problem is manifested in case of kerosene, diesel and fertilizers. Besides, the current system is beset with significant level of adulteration, pilferage and corruption.

Focused Attention: Chronic problems of rural poverty, hunger, child nutrition and food security, among others, need focused attention to significantly develop productivity, production and profitability of farming enterprise by creating enabling environment through enhancing annual public sector investment, arresting imbalance in the flow of farm credit, legal framework for defining tenant farmers' relationship with land in particular

Investment: The Gross Capital Formation [GCF] in agriculture and allied sectors as a proportion to the GDP in the sector stagnated around 14 per cent during 2004-05 to 2006-07. Though it increased to 16.03 per cent in 2007-08 and 19.67 per cent in 2008-09 [provisional] and estimated 20.30 per cent in 2009-10, the GCF in agriculture and allied sectors relative to overall GDP has remained stagnant at around 2.5 per cent to 3.0 per cent. As a result the share of GCF in agriculture and allied sector in total GCF has remained in the range of 6.6 per cent to 8.2 per cent during 2004-05 to 2009-10. To accelerate the process of farm development and achieve inclusive rural growth, policy should focus on critical areas, namely:

1. accelerated investment in rural infrastructure to improve transport, communication, storage, processing and marketing facilities;
2. establishing State of Art Agri-meteorology;
3. expanding irrigation and reclamation of wastelands;
4. strengthening agricultural education, research and extension services and capacity building of farmers to bridge the yield gap between the potential yields and actual yields at field level in rain-fed and irrigated farming systems;

5. development and use of genetically engineered seeds, micro-irrigation systems, greenhouse technology, integrated nutrient and pest management techniques, computer-based modeling to track disease and pest incidence;
6. farm mechanization;
7. remote sensing technology.

Investment in agriculture would facilitate farmers' access to frontier technology, food processing, farm-to-market linkages, agricultural extension, weather and crop forecasting, large-scale development of bio-diesel, mechanization and commercialization of agriculture. Public, private and foreign investment should remedy the situation of investment shortage in agriculture and help transform a 'negative subsidy regime' into a 'capital-intensive positive Agricultural Marketing Service regime' and stimulate Indian producers to access global markets. Government, Agricultural Universities and ICAR Institutes along with industrial, business and commercial houses in close coordination should accelerate their efforts to accomplish this task

Farm Credit: The credit flow to agriculture since 1970 till 2010 has been of the order of Rs. 28,53,261 crore, of which 81.50 per cent was disbursed between 2001-02 to 2009-10. However, its impact on improving crop productivity and output has been low. Despite banking system has been achieving stipulated credit targets announced in the budgets since 2001-02 in absolute terms every year there have been significant disparities in credit flow between States, between districts and between villages. In fact, in absence of appropriate legal frame work tenant farmers, share croppers, oral lessees, landless labourers, households residing in hilly, tribal, desert, drought prone areas in particular do not have easy and reliable access to institutional credit.

Tenant Farmers: India has a large number of tenant farmers whose legal relationship with the landowners and the piece of land they cultivate has yet not been acknowledged

Pattern of Land Leased for Farming by Rural Households by Percentage

State	Landless Labourers	Below 0.5 hectare	0.5 &1.0 Hectare	State	Landless Labourers	Below 0.5 Hectare	0.5 to 1.0 Hectare
Andhra	53.1	30.4	08.5	Madhya	28.5	39.7	10.9
Arunachal	71.3	20.1	04.1	Maharashtra	60.1	19.8	07.0
Assam	34.7	43.6	11.3	Orissa	17.3	71.8	07.9
Bihar	58.0	87.0	06.0	Punjab	23.8	31.9	13.5
Chhatisgarh	26.9	43.5	18.6	Tamil Nadu	72.7	21.3	02.3
Gujarat	63.7	18.8	05.5	Uttar Pradesh	78.0	69.5	13.2
Haryana	24.0	45.4	08.9	West Bengal	14.1	75.1	08.4
Karnataka	55.2	28.3	05.3				
Kerala	50.0	46.2	03.4	All India	35.8	47.5	08.2

through statutory legal framework to facilitate them to access credit from banks and insurance cover from insurance companies. The National Sample Survey [2003] estimated that the area under informal tenancy in India varies between 15 per cent and 35 per cent of the total farm area and 36 per cent of the total households leasing land are landless labourers and 47.5 per cent having land below 0.5 hectare.

Conclusion

Rural households should identify their financial and non-financial needs for income generating activities in rural farm and non-farm sector and infrastructure and demand them from elected representatives. State and Union Government need to allocate adequate financial resources in their annual budgets to tackle issues of poverty, hunger, child nutrition, food security and rural infrastructure. Implementing agencies including banks should have serious concern, commitment and be accountable to achieve expected goals district, State and region-wise. Information about the performance of each programme should be made available to the public every month through local print and electronic media as also through seminars, workshops and conferences at district level.

Women Empowerment for Sustainable Development

Empowerment is a multi-faceted, multi-dimensional and multi-layered concept. Women's empowerment is a process in which women gain greater share of control over resources - material, human and intellectual like knowledge, information, ideas and financial resources like money, access to money and control over decision-making in the home, community, society, nation and to gain 'power'. According to the Country Report of Government of India, "Empowerment means moving from a position of enforced powerlessness to one of power". Empowerment is a process aimed at changing the nature and reaction of systemic forces which marginalize women and other disadvantaged sections in a given context. The need for women empowerment was felt in India long back. Mahatma Gandhi had announced at the Second Round Table Conference that his aim was to establish a political society in India in which there would be on distinction between people of high and low classes and in which women would enjoy the same rights as men and the teeming millions of India would be ensured dignity and justice- social, economic and political.

The country's concern in safeguarding the rights and privilege of women found its best expressions in the constitutions of India, covering fundamental rights and the directive principles of the state policy. Articles 14, 15, 15[3], 16, 39, 42, 51 [A] [e] contain various types of provisions for equal rights and opportunities for women and eliminate discrimination against women in different spheres of life. The Constitution [73 and 74 amendments] act 1992 provides that not less than one third [including the number of seats reserved for belonging to schedule caste and schedule tribe]. Of the total number of seats reserved for women. To make this de-jure equality into a de-facto on, many policies and programmes were put into action from time to time, besides enacting/ enforcing special legislations, in favor of women. Apart from the constructional provisions, a large number of laws have been enacted to protect the Human Rights for women. The important policies which have vital implications for the women are National Policy for Empowerment of Women 2001 and other relating to population, health, sanitation, water, housing credit, science and technology and media etc. Since women empowerment is global issue, UNO has also expressed concern in the matter. The charter of the United Nations declare equal dignity and worth of human person- all types of human rights, civil, political, economic, social and cultural. In 1993, the Vienna Declaration and programme of action proclaimed the rights of women and girl child as "Inalienable, integral and indivisible part-priority objective of the International community". The National commission for Women made a number of recommendations for changes and removal of lacunae in 34 laws and 8 bills. It also made recommendations an Older Persons Maintenance, Care and Protection Bill, 2005. The Compulsory Registration of Marriage Bill, 2005, Protection of Women from Domestic Violence Rules 2005, laws relating to Rape/Sexual Harassment assault etc.

Legislative Support for Women

The Government has given greater focus to issues relating to women through creation of an independent Ministry of Women and Child Development, initiation of legislation that has taken the country closer to complete legal equality for women, gender budgeting and initiation of programmes for greater inclusion of women in all walks of life.

1. The Government initiated the protection of women from *Domestic Violence Act 2005*, which has given more effective protection to women who are victims of violence of any kind occurring within a family and provided them a civil remedy to deal with such violence. It empowers women to file a case against a person with whom she is having a 'domestic relationship' in a 'shared household' and who has subjected her to 'domestic violence'.
2. *Distance Education Programme for Women's Empowerment 2000.* Government had started a certificate course in the Distance Education mode on Women's Group Mobilisation and Empowerment.
3. *Antyodaya Anna Yojana (AAY) 2000* was launched for one crore poorest of the poor families.
4. *National Rural Health Mission (NRHM), 2005* was launched with a strong commitment to reduce maternal and infant mortality, provide universal access to public health services, prevent and control communicable and non communicable diseases, ensure population stabilization, maintain gender balance and revitalize local health traditions.
5. *Janani Suraksha Yojana* (JSY), 2005 is a safe motherhood intervention being implemented with the objective of reducing maternal and neo-natal mortality by promoting institutional delivery among the poor pregnant women.
6. *Indira Sahara,* 2000 was launched to provide Social Security cover extended to the age group 18-50.
7. *Mukhya Mantri Antodaya Pusthaar Yojana,* 2009 was launched to make the State malnutrition free, for Below Poverty Line (BPL) families.
8. The Government initiated the *Hindu Succession Act, 1995* to make Hindu women's inheritance rights in coparcenary property equal to that of men.
9. Amendments initiated by the Government have been enacted prohibiting arrest of women after sunset and before sunrise, medical examination of persons accused

of committing or attempting to commit rape and mandatory judicial inquiry in case of rape while in police custody.

10. *Rashtriya Mahila Kosh* (RMK) was set up in March 1993, to extend credit facilities to poor and needy women in the informal sectors, has disbursed loans of Rs.11.69 crore during 1999-2000 (up to 31.1.2000) for the benefit of 0.47 lakh women.
11. The Government has introduced a bill in Parliament to amend the *Factory Act, 1948* in order to provide flexibility in the employment of women at night while requiring the employer to ensure measures for safety and protection and thereby generate employment opportunities for women.
12. *Apni Beti Apna Dhan Yojana*: Haryana Government's Scheme was launched on 2 October 1994 under an investment Rs. 2500 is made by the Government in Indira Vikas Patra for newly born female child in SC/ST families which becomes Rs. 25000 after 18 years and given to the concerned girl.
13. *Kunwar Bainu Mamerun Scheme:* Gujrat Govt.'s Scheme was launched in 1995 in which an assistance of Rs. 7500 at the time of their daughter's marriage.
14. *Kamdhenu Yojana:* Maharastra Government's scheme provides the financial opportunities of self-employment to disabled, divorced women.
15. *Girls Child Protection Scheme:* A.P. Government Scheme aims protecting the interest of girl child in the society.

Financial Focus

1. The Government has introduced gender budgeting for improving the sensitivity of programmes and schemes to women's welfare. The budgetary outlay for 100 per cent women specific programmes has been rising every year and this year it is Rs. 11,460 crore.
2. Ensuring that at least 33 per cent of the beneficiaries of all Government schemes are women and girl children has been laid down as a key target in the 12the plan.

Women's Reservation

1. A bill for introducing one third reservations for women in legislatures was drafted. In an effort to build a consensus, the Government held meeting with all opposition parties and with all UPA constituent parties. Discussions were also held with women's groups and other stakeholders. The Government has now tabled the new bill in Parliament.
2. The new *Cantonment Act 2006* imitated by the Government has provided for reservation for women for the first time and wards have been reserved accordingly in the elections to cantonment boards scheduled to be held in 2008.
3. *Women's Reservation Bill 2010:* The Women's Reservation Bill has been a political raw nerve for nearly a decade now. The 'Women's Reservation Bill' proposes to set aside 33 per cent of the seats in Parliament to women. Its advocates say the Bill is essential for active political participation of women. The Women's reservation Bill was passed by the Rajya Sabha on 9 March. Women get 33 per cent reservation in gram panchayat (meaning village assembly, which is a form of local village government) and municipal elections. Due to female feticides, infanticide and issues related to women's health, sex ratio in India is alarming at 1.06 males per female. It is expected this bill will change the society to give equal status to women.

Girl's Education: 2,180 residential Kasturba Gandhi Balika Vidyalaya schools have been sanctioned and are providing elementary education to 1,82,000 out of school girls. *Gaun Ki Beti, Kisori Balika Divas Yojana, Ladli Laksmi Yojana, Cycle Praday Yojana etc.* schemes were launched by the Government for empowering the girls in India.

Gender Inequality: Gender Inequality is now receiving greater attention. The principle of gender equality and protection of women's right from the days of independence. Accordingly, the concern of the country in safeguarding the rights and the privilege of women found its best expression in the constitution of India. While article 14 confers equal rights and opportunities on men and women in the political, economic and social citizen on the grounds of sex, religion, race, caste etc. and Article 15 (3) empowers the state to make affirmative discrimination in favor of women. Similarly Article 16 provides an equality of opportunities in the matter of public appointments for all citizens, yet, another Article 39 mentions that the state shall direct its policy towards providing men and women equally, the right to means of livelihood and equal pay for equal work. Article 42 directs the state to make provisions for ensuring just and humane conditions of work and maternity relief. Article 51 (A) (e) imposes a fundamental duty on every citizen to renounce the practices derogatory to the dignity of women. To make this de jure equality into a de facto one, special legislations have been enacted from time to time in support of women.

On 8 March 1996, on the occasion of *International Women's Day*, the parliament passed resolution to set up a standing Committee for the "improvement of the status of women" in India and the Committee on Empowerment of women was constituted in April 1997. *National Commission for Women [NCW]* a statuary body set up in 1992, safeguards the rights and interests of women. It continue to pursue its mandated role and activities viz; safeguarding women's rights through investigations into the individual complaints of atrocities, sexual harassment of women at work place conducting *Parivarik/Mahila Lok Adalats* legal awareness programmes/ camps, review of both women specific and women related legislations, investigates into individual complaints, atrocities, harassment, denial of rights etc.

Milestones and Challenges

Empowerment is now increasingly seen as a process by which the one's without power gain greater control over their lives. This means control over material assets, intellectual resources and ideology. It involves power to, power with and power within. The questions surrounding women's empowerment the condition and position of women have now become critical to the human rights based approaches to development. The Cairo conference in 1994 organized by UN on Population and Development called attention to women's empowerment as a central focus and UNDP developed the Gender Empowerment measure (GEM) which focuses on the three variables that reflect women's participation in society – political power or decision-making, education and health. 1995 UNDP report was devoted to women's empowerment and it declared that if human development is not engendered, it is endangered a declaration which almost become a lei motif for further development measuring and policy planning. Equality, sustainability and empowerment were emphasized and the stress was, that women's emancipation does not depend on national income but is an engaged political process. People's choices have to be enlarged and they must have economic opportunities to make use of these capabilities. Women are as capable as men of exercising will, controlling desires and taking decisions but males enjoy support of social institutions and women are excluded as the 'other'. Women are often not treated as "ends in themselves" persons with dignity who deserve respect from laws and institutions instead they are treated instrumentally as reproducers, caregivers, sexual receivers, agents of family's general prosperity. Human development report since 1999 demonstrate that practically no country in the world treats its women as well as men according to the measures of life expectancy wealth and education. The intervention strategy for empowering women to have informed and effective choices on their health and nutrition and for the development of children and adolescents has to be multi-pronged. Such as:

1. *Convergence of service delivery at village levels:* There are two main programmes in the Department of Women and Child Development, which aim at convergence of services delivery at the village level, namely, Integrated Child Development Scheme (ICDS) and Integrated Women.'s Empowennent Programme (IWEP). The ICDS network

through Anganwadi Centres reaches 85 per cent of the villages and hamlets in the country. The IWEP (erstwhile Indira Mahila Yojana) which extends to 650 blocks operates through the self help groups of women. Both these programmes can be effective vehicles for the implementation of the National Population Policy. It is therefore critical that both the schemes are universalized.

2. *Nutrition:* The Supplementary Nutrition provided under the ICDS Scheme is one of the most vital components under Basic Minimum Service Programme aimed at eradication of the menace of malnutrition of children and women. The success of the programme however depends largely on adequate provision of funds to the States and UTs. An Action plan needs to be drawn up for taking up nutrition in a mission mode to cover infants, adolescent girls, pregnant and lactating mothers - the three critical links in the inter-generational cycle of malnutrition. One intervention that has successfully worked in improving nutrition levels as well as impacting favorably on retention of children in schools is the mid-day meal scheme. This has shown positive results in programmes like TINP and needs to be replicated widely.
3. *Formation of Self-Help Groups:* The formation of self-help groups as a basis for the social and economic empowerment of deprived and disadvantaged women has been found to be a successful mechanism for the organisation, mobilization and self development of women. This has been tested through the IMY and Swa Shakti projects of the Department of Women and Child Development and is being replicated in a number of programmes of other Departments. These groups can facilitate the process of economic empowerment through thrift and savings, training and skill up gradation and access to credit and other productive resources. They can also be instruments of social empowerment through awareness generation and convergence of delivery of schemes. With the feeling of ownership and management

of their own resources and savings, poor women have been able to choose their priorities and have even been found to cover the cost of additional nutrition and health gaps. The success of this approach has resulted in universalization of this mode of organisation in all the southern States. There is a need to replicate this mode throughout the country.

4. *Access to Resources:* The issue of improved health and nutrition is intimately linked to access to and control over local, social, and economic structures. For women to be empowered we need to ensure:
   - *(a)* Equitable access and distribution of resources like land, credit etc.
   - *(b)* Access to education.
   - *(c)* Access to health /nutrition.
   - *(d)* Access to water and sanitation.

   This implies that resources should flow into these areas to bridge the gender gap and that systems be developed to plan, implement and monitor the 'bridging' of the gap. Ownership of land tends to reduce fertility by providing an alternate means of security. Similarly education has its own impact on reproductive behavior of both men and women. Improving the access of women/households in rural areas and urban slums to safe sources of drinking water will free them from the drudgery of fetching water and in decreasing the morbidity resulting from water-borne diseases such as diarrhoea and cholera. This will impact positively on the health and energy levels of women. Access to technologies which can reduce the drudgery of women on the various works performed by them both within and outside the household is also a very useful intervention for empowering the women.

5. *Women Component Plan:* While the Planning Commission has already incorporated the concept of Women's Component Plan in the 9th Five Year Plan whereby 30 per cent of funds/ benefit on every women related sector

actually flow to women, it is important that guidelines are finalized early so that this could be implemented effectively.

6. *Development of Gender Disaggregated Data System:* One of the constraints in the preparation, implementation and monitoring of plans for the development of women is the absence of gender segregated data on various indices of development at the State, district and sub district levels. These lacunae in our statistical system should be addressed on a priority basis.
7. *Legislation:* Laws should be gender sensitive and ensure equal provision and access to resources for men and women. Also there needs to be a much broader focus on implementation issues. Many of the existing statutes such as Indecent Representation of Women's Act, Minimum Wages Act, Equal Remuneration Act, and Pre-natal Diagnostic Act, Maternity Benefit Act, etc., are implemented more in their violation. A number of these Acts are under review in order to strengthen their provisions. The Maternity Benefit Act needs to be strictly implemented and expanded to cover women in the informal sector, along with provision of paid leave for a longer period.
8. *Freedom from Violence:* Women and girls face violence in various forms at various stages of their life cycle. This takes the form of female foeticide and infanticide, rape, dowry death and more indirect forms such as desertion or abandonment of older women. This calls for a multipronged strategy of implementation of laws, awareness, community sanctions etc.
9. *Participation in Political Life:* For empowerment, women need to have a voice in decision making and planning through adequate representation. Reservation of women in the rural and urban local bodies had enabled representation of nearly a million women at the grassroots who play a very important catalytic role in

transforming the society. Similar representation in State Legislature and Parliament would further strengthen the process of empowerment of women.

10. *Sustained Media Campaign:* One of the most effective interventions that can take place to address the issues of attitude and mind sets of men and women of the community and also of the functionaries of the government - the bureaucracy, police and judiciary is media campaigns. A sustained campaign through the print, electronic and folk media is necessary on various issues related to empowerment of women, health and nutrition, laws, value of the girl child, violence against women etc.

Non-governmental organisations, community-based organisations and self help groups can be very effective in the process of empowerment through participatory communication. Participatory communication can help women to change their attitudes, behaviours and styles of communication. Empowerment is a complex term and may be measured in terms of women's freedom to shape their lives, their control over resources, their access to basic facilities, their level of political participation, their ability to take their own decisions and their ability to remove hindrances in their path to progress. Self-help groups of women have been found to be very effective grassroots institutions in facilitating access for women to means of development be it information, financial and material resources or services. The 'self-help group' mode should be encouraged, so that the groups become dynamic change agents in bringing about empowerment and socio-economic development of women. Organizing women into self-help groups marks the beginning of a major process of empowering women by strengthening their capacity for collective decision making and entrepreneurship development. Gender sensitization training has been developed to initiate the task of attitude change within male-dominated extension and research bureaucracies and donor agencies.

Conclusion

Indisputably, India is committed to the cause of empowerment of women. However, the journey towards progress in long and arduous. India has witnessed great change in the last two decades. Age old prejudices and gender based biases are giving way to gender equality and harmonious development. Policies to be raise women's age at marriage enhance their educations and open greater employment opportunities will also help to empower them, at least in some respects. We choose to focus particularly on women, because in every society they struggle against gender norms that limit their resources and opportunities for improvement and because we know that women empowerment is a tremendous resource for social change and a broader fight against global poverty. Our goal is to cause policy, institutional and individual change that will improve the lives of women and girls everywhere.

Government Programmes and Women Empowerment *Areas of Serious Concern*

Asian and Pacific Centre for Women and Development [APCWD] define *"Empowerment as a process that aims at creating the conditions for the self-determination of a particular people at creating the conditions for the self-determination of a particular people or group"*. "Empowerment with women" is the central issue that has been pervading the development debate after the 80s. Improving their status and empowering them would go a long way in accomplishing egalitarian gender relations in society. Women who are hitherto constrained by their social structure for their self-expression constitute the target of most of the development programmes, which aim at bringing them into the mainstream of the development.

Constitutional Guarantee: The Constitution of India guarantees to all women equality [Article 14]; no discrimination by the State [Article 15 (1)]; equality of opportunity [Article 16]; equal pay for equal work [Article 39(d)]; renounce practices derogatory to the dignity of women [Article 51 (a) (c)] The Constitution also allows the State to make special provision in favor of women and children [Article 15(3)]; and securing just and humane conditions of work and maternity relief [Article 42]. Acknowledging the world-wide significance of women empowerment the Government of India declared 2001 as the *"Year of Women's Empowerment"* and the National Policy for the Empowerment of Women came into force from 2001.

Women Empowerment Indicators: Draft Country Paper of India for the 4th World Conference on women held in Beijing in 1995 proposed certain qualitative and quantitative indicators for evaluating women's empowerment. The qualitative aspects included self-esteem and self-confidence, articulation, leisure time, workloads, roles and responsibilities, domestic violence, women economic contribution and decision making. Quantitative aspects included demographic trends, number of women in participation, access and control over resources, physical health status, literacy levels and political participation at the local level.

Government Programmes for Women Empowerment: Government of India has been implementing various programmes through its different departments to bring about women's development and their empowerment. For lack of an overarching policy that would have provided a common understanding and a unified vision, each department has defined and operationalized empowerment through its own prism and from its own perspective and understanding. In the case of some departments, the stated goal is not to bring about women's empowerment, but rather, the emphasis is on bringing about their overall efficiency and economic development. For example:

1. Social Welfare Board aims at bringing about women's development and empowerment through partnerships with NGOs.
2. Department of Rural Development focuses on economic self-reliance as an indicator of women's development.
3. Agriculture Department endeavors to make women better agricultural workers by increasing their understanding about the use of technology in agriculture.

4. Horticulture Department aims at providing training to women for vegetable and fruit production, preservation and link them to the market so that they can become economically self-reliant.
5. Dairy Department, in the name of Women's Dairy, has started a new scheme whereby women are given training in animal care, a traditional occupation followed by them and are encouraged to set up their own dairy and thereby become economically self-reliant.
6. Social Welfare Department offers various scholarships and pension schemes and thereby provides economic support to certain vulnerable groups to bring about their upliftment.
7. Education Department, in order to bring about gender equality, has initiated special programmes for girls whereby they can be mainstreamed with the existing programmes.
8. Adult Education programme of the Education Department considers women's literacy as the first step towards their empowerment and is pursuing the Continuing Education programme through the self-help groups (SHGs) in order to bring about their economic self-reliance.
9. The Department of Women's Empowerment and Child Development is running various schemes and programmes for the empowerment of women by setting up self-help groups (SHGs) with the help of NGOs.

Welfare Schemes for Women and Girls: Most of the schemes currently implemented by the Department of Women's Empowerment and Child Development and those by the State Social Welfare Board and Department of Health fall in following category:

Department of Women Empowerment and Child Development implements programmes viz.

1. *The Integrated Child Development Services (ICDS) programme:* This is a flagship programme of the department. While

providing *'Anganwadi'* (crèche) services and health and nutritional supplements to infants, ICDS also provides pre and post-natal care for pregnant and lactating mothers. The *anganwadi* workers have to dispense iron tablets and iodine-fortified salt to pregnant and lactating mothers. The pregnant and lactating mothers also have to receive dry rations from the anganwadi workers.

2. *Kishori Balika Yojana* (scheme for the adolescent girls): As part of the ICDS programme, a special scheme for the adolescent girls was initiated from 2001 onwards, with assistance from the Government of India as well as from the World Bank. The scheme is intended for adolescent girls in the 11-18 age group who belong to the BPL (below poverty line) households. The scheme intends to provide training to these girls in order to bring about their overall development. The areas in which training would be provided would include information about how to take care of their bodies, the meaning of a balanced diet, importance of family welfare, besides providing them interpersonal skills and making them self-confident and training them in vocational skills so that they can become independent. During 2005-2006, besides starting the scheme in 40 blocks, 59 additional blocks received sanction from the Government of India. The ICDS programme is run by the Department itself. The other programmes of the Department include:
    - *(a)* *Old Age Pension Scheme:* This scheme is applicable to both men and women and is meant for both urban as well as rural areas and provides Rs 400 per month to those who are above 60 years of age.
    - *(b)* *Pension scheme for widows/homeless/aged/disabled:* The scheme is applicable only in rural areas and is implemented by the District Social Welfare Officer on the basis of the recommendation received from the Pradhan of the Gram Panchayat as well as the Minister, Panchayats, and forwarded through the Block office.

(c) *Financial assistance to destitute widows:* Destitute widows are entitled to receive a sum of Rs. 400 per month. This is a scheme for rural areas and is being implemented by the Gram Panchayats.

(d) *Financial assistance for re-marriage of widows:* A sum of Rs. 11,000 is provided for the re-marriage of a widow below the age of 35 years.

(e) *Grant to female student who has passed intermediate from BPL (below poverty line) family to enable her to pursue her studies:* A onetime grant of Rs. 25,000 is being given since 2006-07 to a female student to enable her to complete her graduation.

Social Welfare Board set up in 2003 receives funding from the Central Government to run its schemes. The state government has the responsibility for the day-to-day functioning of the Board. All the schemes of the Board are implemented through the NGOs. These schemes include:

1. *Hostels for working women*
2. *Women's Helpline Family Counseling Centres*
3. *Campaign against female foeticide*
4. *Vocational training programmes*
5. *Creches*
6. *Condensed courses for women*
7. *Short-stay homes for women*

Department of Health: In order to reduce the maternal and infant mortality rates, there is a scheme for the safe delivery of pregnant mothers as well as care of their infants. The scheme is applicable to women who belong to the BPL (Below Poverty Line) households and who are taken to the government health centre or hospital for their delivery. A pregnant woman can be accompanied by an ASHA (health) worker or by the local 'dai' (midwife) and an allowance is paid to this person. In case a pregnant woman delivers her baby in a hospital in the rural area, she is paid an amount of Rs. 1400/ and Rs. 1000 if she is taken to a hospital in the urban area. The pregnant woman is also provided the tetanus injection and newly born infant is provided vaccinations against six dangerous diseases at periodic intervals.

Department of Education: [Empowerment and Gender Equity Schemes]: Under the *Sarva Shiksha Abhiyan* (Education for All), Department of Education has initiated schemes to reduce the gender gap in the education of children, viz.

1. *Early Child Care Education Centres*: These Centres are set up to ensure better enrolment and retention of girls in the primary schools. Since the girl-child has the responsibility to look after the young siblings and is therefore deprived of school education, an ECCE centre attached to the school would ensure that girls would come to school. It is intended that if school-going girls have access to such centres, they would get enrolled in schools, and would be retained in schools. The scheme also envisages provision of good quality education to such girls. At the ECCE centers, the physical and psychological growth and development of all children in the 3-6 age group, is provided for. The education department at the district level has the responsibility for Sarva Shiksha Abhiyan and Department of Social Welfare (through the Integrated Child Development Services Programme) have the responsibility for running the ECCE Centers.
2. *National Programme on Education for Girls at Elementary Level (NPEGEL)*: Since education is a concurrent subject, this national programme is also being implemented at the state level in some select districts and blocks since 2003. It is intended to increase the enrolment rates of girls belonging to SC/ST communities at the elementary stage. The scheme intends to focus attention on the educationally deprived sections and to encourage the enrolment, retention and quality education of the girls belonging to the SC/ST communities. It offers materials incentives such as stationery and introduces additional incentives like awards, remedial teaching and bridge courses as well as development of a model upper primary school in each cluster.

3. *Kasturba Gandhi Balika Vidyalaya (KGBV):* The scheme draws its legitimacy from the thrust in national policy documents as well as international discourse that refers to bridging the 'gender gap.' Following this thrust, the scheme is being implemented in educationally backward blocks with a wider gender gap. The scheme is intended for girls belonging to the scheduled castes (SCs), scheduled tribes (STs), other backward classes (OBCs), religious minorities and below poverty line (BPL) households. Funded by the Government of India, under the *Sarva Shiksha Abhiyan* , the basic idea behind the scheme is to give a second chance for mainstreaming rural girls belonging to deprived social backgrounds who could not study up to or beyond class V. The second opportunity consists of the facility to stay in a hostel while studying for the upper primary stage of elementary education namely classes VI to VIII. They are set up in areas where there are a minimum of 50 school going girls who are school drop-outs. As all the girls are primary school drop-outs, they are above 10 years of age and are mostly in their teens.
4. *Innovative scheme for the adolescent girls:* In order to create and sustain the interest of girls in education, they are trained to produce items that can be used in their daily lives. They are also offered components of empowerment strategies such as personal development, confidence building abilities, and life-skills oriented education.
5. *Mahila Samakhya* (Education for Women's Equality) was the first major scheme launched by the Central government that owed its genesis to the National Policy on Education (1986) recognizing the empowering potential of education and education as an agent of basic change in the status of women. The basic objectives of *Mahila Samakhya* are:
   (a) As a gender-based programme, to create an ambience in the society for tolerance and mutual respect for women.

(*b*) To ensure that education becomes accessible to the socially and economically marginalized women and girls.

(*c*) To encourage and promote a gender-based discourse in society.

(*d*) To enhance the self-image and self-confidence of women and enable them to critically analyze their role as individual women and as members of society so that they can begin to challenge that role collectively and initiate a process of social change.

(*e*) To collectively participate in decision making and seek equal rights and opportunities for a more egalitarian society.

(*f*) To enhance participation of women and girls in formal and non-formal education programmes.

Education Department of the Ministry of Human Resource Development, Government of India, launched *Mahila Samakhya* as a major programme for bringing about women's development as well as empowerment in 1989 on a pilot basis in 6 states of India, with funding from the Netherlands Government.

Department of Horticulture: The Horticulture Department has a special scheme for training women in fruit preservation, viz. pickles, jams, chutneys, fruit juices, etc. The aim is to give fillip to local production and to ensure that women become economically self-reliant.

Dairy Department: Women dairy development scheme originated in 1994-95 and its main aim was to bring about rural women's economic and social development as well as ensure that they assume leadership positions. The scheme envisages 100 per cent participation of women and ensures that the women's milk cooperative would be run and managed entirely by the women themselves. For the Women's Dairy Development scheme, women are formed into groups at the village level by the department. A milk collection centre is then opened at the village level and it is the responsibility of the women's group to ensure that the milk that is collected at the centre is then sent to the dairying plant. The department arranges for the technical training of the women's group that includes how to measure the fat content in the milk, how to measure the purity of the milk (with the use of Lactometer). Each group has a President and a Secretary and it is their responsibility, in addition to measuring the fat content and the milk purity, to maintain daily accounts and at the end of the month, to submit the accounts to the department. It is they who also make the payment to each member of the group. As cattle- rearing is an occupation traditionally followed by the hill women dairying is linked to their traditional occupation to make it economically attractive to women. Aside from dairying, rural women are also provided training in such related issues such as first aid for the cattle, grass cultivation, seed production, setting up kitchen garden, use of smokeless *chullah* (stove), production of organic manure, setting up *'sulabh sauchalayas'* (community toilets), as well as health related issues that are relevant to the lives of women.

Emerging Trends: A synoptic overview of what is happening with regard to women's empowerment programmes in India is briefly presented here. Some of the emerging trends are:

1. *Percolation of the discourse of empowerment to the ground level:* There are two distinct strands in the women's programmes in India. These are welfare programmes and gender equity and women's empowerment programmes. As the term 'empowerment' is widely used it has led to its dilution. But on the other hand, it has raised awareness levels among women on various issues such as their legal rights, their entitlements under the different government schemes, about how they can better their social and economic conditions and so on.
2. *SHGs form the mainstay of women's empowerment programmes:* SHGs have grown phenomenally in recent years in the country. Women's collectives as forums of women's empowerment have not been a new phenomenon in the

country. Thus, Mahila Mandals as part of community development initiatives dates back to the 1950s However, it was NGOs such as SEWA (Self Employed Women's Association) and the WWF (Working Women's Forum) that gave fillip to formation of women's collectives by linking them to credit. Experience of SEWA and of WWF showed that women were not defaulters with regard to repayment of credit. The collective ensured that there was peer pressure on women to repay loans and the resulting high repayment rates meant that lenders were willing to forego collateral.

3. *Is Empowerment a top-down or a bottom-up process?* As mentioned in the theoretical debate on empowerment, empowerment is itself a form of power. In feminist literature, 'power' is disaggregated into 'power over' (domination), 'power to' (capacity), 'power within'(inner strength), and 'power with' (achieved through cooperation and alliance). In feminist use of empowerment, the emphasis is clearly on 'power to' and 'power with' and not on "power over.' If conceived thus, empowerment has to be a bottom up rather than a top-down process. If women are considered powerless, then the idea of empowering women can imply a top-down approach. On the other hand, if it is argued that despite patriarchal considerations, women have power, then empowerment would be perceived as a bottom up process. A question that needs to be asked about the NGOs that are involved in the women's empowerment programmes is whether empowerment is perceived as capacity building to cope with the requirements of life as opposed to capacity building to transform the conditions of life and assert alternative gender roles. Since NGOs receive funding from government and have already indicated the compromises they are required to make to ensure continuity of funding, it appears highly likely that a majority of them are engaged in capacity building in order to promote status-quo and not address social justice and equity issues.

4. *Empowerment of individual women to improve their efficiency and productivity rather than organizing and building a movement for women's equality:* There was a tendency to focus on the efficiency dimension of empowerment of individual women. Thus women had to become aware, self-confident, independent, and capable of taking decisions. While these are important dimensions of empowerment, the transformative potential of empowerment that could be brought about through women's organizations was not part of the consciousness of a large number of NGOs.
5. *Are SHGs really reaching the poor women?* Since a majority of NGOs indicated that they worked with a mixed group of women belonging to different socio-economic background and varied caste groups, a question can be raised whether SHGs are really inclusive of poor women. 'One of the realities of micro-credit phenomenon that has been established by studies is that it fails to include in its fold the very poor'. While the poor are the target, in order to ensure economic sustainability of the programme, whoever can pay becomes part of the programme. In other words, realities of micro-credit demand a certain capacity to pay and to save, thereby creating exclusions right from the group's inception.
6. *Use of technology in women's training programmes:* this is an ICT era. Thus various information tools such as community radio, community television, community newspaper should be used to empower the rural women.

Necessary Dimensions for Attention to Facilitate Meaningful Women Empowerment: Dimensions to facilitate women empowerment include:

1. *Economic empowerment:* The fact is that women though largely absent from the format workplace and hence from official labour statistic are nevertheless heavily engaged in subsistence agricultural and informal sector of economy. There is a constant effort to put women's income in bracket in order to consolidate the position that women are only reproducers and not producers. This idea needs to be changed. Women's economic right is definitely an

important indicator for enhancement of their status. So, women labour needs to be recognized. Education, more employment avenues, political awareness etc. would all lead to women's economic emancipation.

2. *Social empowerment:* A major limitation to the advancement of women is the intuitional set of social prescriptions that limit their participation in socio-economic activities and their input in decision making efforts to increase the potential for women's social participation extend down to the level of the household.
3. *Physical Empowerment:* most women in the third world countries work very long hours at numerous tedious tasks as well as take care of their children and homes. Until we recognized the physical hardships endured by women from meeting their productive and reproductive responsibilities and make concerted efforts to improve upon their health status, other advancements will have limited impact for them. Physical empowerment is dependent upon each of the other dimensions as all have contributory effects.
4. *Psychological Empowerment:* it is a common occurrence for women in third World Countries to belittle their own position in the society and their contribution to the economy. When asked of their occupation the majority of rural women will say they have none, despite the fact that they may engage in three or more income generating and productive activities to help meet the needs of their families due to cultural view of the low position of women in many societies the women themselves often have a negative view of their potential and importance.

Need for: Full potential of benefits envisaged under various Government programmes meant for women socio-economic welfare and empowerment can be harnessed if areas of serious concern are timely attended, viz.

1. *Education:* Studies confirm that female literacy has a significant influence in improving social and economic status of women. The female literacy rate is woefully

lower than that of male. Compared to boys, far fewer girls are enrolled in schools and many of them are drop out. According to the National Sample Survey data of 2011, only Kerala and Mizoram have approached universal female literacy rate. According to the U.S. Department of Commerce, the chief barriers to female education in India are inadequate school and sanitary facilities, shortage of female teachers and gender bias in curriculum.

2. *Work participation:* Though the country has a large percentage of women workers, there is a serious underestimation of women's contribution as workers to nation's economy. There are, however, fewer women in the paid work force than those of men. In rural areas, agriculture and allied sector employed as many as 89.5 per cent of total female labour. Women's average contribution, in overall farm output, is estimated at 55 per cent to 66 per cent of the total labour. According to 1991 World Bank report, women accounted for 94 per cent of total employment in dairy sector. Women contributed 51 per cent of total employment in forest-based small-scale enterprises.
3. *Female-headed Households:* According to 2010-11 year data, while only 12 per cent of households in India were female-headed, about 88 per cent of the households below poverty line were female-headed.
4. *Land and Property Rights:* In most Indian families, women do not own any property in their own names and do not get a share of parental property. Some of the laws discriminate against women, when it comes to land and property rights. Married daughters, when faced with marital harassment, have no residential rights in the ancestral home. Christian women have yet not received equal rights of divorce and succession.
5. *Talaq System:* Many Muslim women have questioned the Fundamentalist Leaders' interpretation of women's rights under the *Shariat* Law and have criticized the Triple *Talaq* System.

Full potential of country's socio-economic development can be harnessed when women who constitute about half of our population are empowered to exercise their authority and take decision to implement Government programmes for women's welfare. As long as this does not happen, half the talent, half the progress and half the development would be lost. We as a nation cannot afford to do that. For a chariot to move forward both wheels have to be equally strong and if one is weak it cannot move forward. So to move the chariot of our country's socio-economic growth forward both the wheels- men and women- have to be equally strong and to move ahead jointly. To express the aspirations of Indian women, I will quote a stanza:

"He took the lightness of the leaf and
The glance of the flaws
The gaiety of the sun's rays and tears of the mist,
The inconsistency of the wind
And timidity of hare, the vanity of peacock and
The softness of dawn on the throat of swallow
He added the harshness of the Diamond
The sweet flavour of honey, the cruelty of tiger,
The warmth of the fire and the turtle dove
The chill of show and chatter of joy"
He melted all these and formed women.

It can be concluded that women are the most beautiful creation of God and He gave all the emotions and a lot of patience with softness and a lot of hardness to live and survive in the world.

Indira Gandhi Matritva Sahyog Yojana (IGMSY)

A Conditional Maternity Benefit Scheme

The vulnerable condition of the pregnant women belonging to poor and economically deprived families across the country is well recognised. In the Eleventh Five Year Plan document, the Planning Commission has noted that:

> *"Poor women continue to work to earn a living for the family right upto the last days of their pregnancy, thus not being able to put on as much weight as they otherwise might. They also resume working soon after childbirth, even though their bodies might not permit it preventing their bodies from fully recovering, and their ability to exclusively breastfeed their new born in the first six months. Therefore, there is urgent need for introducing a modest maternity benefit to partly compensate for their wage loss".*

Under-nutrition, especially in infant and young children, adolescent girls and women results in increased susceptibility to infections, slow recovery from illnesses, cumulative growth and development deficits leading to reduced productivity and a heightened risk of adverse pregnancy outcomes for women. A woman's nutritional status has important implications for her health as well as the health and development of her children. A woman with poor nutritional status, as indicated by a low body mass index (BMI), short stature, anaemia, or other micronutrient deficiencies, has a greater risk of obstructed labour, having a baby with a low birth weight and adverse pregnancy outcomes resulting in death due to postpartum hemorrhage, illness for herself and her baby and adversely affecting lactation. In India, high levels of under-nutrition and anaemia in adolescent girls and women are compounded by early marriage, early child bearing and inadequate spacing between births. Girls and women often face an inter-generational cycle of under nutrition compounded by multiple deprivations - gender discrimination, poverty and exclusion. This vicious cycle needs to be addressed through multisectoral interventions. Due to increased nutritional needs during pregnancy and lactation, the pregnant and lactating mothers require greater nutritional support, especially in settings where levels of under nutrition and anaemia are already high. During this period, mothers require access to health care services, enhanced food and nutrient intake, family care, skilled counselling support and a hygienic environment. Therefore, improvement in nutritional status of women especially during pregnancy and lactation, requires multi-sectoral, concerted, convergent and supportive actions.

Maternal under-nutrition is a major challenge in India with more than one third (35.6%) having low Body Mass Index (BMI). Early marriage, early child bearing and frequent pregnancy adversely affect the maternal nutritional status. According to the NFHS-III, 58 per cent women were married before the legal age of 18 years and three quarters (74%) were married before reaching the age of 20 years. Around 30 per cent women aged 25-49 years gave first birth before the age of 18 years and 50 per cent gave first birth when they were at the age of 20 years. The prevalence of anaemia for ever-married women has increased from 52 per cent in NFHS-2 to 56 per cent in NFHS-3. According NFHS-3, 69.5 children aged 6-59 months reported any anaemia with 26.3 per cent having mild anaemia, 40.2 per cent moderate anaemia and 2.9 per cent severe anaemia. Anaemia tends to increase with the number of children ever born and decreases with education and the household's wealth. Anaemia is more prevalent for women who are breastfeeding (63%) and women who are pregnant (59%) than for other women (53%). Therefore, the anaemia situation has worsened over time for both women and young children. The promotion of early and exclusive breastfeeding for the first six months and appropriate complementary feeding continue to be major challenges. According to NFHS-III, only about 25 per cent of the babies are initiated into breastfeeding within one hour of birth. Only 46 per cent of children under five months of age are exclusively breastfed. It is significant that complementary feeding has increased substantially. The percentage of infants (between 6 to 9 months) receiving complementary feeding, along with breast milk, increased significantly from 33.5 per cent to 55.8 per cent during the period 1998-99 (NFHS-II) to 2005-06 (NFHSIII). According to Lancet 2003 - India Analysis, 16 per cent of under 5 child mortality in India can be averted by ensuring universal exclusive breastfeeding for the first six months of the infant's life. Another 5 per cent can be reduced by promoting the universal practice of appropriate complementary feeding.

Maternal mortality is defined by NFHS-III as the death of a woman during pregnancy or delivery or within 42 days of the end of pregnancy from a pregnancy - related cause. Approximately 30 million women in India are pregnant annually, and 27 million have live births. Of these, nearly 136,000 maternal deaths occur annually, most of which can be prevented. According to data from the Registrar General of India quoted in Special Bulletin in Maternal Mortality in India (April 2009), maternal mortality ratio in India is 254 as reported between 2004 and 2006. This is derived as the proportion of maternal deaths per 100,000 live births reported under SRS.

Infant and Child Mortality: Around 1.7 million children in India do not reach their first birthday, of these 1.2 million die within the first month. According to the NFHS-3, infant mortality in India has declined from 77 deaths per 1,000 live births in 1991-95 (10-14 years before the survey) to 57 deaths per 1,000 live births in 2001 11 (0-4 years before the survey), thus implying an average rate of decline of 2 infant deaths per 1,000 live births per year. All other measures of infant and child mortality also show declining trends during the years before the survey. By comparing the estimates for the period 10-14 years before the survey with the estimates for the period 0-4 years before the survey, it is seen that the neonatal mortality rate has decreased by 12 deaths per 1,000 live births (from 51 to 39), the postneonatal mortality rate has decreased by 7 deaths per 1,000 live births (from 25 to 18), and the child mortality rate (at age 1-4 years) has decreased by 14 deaths per 1,000 children age 1 (from 32 to 18).

Antenatal care: Among mothers who gave birth in the five years preceding the NFHS-III survey, almost three-quarters received antenatal care from a health professional (50% from a doctor and 24% from other health personnel). Younger women were more likely than older women to receive antenatal care, as were women with more education and women having their first child. Less than half of women received antenatal care during the first trimester of pregnancy, as is recommended. Another 22 per cent had their first visit during the fourth or fifth month of pregnancy. Just over half of mothers had three or more antenatal care visits; urban women were much more likely to receive three or more visits than women in rural areas. For 65 per cent of births, mothers received iron and folic acid supplements, but only 23 per cent consumed them for the recommended 90 days or more. Three in four mothers received two or more doses of tetanus toxoid vaccine.

Immunisation of children: As per National Family Health Survey (NFHS-3).

Less than half (44%) of children 12-23 months are fully vaccinated against the six major childhood illnesses: tuberculosis, diphtheria, pertussis, tetanus, polio, and measles. However, most children are at least partially vaccinated: only 5 per cent have received no vaccinations at all. 78 per cent of children have received a BCG vaccination, and the same have received at least the recommended three doses of polio vaccine. However, only 59 per cent have been vaccinated against measles and only 55 per cent have received all the recommended doses of DPT. In view of the above situations, there is an emergent need to address the nutritional deficits of the pregnant and lactating mother. This could be promoted by providing maternal support, counseling and services in an enabling environment with a view to enhance the demand and utilization of existing maternal and child care services. Such a support could also be through a direct cash transfer system on achieving certain conditionalities which could be used by the beneficiary for her own care and that of her child.

Maternity Benefit in India

1. **Constitutional Provisions:** Article 47 requires that the State should, as its primary duty, raise the level of nutrition and the standard of living of its people and improve public health. Article 42 requires that the State should make provision for securing just and humane conditions of work and for maternity relief. Article 43 mentions that the State shall endeavour to secure to all workers agricultural, industrial, or otherwise, a living wage, such conditions of work that ensure a decent standard of life.
2. **Maternity Benefit Act 1961:** The rights of mothers to maternity benefits were recognized long ago in India with the introduction of the Maternity Benefit Act in 1961. The Act regulates employment of women in certain establishments for a certain period before and after childbirth and provides for maternity and other benefits. Such benefits are aimed to protect the dignity of motherhood by providing for the full and healthy maintenance of women and her child when she is not

working. The Act is applicable to mines, factories, circus industry, plantations, shops and establishments employing ten or more persons, except employees covered under the Employees' State Insurance Act, 1948. It can be extended to other establishments by the State Governments.

3. **Employees' State Insurance Act, 1948** provides for certain benefits to employees in case of sickness, maternity and employment injury and to make provision for certain other matters in relation thereto. It provides for periodical payments to an insured woman in case of confinement or miscarriage or sickness arising out of pregnancy, confinement, premature birth of child or miscarriage. The Act prohibits employers from dismissing, discharging, or reducing or otherwise punishing an employee during the period the employee is in receipt of sickness or maternity benefit. It also prohibits dismissal, discharge or reduction or otherwise punishment to an employee during the period s/he is absent from work as a result of illness duly certified in accordance with the regulations to arise out of the pregnancy or confinement rendering the employee unfit for work.

4. **Central Civil Services (Leave) Rules 1972** guarantees maternity leave by an authority competent to grant leave for a period of 135 days (now 180 days as per Sixth Pay Commission) from the date of its commencement to a female Government servant (including an apprentice) with less than two surviving children. During such period, she shall be paid leave salary equal to the pay drawn immediately before proceeding on leave. It also provides for maternity leave not exceeding 45 days may also be granted to a female Government servant (irrespective of the number of surviving children) during the entire service of that female Government in case of miscarriage including abortion on production of medical certificate. On the recommendations of the Sixth Central Pay Commission, the Central Government through an order

in September 2008 has provided for granting two years (i.e.730 days) Child Care Leave to women employees having minor children during the entire service for taking care of up to two children.

5. **Infant Milk Substitute, Feeding Bottles and Infant Foods (Regulation of Production, Supply and Distribution) Act, 1992 IMS Amendment Act, 2003:** The Ministry of Women and Child Development, Government of India legislated IMS Act to protect, promote and support breastfeeding. In pursuance of the International Code, India framed and adopted the Indian National Code of Marketing of Breast Milk Substitutes in 1983. As the National Code was not found adequate in the absence of legal back-up, the Government of India enacted the 'Infant Milk Substitutes, Feeding Bottles and Infant Foods (Regulation of Production, Supply and Distribution) Act, 1992'. This Act was further amended in 2003 and called the Infant Milk Substitutes, Feeding Bottles and Infant Foods (Regulation of Production, Supply and Distribution) Amendment Act, 2003. India is the first such country in the world having given a legislative framework to the WHO resolution to promote exclusive breastfeeding for the first six months of life, as well as continued breastfeeding together with complementary foods for the first two years, in harmony with the global strategy on infant and young child feeding. The National Guidelines on Infant and Young Child Feeding, MWCD-GOI 2006 support operationalization of the IMS Amendment Act and emphasizes enhanced maternal care and nutrition.

6. **National Maternity Benefit Scheme (NMBS):** Introduced in 2001 to provide nutrition support to pregnant BPL women through a one time payment of Rs. 500/- eight to twelve weeks prior to delivery. In the year 2005, the Government of India launched the Janani Suraksha Yojana under the National Rural Health Mission to provide cash incentives for women to have an institutional delivery.

The NMBS was merged into the JSY and with the intervention of the Supreme Court the benefits under the NMBS retained, irrespective of place of delivery.

7. **Janani Suraksha Yojana (JSY):** It was launched in 2005 with an objective to increase institutional deliveries. Under the scheme, the government provides a cash incentive for pregnant mothers to have institutional births as well as pre- and ante-natal care. The JSY primarily aims at promoting institutional delivery while NMBS component (payment of Rs. 500/-) within the Scheme is fairly limited. According to the October 2006 JSY guidelines, all women in Low Performing States (LPS) receive cash assistance if they have their baby in a government health centre or accredited private institution. In rural areas they receive Rs. 1400 and in urban areas Rs.1000. The money is to be dispersed at the time of delivery in the institution. The cash assistance to the mother is mainly to meet the cost of delivery. Under JSY, below poverty line pregnant women above 19 years of age also receive Rs. 500 cash assistance for their first two births if these deliveries are at home. The cash is to be given at birth or around 7 days before for "care during delivery or to meet incidental expenses of delivery." The Scheme *"Indira Gandhi Matritva Sahyog Yojana (IGMSY)" – Conditional Maternity Benefit (CMB) Scheme* would be implemented through the platform of Integrated Child Development Services(ICDS) Scheme. The focal point of implementation would be the Anganwadi Centre (AWC) at the village.

Objectives

To improve the health and nutrition status of pregnant & lactating women and infants by:

1. Promoting appropriate practices, care and service utilisation during pregnancy, safe delivery and lactation.
2. Encouraging the women to follow (optimal) IYCF practices including early and exclusive breast feeding for the first six months.

3. Contributing to better enabling environment by providing cash incentives for improved health and nutrition to pregnant and lactating mothers.

Target Groups: Pregnant Women of 19 years of age and above for first two live births (benefit for still births would be as per the guidelines of scheme) *All Government/PSUs (Central & State) employees would be excluded from the scheme as they are entitled for paid maternity leave.*

The beneficiaries: Pregnant and lactating women In order to estimate the number of pregnant and lactating women that would be covered under the IGMSY, the surveyed population of P & L Women under ICDS(225 lakh) has been taken into consideration. 75 per cent percent of women in the 52 selected districts have been estimated to avail benefits initially under IGMSY, since it is a self selecting scheme. Based on these calculations, the scheme would cover around 13.8 lakh pregnant and lactating women from these selected districts.

Programmes and Services Using the framework of existing ICDS programme, the IGMSY would be implemented as a pilot intervention in selected 52 districts. It would be implemented through the existing District ICDS Cell. Thus, the District ICDS Cell would have the nodal responsibility for the implementation of the IGMSY in all the selected districts, while at the state level the implementation of the scheme would be undertaken through the State ICDS Cell supported by the additional staff provided under the IGMSY at state and district level. ii. Cash transfer would be provided to all pregnant and lactating women in selected districts to contribute towards supporting their health and nutritional needs. The scheme would contribute to partly compensate the woman for the wage loss that she might incur while caring for herself and the child. It would also increase the demand for mother and child health services by providing incentives based on fulfillment of specific conditions relating to health and nutrition of the mother and child. Each pregnant and lactating mother would receive a total cash incentive of Rs.

4000/- between the second trimester till the child attains the age of 6 months subject to fulfillment of following conditions:

The rationale and benefits of the conditions can be explained as under:

1. **Care during pregnancy and delivery:** The focus of IGMSY is to improve nutritional and health status of pregnant and lactating women across the country by partly compensating for their wage loss and encouraging increased access to supplementary nutrition under ICDS Scheme:

   (a) **Early Identification and Registration of pregnancy:** Early registration of pregnancy is essential for availing facilities offered by the health care services to assess the health and nutritional status of the pregnant woman. It also helps to screen for complications early in the pregnancy. Early identification and registration of pregnancy is being promoted by the Government of India primarily through National Rural Health Mission (NRHM) and *Janani Suraksha Yojana* (JSY). IGMSY would also facilitate early registration of pregnancies in target districts through conditional cash transfer. Although, registration of pregnancy should ideally be within two months, under IGMSY registration within four months of pregnancy would be the first milestone for receiving cash benefits of Rs. 1500/- at the end of second trimester. Every registered mother under the IGMSY would have a Mother and Child Protection Card. Early registration at the AWC would also ensure that the woman gets the benefit of Supplementary Nutrition(SNP) and regular counseling under ICDS during the pregnancy. The woman should have attended at least one counseling session at the AWC or VHND for the condition to be fulfilled.

   (b) **Antenatal Care (ANC):** During the ANC at the health center, vital milestones of pregnancy are

noted. Ideally, apart from the ANC at registration, three ANCs are necessary and are mandated under NRHM. Periodic antenatal check-ups help in early detection, management of complications, timely advice and appropriate referral. This can help improve maternal and neonatal survival. ANC is a key entry point for a pregnant woman to receive a broad range of health promotion and preventive health services, including nutritional support and prevention and treatment of anemia and other infectious diseases associated with reproductive health Under the NRHM, the Village Health and Nutrition Day (VHND) is organized once every month at the AWC in the village. On this day, AWWs, ASHAs and other health workers mobilize the villagers, especially women and children, to assemble at the AWC. The ANM and other health personnel are also required to be present at AWC on this day to provide maternal health care to pregnant women from the community. ASHA and other health workers should ensure that every pregnant woman registered under the IGMSY receives the required ANCs. In order to receive the cash benefits under the IGMSY, every pregnant mother would have to mandatorily attend at least one ANC. Monthly supply of Iron and Folic Acid (IFA) tablets would be given to every pregnant woman at the AWC or Health centre or during ANC during this period, along with tetanus vaccination due. Nutrition and health education would also be carried out by the AWW and the health functionary who would also facilitate the above services to the beneficiary. The details of the services availed would be duly recorded in the Individual Mother and Child Protection Card common to ICDS and NRHM.

(c) **Institutional Delivery:** One of the accepted strategies for reducing maternal mortality is to promote deliveries at health institutions by skilled personnel like doctors and nurses. The Janani Suraksha Yojana (JSY) provides cash assistance for Institutional Delivery. The benefits under JSY are linked to pregnant women getting the delivery conducted in health centres/hospitals. *[Early initiation of breast feeding and colostrum feeding may also be ensured]*. No cash transfer has been envisaged under IGMSY at the time of delivery since it is covered under JSY.

2. **Infant Care**

(d) **Immunization:** Immunization of pregnant women and infants protects children from six vaccine preventable diseases - poliomyelitis, diphtheria, pertussis, tetanus, tuberculosis and measles. These are major preventable causes of child mortality, disability, morbidity and related malnutrition. Immunization of pregnant women against tetanus also reduces maternal and neonatal mortality. This service is delivered by the Ministry of Health and Family Welfare under its Reproductive Child Health (RCH) programme. In addition, the Iron and Vitamin "A" Supplementation to children and pregnant women is done under the RCH Programme of the Ministry of Health and Family Welfare. Recognizing the fact that malnutrition and the cycle of ill health often starts with the mother, IGMSY would strive to ensure the optimal immunization of every pregnant woman in close collaboration with the health workers. The scheme would also ensure accessing provisions for counseling, iron and folic-acid supplements that are vital for the health of both the mother and the child.

(e) **Growth Monitoring:** Growth monitoring consists of routine weighments & watching developmental milestone to observe pattern of growth, combined with preventive action when deviations are detected. Under the ICDS Scheme, growth monitoring of children is one of the important activities. Children under three are weighed once a month and children 3-6 years of age are weighed quarterly. Mother and Child Protection Cards are provided to mothers to track the nutritional status, immunization schedule and developmental milestones for both the child and the pregnant and lactating mothers. Through discussion and counseling, growth monitoring also increases the participation and capabilities of families to understand and improve childcare and feeding practices. It helps families understand the linkage between child growth and the dietary intake, health care, safe drinking water and environmental sanitation etc. Keeping the importance of the growth monitoring in view, it would be mandatory for all the IGMSY beneficiaries to regularly attend the growth monitoring sessions at the AWCs. The AWWs would be responsible for maintaining the weight-for-age growth charts for all infants and young children as per WHO Child Growth Standards included in the Mother and Child Protection Card. This condition would contribute towards improving health and nutrition seeking behaviour.

(f) **Infant and Young Child Feeding (IYCF):** IYCF is a critical care practice that can accelerate child survival and development. Research studies (LANCET, 2004) around the world highlight that globally, the universal practice of exclusive breastfeeding for the first six months of life reduces young child mortality by 13 per cent. Together, universal optimal IYCF practices can prevent around one-fifth of young child mortality in India. The promotion of colostrum feeding is critical because it is the baby's first immunization, ideal nutrition for the newborn that builds resistance to infection, aids recovery from infection and accelerates growth. This would ensure and encourage: *(i)* Colostrum feeding; *(ii)* Initiation of breastfeeding within one hour of birth; *(iii)* Exclusive breastfeeding for the first six months; *(iv)* Introduction of appropriate complementary feeding at six months along with continued breast feeding for two years.

The milestone under IGMSY for receiving cash benefit of Rs. 1000/- after six months of birth of the child by ensuring exclusive breastfeeding for six months and introduction of complimentary feeding as certified by the mother and the child receiving OPV and DPT at 14 weeks along with attending at least 2 growth monitoring session of the child and IYCF counseling sessions by the mother between 3rd and 6th months of delivery.

Incentives to Anganwadi Workers (AWWs) and Helpers (AWHs): AWW would receive a cash incentive of Rs. 200/- per pregnant and lactating woman after all the due cash transfers to the beneficiary is complete. Similarly, a cash incentive of Rs. 100/- would be provided to AWH per beneficiary. This would ensure effective implementation of the scheme, since the cash incentives would act as a catalyst to motivate the AWW and AWH to service the beneficiaries efficiently and also encourage more women to participate in the scheme.

The success of the IGMSY largely depends on the successful convergence of ICDS and NRHM. The IGMSY would enhance the demand for services offered by NRHM and the health system. It is therefore expected that health functionaries especially at the District, Block and Village level would support fulfillment of scheme objectives. With adequate information dissemination, this scheme would enhance demand at all levels. Medical personnel at the CHC and the PHC level would have to ensure that demand for services is met adequately. Furthermore, the ANM and ASHA need to positively contribute to the success of the scheme by encouraging enrolment under the scheme and facilitating fulfillment of conditions prescribed along with the AWW. The role of ANM and ASHA would be crucial right from the stage of registration of pregnancy until the disbursement of the final cash transfer after fulfillment of the prescribed conditions.

Rural Women and Their Nutritional Health

Where women are respected there God's delight and where they not, there all work and efforts come to naught" There is no hope of rise for that family or country where they live in sadness. But in India, women project picture which depicts the gravity of total situation, illiteracy, ignorance, non perception of role, shyness, poor health and nutrition, socio economic barriers, low level of development of skill and indifferent socio-economic life style which make the life of women more pitiable grave. Women are the base for all round development venture. No nation can develop without the development of women. Women, the reservoir of productive human resource constitutes almost half of the country's total population. Women perform a multiplicity of roles to make critical contribution to family, health and sustainable development in our country. As a mother, she shapes the personality and character of her children and thereby the character of the nation. As a house wife, she maintains the productivity of the human capital with in her household through proper home management. She is pivotal in society's social, cultural, educational and economic programmes. By catering to physical, emotional and moral needs of the members' women gives meaning to life, provides a suitable environment for the growth of personality and refines the life of citizens. In India, women are the central figure of family life. Women have strong potential role in many aspects of economic development, in relation to their family responsibilities as well as their agricultural production activities. World economic profile of women shows that women represent 50 per cent of total population, make up 30 per cent of official labour force, and utilize 60 per cent of all working hour, but receive 10 per cent of world income and only one per cent share in property income. It is a fact that women cannot contribute meaningfully in the process of development, until their own development is taken care of. Though women in urban areas have excelled in all fields-political, social and economic, the rural counterparts are denied of even the basic amenities like health and education.

Status of Women in India

Women's status is the pure indicator of progress of any nation. Women are the laps in which a new seed of life grows up, but in the country like India, condition of women is still so good. Pt. Jawahar lal Nehru rightly states:

> *"The status of women indicates the character of country".*

In India the status of women has many ups and downs since the ancient Vedic times to the present day. Status and development of women influence the country development as they not only constitiute half of its population but also influence growth of the remaining half of its population. As late Pt. Jawahar lal Nehru said:

> *"In order to awaken the people it is the women who have to awaken. Once she is on move, the family moves, the village moves, the nation also moves".*

Literacy Rate Among the Rural Women

The women in rural area are deprived of minimum facilities of enlightenment and education. Women's education in India plays a very important role in the overall development of the country. It not only helps in the development of half of the human resources, but in improving the quality of life at home and outside. The literacy rate in women is very low. According to Census 2001, female literacy rate is 54.16 per cent and the female illiteracy rate is 62 per cent whereas, male illiteracy rate is 42 per cent. There is a proverb saying *"Educate a man, you will educate but one, educate a women, you will educate a nation."* It is to remember developmental trilogy Nutrition, Health and Education depend on Women to a large extent.

Health Status of Women

Maternal Mortality Rate (MMR) was 301 per 1000,000 live births during 2001-03 mainly among pregnant women and under nourished, malnourished women. Frequent pregnancies, coupled with poor diets result in anaemia and women fall ill more frequently than men, but avail of medical facilities more infrequently. All these result in a reduced life span of women. The most vulnerable groups who suffered from these nutrient deficiencies and their consequences were preschool children, pregnant and lactating women especially in rural area. Pregnancy is crucial stage in women's life from the nutrition point of view. During pregnancy a woman is responsible to provide good nutrition for two individuals. The growing baby gets all its nourishment from its mother through the umbilical cord, so diet is very important. If the mother is lacking in any vitamin and nutrients, her baby might like them too. Women who consumed minimal amounts over the eight week period had a higher mortality or disorder rate concerning their offspring than women who ate regularly, because children born to well-fed mothers had less restriction within the womb. According to World Bank (1993) about one third of the total disease burden in developing country of women between 15-45 years of age is linked to health problems related to pregnancy, child birth, abortion and reproduction tract infection. Not only are physical disorders been linked with poor nutrition before and during pregnancy, but neurological disorders and handicaps are a risk that is run by mothers, who are mal-nourished, a condition which can also lead to the child becoming more susceptible to later degenerative diseases. Poor nutrition that continues into pregnancy and lactation leads to low birth weight (LBW) babies, infant's death, and progressive growth retardation of children. According to the diet survey, there is a shortage of the nourished diet in the women of rural area. In reference of Indian Council of Medical Research the comparison of the figure of pregnant women is very low and irrelevant nutritive rate is very high, which results to a delivery of unhealthy and low weight baby. Consequences of anaemia during pregnancy include increased risk of maternal and infant death, premature delivery and LBW. There is a higher risk for both mother and child if the mother has little education, a poor household and rural residence. Impact of various micronutrient deficiencies in India has second rank for low birth weight baby. Low birth baby include infants born prematurely or with intrauterine growth retardation. Maternal illiteracy and low socio economic status have been shown to be major risk factor for intrauterine growth retardation. Maternal weight, Maternal undernutrition, Maternal body mass Index, are associated with high low birth weight, LBW is associated with poor growth during infancy and childhood and high non communicable disease in adult life.

Micronutrient deficiencies are widespread; more than half of the women in the reproductive age group of 15-45 years suffer from under nutrition, micronutrient deficiencies and are Anaemic having Vitamin A deficiency and Iodine Deficiency. Micronutrient deficiencies are a significant cause of malnutrition and associated ill health throughout the world. This is particularly true in the developing countries like India, deficiency in iodine, iron and vitamin A are known to be especially prevalent and are associated with a range of mild to severe effects. The main dietary deficiencies of nutrients observed to different extent among moderate and severe cases of malnutrition were energy, Vitamin like A, B, B_{12}, and folic acid, riboflavin mineral like iron and calcium and trace metals like Zinc and selenium. *Ministry of Health and Family welfare of India (2000)* reported 25 per cent of pregnant women had knowledge about anaemia. Consequently, anaemia is high among vulnerable group. Given natural biological advantage, similar nutrition and health care should result in a higher proportion of females to males. Pregnant women are deficient of calories and iron which are necessary for them and their offspring. More than 320 million people suffering from iron deficiency- anaemia, prevalence being highest among women and children (40-88 per cent of pregnant women, 60-70 per cent of children, 50 per cent of adolescent girls), seriously affecting the health and productive faculties. The highest concurrent prevalence of two, three, four and five micronutrient deficiencies were of zinc and iron (54.9%); zinc, magnesium and iron (25.6%) zinc, magnesium, iron and folic acid (9.3%) and zinc, magnesium, iron, folic acid and iodine (0.8%). Zinc deficiency is a major public health problem in many developing countries. However, its prevalence is still unknown in most populations. Women of reproductive age in developing countries are highly vulnerable to nutritional deficiencies, including that of zinc. India is one of the major iodine deficiency endemic countries in the world. Iodine deficiency disorder (IDD) exists as a public health problem in India. The prevalence of IDD in the pregnant women, as apparent from urinary iodine excretion (UIE) less than 10 mg/dl, has been found to be 22.9 and 9.5 per cent in the states of Delhi and Himachal Pradesh respectively 12, 13, whereas, in Uttarakhand a median UIE of 9.5 mg/dl was found in adolescent pregnant women indicating the presence of IDD14. Under nutrition occurs due to lack of nutrient perceived from Recommended Dietary Allowance (RDA). It is essential that appropriate diet Recommended Dietary Allowance (RDA) for Indians are evolved, especially as the country is entering an era of dual disease burden of micronutrient and infections on one hand and of obesity on the other. 52.2 per cent of women are suffering from under nutrition in tribal population of Bankura District, West Bengal, India. The data collected by NNMB over a period of time has shown that in spite of phenomenal increase in food production through 'green', 'white' and 'yellow' revolutions, the problem of undernutrition in India continues to be a public health problem. Though severe forms of undernutrition is decreasing considerably, significantly higher proportion of populations suffer from mild to moderate forms of undernutrition. The increase in population size, low literacy level, recurrent drought conditions, increasing unemployment and decreasing household food security status could be contributing of the dilution of the effects of development trickling down to the grass root level. Therefore, there is a need to strengthen the existing nutritional education to rural women. There is sufficient evidence that majority of pregnant women suffer from under nutrition and they have low birth baby. The problem of malnutrition and undernutrition is widely prevalent in India, especially amongst the vulnerable group of population.

Government Interventions

Improvement in the health status of the people has been one of the major thrust areas for the social development programmes of the country. Starting with the Bhore Committee Recommendations 1940, the Government of India has laid foundations of Comprehensive rural health services through the Concept of Public Health Care. In compliance with the National Population Policy, 2000 and National Health Policy, 2002 and the recent Millennium Development Goals in which out of the eight goals three of them are health oriented goals were also kept in the mind as the goal under NRHM as, NRHM address two of the major health problems identified in UN millienum development project. MDGs are eight goals to be achieved by 2015 that respond to the World's main development challenge. India is one of the 189 which was signed by 147 heads of states and Governments during the Un Millennium Summit in September, 2000.

The United Nation's Millennium Development Goals focus on democratically elected Governments of developing countries to acknowledge basic human needs and fundamental rights that every individual should be able to enjoy, such as freedom from extreme poverty, hunger and malnourishment; access to quality education, better health services and improved shelter; opportunity for productive, decent and environment-friendly employment; the right to women for safe delivery without risking their lives; and a world where women and men live in equality and environment sustainability is accorded top priority. The Millennium Development represents the most important promise ever made to the world's most vulnerable people in 2000 and to fulfill it within a period of 15 years i.e. by 2015. The MDG framework for accountability emerged from its Declaration in 2000 has endorsed an unprecedented level of commitment and partnership in rebuilding hassle free and healthier lives for billions of people hitherto neglected and in creating an environment that contributes to inclusive growth, all round development, peace, harmony and security.

The various health programmes introduced by the Government for rural health like Integrated Management of Neonatal and Childhood illnesses (IMNCI), Reproductive Child Health and National Rural Health Mission are all focusing on improving the child and women health. Union Budget 2007-08 emphasizes on the mother and child care and on prevention and treatment of communicable diseases like TB and Malaria. Rural India is infected by communicable diseases which are water borne, vector borne, airborne and by sexual transmission.

National Rural Health Mission (2005-2012)

Since independence Govt. of India has created a vast network of health infrastructure such as sub centers PHCs and Community Health centers with qualified doctor's nurses and paramedical staff. This infrastructure available at different levels of is able to cater 20 per cent of the health care needs of the population while the 80 per cent of the Health care needs are still being provided by the private sector. Against this backdrop the Government of India lunched National Rural Health Mission (NRHM) in April 2005 to provide effective health care to rural population throughout the country with special focus on 18 states, which have week public health infrastructure and very poor performance in respect of demographic and health indicators. These states are Aruanchal Pradesh, Assam, Bihar, Chhattisgrarh, Himachal Pradesh, Jharkhand, J &K, Manipur, Uttarakhand and Uttar Predesh.

The NRHM will cover all villages through approximately 2.5 lakh village based "Accredited Social Health Activities" (ASHA) who would act as link between villagers and health centers. One ASHA will be farmed in every village or cluster of village across 18 states to advise villagers about sanitation, hygiene, contraception and immunization. They also provide primary medical care for diarrhea, minor injuries fever and also escort the patients to medical centers. The Government is committed to invest 5 -6 per cent on Health Services. An amount of Rs. 67 billion was provided in the Budget during 2005-06. A national Health Insurance Scheme has also been launched for BPL families to ensure annual health coverage of RS. 30,000/ for family or an individual. An amount of Rs. 1,00,000/- will be paid to the families of those who die in accident and same amount is paid in case of disability. An amount of Rs. 50,000/- is paid in case of partial disability.

Goal and Strategies of NRHM

1. Reduction in IMR and MMR.
2. Universal access to integrated comprehensive Public Health Services.
3. Child Health, Water, Sanitation and Hygiene.
4. Prevention and control of communicable and non-communicable disease including local endemic diseases.
5. Health plan for each village through village health committee of GP.
6. Train and hence capacity of PRIs to own, control and manage public health services.
7. More multi-purpose workers to provide health care services.

8. Preferences of district health plan and its implementation.
9. Integrating vertical health and family welfare programmes at national, state district and block level.

Sub Health Centres

It is the first contact point between the community and public Health System manned by an ANM (Auxiliary Nurse Midwife) and a male health worker. Each sub health center covers a population of 3000-5000. There is a provision of Rs. 10000/- fund per year to each Sub centre. Availability and flexibility in utilizing the fund for improving the services as per local; needs will empower the ANM and PRI (Panchayati Raj Instutions). Sub- Centers are assigned tasks relating to interpersonal communication in order to bring about behavioral change and provide services in relation to maternal and child health, family welfare, nutrition, immunization and control of communicable diseases programmes. The sub-Centers are provided with basic drugs for minor ailments needed for taking care of essential health needs of men, women and children. There are 1,45,272 sub Centers functioning in the country as on March 2007.

Community Health Centre: the NRHM aims at ensuring a functional 30-bedded rural hospital at the CHC level to provide 24 x 7 hr. hospital services with seven medical specialist including a Surgeon, Physician, Gynecologist and Pediatrician supported by 21 paramedical and other staff including 9 staff nurses. It is a referral Unit for 4 PHCs. A CHC covers a population of 9,0000-12,0000. A separate AYUSH set up also is provided in every CHC. The population coverage norms depends upon whether the centre is in a hilly, tribal, difficult area or in the plains. As on March, 2007, there are 4,045 CHCs functioning in the country.

Women Health Volunteers (WHVs)

Also called as the Accredited Social Health Activist (ASHA), a central functionary of NRHM is appointed for every 1000 population. NRHM aims to increase the availability and accessibility to health care by providing over 40,0000

ASHAs and the aim is already at the verge of fulfilling. A female resident preferably the daughter-in- law of the village between the age group of 25-45 years and a minimum of 8th class education is selected as ASHA BY THE VILLAGE Panchayat Health Committee. She will be trained on the job for three weeks spread over a period of 12 months where she will be paid Rs. 50/- per day during her training. She will ensure better access to Universal immunization, safe delivery, newborn care and prevention of water borne and other communicable diseases. She would be given performance-based compensation.

Conclusion

Implementation of NRHM focusing MDGs can effectively be improved by integrating it with Self-Help groups, which are promoted, nurtured and linked with banks to socially, economically and politically empower rural poor, particularly women and lifting them above poverty line through continuous generation of assured income. While designing innovative health insurance products by insurance companies and improvement in infrastructure a continuing process, commitment, dedication and involvement of staff for the cause of rural poor, women and children is a must.

Women Empowerment Through Microfinance and SHGs

It was expected that women will equally benefit along with men. This has been believed by actual development. The ninth plan document recognizes that inspite of development measures and constitutional legal guarantees- women have lagged behind in almost all sectors. In India, the emergence of liberalization and globalization in early 1990's aggravated the problem of women workers in unorganized sectors from bad to worse. The women who were engaged in various self employment activities have lost their livelihood. Despite in tremendous contribution of women to the agriculture sector, their work is considered just an extension of household domain and remains non-monetized. Microfinance is emerging as a powerful instrument for poverty alleviation in the new economy. In India, Microfinance scene is dominated by Self Help Group (SHGs)-Bank Linkage Programme as a cost effective mechanism for providing financial services to the "Unreached Poor" which has been successful not only in meeting financial needs of the rural poor women but also strengthen collective self help capacities of the poor, leading to their empowerment. Rapid progress in SHG formation has now turned into an empowerment movement among women across the country. Economic empowerment results in women's ability to make decisions, increased self confidence, better status in society, role in household etc. Micro finance is necessary to overcome exploitation, create confidence for economic self reliance of the rural poor, particularly among rural women who are mostly invisible in the social structure.

Empowerment can be viewed as a means of creating a social environment in which one can take decisions and make choice either individually or collectively for social transformation. It strengthens the ability by way of acquiring knowledge power and experience. Empowerment is a multi-dimensional social process that helps people gain control over their own lives communities and in their society, by acting on issues that they define as important. Empowerment occurs within sociological psychological economic spheres and at various levels, such as individual, group and community and challenges our assumptions about status quo, asymmetrical power relationship and social dynamics. Empowering women puts the spotlight on education and employment which are an essential element to sustainable development.

Empowerment: Focus on Poor Women

In India, the trickle down effects of macroeconomic policies have failed to resolve the problem of gender inequality. Women have been the wounded section of society and constitute a sizeable segment of the poverty-struck population. Women face gender specific barriers to access education health, employment etc. Micro finance deals with women below the poverty line. Micro loans are available solely and entirely to this target group of women. There are several reason for this: Among the poor , the poor women are most disadvantages – they are characterized by lack of education and access of resources, both of which is required to help them work their way out of poverty and for upward economic and social mobility. The problem is more acute for women in countries like India, despite the fact that women's labour makes a critical contribution to the economy. This is due to the low social status and lack of access to key resources. Evidence shows that groups of women are better customers than men, the better managers of resources. If loans are routed through women benefits of loans are spread wider among the household. Since women's empowerment is the key to socio economic development of the community; bringing women into the mainstream of national development has been a major concern of government. The ministry of rural development has special components for women in its programmes. Funds are earmarked as "Women's component" to ensure flow of adequate resources for the same. Besides Swarnagayanti Grameen Swarazgar Yojona (SGSY), Ministry of Rural Development is implementing other scheme having women's component .They are the Indira Awas Yojona (IAY), National Social Assistance Programme (NSAP), Restructured Rural Sanitation Programme, Accelerated Rural Water Supply programme (ARWSP) the (erstwhile) Integrated Rural Development Programme (IRDP), the (erstwhile) Development of Women and Children in Rural Areas (DWCRA) and the Jowahar Rozgar Yojana (JRY).

Conceptual Framework

Rural development implies increase in per capita income and the achievement of various economic and social attributes of development societies such as increased use of capital, productive activities based on science and technology, expansion of infrastructural facilities, increase in per capita income, expansion of education levels, reduction in mortality and fertility rates etc. rural development makes people stand on their own feet and break away from all structural disabilities which chain them to a static condition in which they have to live in. the problem of development in India is anonymous with the problem of rural development as two third of its population lives in the rural area. Rural development involves raising the socio economic status of rural people on a sustainable basis through optimum utilization of local resources. The essence of rural development is not providing but in promoting rural sector. Thus the life of the rural development should be on self-reliance and in improving the quality of life of rural people. According to World Bank Rural development is a strategy designed to improve the economic and social life of a specific group of people, the rural poor. Rural development implies both on the economic betterment of the people as well as grater social transformation. Rural development in India is essentially an aspect of planned development launched by the Government of India in terms of succession of programmes and strategies formulated in the 5 years plan of Nation development. Thus a point to be stressed in this context is that RD is viewed as an integral aspect of National Development.

Concept and Features of Micro Finance

The term micro finance is of recent origin and is commonly used in addressing issues related to poverty alleviation, financial support to micro entrepreneurs, gender development etc. There is, however, no statutory definition of micro finance. The taskforce on supportitative policy and Regulatory Framework for Microfinance has defined microfinance as "Provision of thrift, credit and other financial services and products of very small amounts to the poor in rural, semi-urban or urban areas for enabling them to raise their income levels and improve living standards". The term "Micro" literally means "small". But the task force has not defined any amount. However as per Micro Credit Special Cell of the Reserve Bank Of India, the borrowal amounts upto the limit of Rs. 25000/- could be considered as micro credit products and this amount could be gradually increased up to Rs. 40000/- over a period of time which roughly equals to $500 – a standard for South Asia as per international perceptions. The term micro finance sometimes is used interchangeably with the term micro credit. However while micro credit refers to purveyance of loans in small quantities, the term microfinance has a broader meaning covering in its ambit other financial services like saving, insurance etc. as well. The mantra "Microfinance" is banking through groups. The essential features of the approach are to provide financial services through the groups of individuals, formed either in joint liability or co-obligation mode. The other dimensions of the microfinance approach are:

1. Savings/Thrift precedes credit
2. Credit is linked with savings/thrift
3. Absence of subsidies
4. Group plays an important role in credit appraisal, monitoring and recovery.

Basically groups can be of two types which are:

1. **Self Help Groups (SHGs):** The group in this case does financial intermediation on behalf of the formal institution. This is the predominant model followed in India.
2. **Grameen Groups:** In this model, financial assistance is provided to the individual in a group by the formal institution on the strength of group's assurance. In other words, individual loans are provided on the strength of joint liability/co obligation. This microfinance model was initiated by Bangladesh Grameen Bank and is being used by some of the Micro Finance Institutions (MFIs) in our country.

The Origin of SHGs

Dismayed by the poor performance of formal institutions in providing financial services to the poorer sections of society the Government of India contemplated in the early eighties to promote another apex bank to take care of the financial needs of the poor, informal sector and rural areas. During this time, NABARD initiated a search for alternative methods to fulfill the financial needs of the rural poor and informal sector. The decline of cooperatives in the sixties and seventies is widely attributed to the government's direct promotional role, their artificial propping up through subsidies and undue interference in management. As a result, NABARD wanted to develop a new channel to reach the poor free from government subsidies and interference. Simultaneously during this period, development workers across the country also began targeting "groups" of the poor and disadvantaged as a bulwark against social inequities. The consequent social capital was the only capital that the poor could rely on and use (not without cost) as a hedge against their resource deficient condition and powerlessness. Despite the decline of the cooperatives, the search for an appropriate community-based structure continued and women's groups called self-help groups (SHGs) emerged in the late eighties and the early nineties around rotating mutual savings and credit, as a stable and viable alternative. It was a development innovation in its own right. In fact, According to the views of MYRADA, an NGO engaged in the promotion of the SHG movement in the late eighties, SHGs were the "real cooperatives" needed to replace the existing inefficient ones that were failing due to excessive government interference. Thus as a result, by 1986 MYRADA formed about 300 SHGs which it called Credit Management Groups. To ensure that these groups remained independent over their own decision making, MYRADA designed the group structures to ensure that:

(a) all decisions would made within the group; hence, even decisions related to savings and loans intervention in society would be made by the group;

(b) decisions would also be made in a transparent and participatory manner;

(c) the management of credit rather than the mere provision of credit would be the empowering tool – hence the groups would be more participative (inclusive) rather than representative in nature and lastly, the groups would be externally facilitated but linked by internal relationships and common/shared social features (homogeneity, affinity).

Thus, in its search for alternative channels to reach the un-reachable, NABARD found SHGs an interesting and effective means to provide banking services to 'so called' 'un-bankable' people and as a result, initiated an experiment with MYRADA on SHG lending. Encouraged by the results, NABARD initiated a pilot project of SHG bank linkage in 1992. Overtime, this form of financial provision to SHGs became a regular banking programme and an important component of priority sector lending. Since then, the growth of bank linkage has been phenomenal. The number of groups linked has doubled every year for about a decade and the loan amount has doubled every year for more than a decade.

Self Help Groups [SHG]

Self Help Group (SHG) is a small voluntary association of usually not exceeding 15 to 20 local people who are financially weak and from the same socio economic background. They come together for the purpose of solving their common problems through self help and mutual help who do not have access to formal financial institutions. The SHG promotes small saving among its member and which are kept in a bank. The SHG provides saving mechanism which suits the needs of the members. It also provides the cost effective delivery mechanism for small credits for its members. The SHGs significantly contribute to the empowerment of the poor. The SHGs are the platform or forum to the members to come together for emergency, disaster, social reasons, economic support to each other have ease of conversation, social interaction and economic interactions. The major objective of SHGs are: To save their income, avail the loan from the common fund of the group, create confidence and capability of the members, help the members by collective decision making, motivate the members by taking up of the social responsibilities, to discuss the women related issues, dowry, health related like HIV/AIDS, etc.

Self Help Groups in India

It is probably the world's largest and most successful micro-finance programme for the rural poor outstanding for its emphasis on self on self-reliance and local autonomy of the very poor. NABARD proposes to reach 100 million of India's rural poor with saving and credit by 2008. NABARD has brought out a publication on some basic data on SHGs (NABARD, 1999-2000). According to this, the number of SHGs availing credit has increased from 3,841 in 1997 to 81,780 in 2000. The total number of SHGs linked to the banks stand at

1,14,755 in March 2000. Eighty five per cent of them are women groups. The number of financial institutions extending credit to SHGs has increased from 120 in 1997 to 266 in 2000. Out of the 266 financial institutions, 27,13,165 and 61 are public, private, regional, rural and cooperative banks respectively. These SHGs are operating in 362 districts of 24 states and Union Territories. The number of NGOs dealing with the SHGs has increased from 220 in 1997 to 718 in 2000. Bank loan to these groups has increased from Rs.118 millions in 1997 to Rs.1,930 millions in 2000. The number of families assisted increased from 0.15 million in 1997 to 1.90 millions in 2000. The achievement of rural microfinance during 2004-05 according to NABARD is given below:

Credit Operations

1. Short term credit limits sanctioned during 2004-05:
   (a) For Scheduled Commercial Banks [SCBs], RRBs seasonal agricultural operations-Rs. 101.85 bn.
   (b) *For RRBs:* Other than seasonal agricultural operatiobnns-Rs. 2.17 bn.
   (c) *For SCBs:* Financing Weaver's Cooperative Societies. Rs. 3.49 bn.
2. Long term loans sanctioned to seven state Governments for contributing to the share capital; of cooperative credit institutions aggregating Rs. 329 bn.
3. Liquidity support to SCBs Rs. 19.14 bn.
4. Liquidity support to RRBs: 1.58 bn.
5. Investment Credit to CBs, SCARDBs, SCBs, RRBs and other eligible institutions Rs. 7605 bn.

Why Self-Help Groups

1. **Access to Credit**: the poor have limited access to credit. The poorest of poor have little access to formal credit. Informal credit too is not easily available to such people because of their status. Even if it is available, it is prohibitively costly so much so that it is availed only in life threatening situations. By joining a group people

become stronger in dealing with formal institutions and accessing credit. In most of the groups, access to economic resources has been powerful motivators.

2. **Lender of the Last Resort:** the formal credit structure does not recognize credit needs that are emergent or that are necessary, if they are not for productive purposes. The emergencies that befall ones life countless. The poorer one is, the more is the available. Unless a person's emergent needs are met they would not undertaken productive efforts. If a system exists that takes care of consumption loans. Subsequently a shift is seen towards productive loans.
3. **Equality:** the poor have always been made to feel poorer and unequal and decisions regarding his recourses needs are taken by the "wise" and "elite". They feel helpless before the educated and capable, running the formal and informal socio economic systems. Only in SHGs these treated as equals. For the first time perhaps in their life, they enjoy such equal treatment. This sense of equality attracts people to SHGs where they can have access to resources with their "self-worth".
4. **Improved Loan recovery:** The peer pressure based on joint liability brings about a remarkable improvement in loan recoveries, leading to improved loan recycling and continues access of borrowing.

Definition of Self-Help Groups

1. **Purpose:** Its express, primarily purpose is to provide help and support for its members in dealing with their problems and in improving their psychological functioning and effectiveness.
2. **Origin and Sanction:** Its origin and sanction for existence rest with the members of the groups themselves, rather than with some external agency or authority.
3. **Source of Help:** It relies upon its own member's efforts, skills, knowledge and concern as its primary source of help, with the structure of the relationship between

members being one of peers, so far as help giving and support are concerned.

4. **Composition:** it is generally composed of members who share a common core of life experience and problems.
5. **Control:** its structure and mode of operation are under the control of members although they may, in turn, draw upon professional guidance and various theoretical and philosophical frameworks.

Aims and Objectives of SHGs in General:

1. Micro-finance/SHGs especially important for women and households headed by women, who often have difficulty in getting credit.
2. Micro- finance intuitions locally mobilize voluntary saving the households as an enterprise gets benefit.
3. Micro-finance programmes, which build social capital, can indeed make significant contributions of women's empowerment.
4. SHGs have emerged as alternative development strategy to promote the common interest of the weak and the vulnerable sections of the society.
5. The key strength of micro-finance programme is the knowledge that loans will be available in time of need, making it possible for households to dispense with less effective and less desirable strategies like child labour.
6. Ability to turn individual's problems into collective one.
7. Develop human dimension of sharing.

The Four-in-one Role of SHGs

1. **A moneylender:** Providing quickly small emergent loan but without charging exploitative rate of interest.
2. **A development Bank:** Providing small production and investment credit to the poor for their economic upliftment but without going through the long procedures, documentation, security requirements etc. and at lesser transaction cost.

3. **A Cooperative:** following participative approach and joint pressure, without the ills of selfish interest, interference of the big brothers/Government department officials etc. and with a lot of flexibility
4. **A Voluntary agency**: helping each other through their common and social upliftment among the poor people.

Features of SHG

The SHG have special features with cooperative philosophy which are discussed below:

1. **Homogeneous membership**: As far as possible, the membership of an SHG may comprise people from comparable socio-economic background. Though difficult to define in clear terms, a major indicator of homogeneity in membership is absence of conflicting interests among members.
2. **No discrimination**: There should not be any discrimination among members based on caste, religion or political affiliations.
3. **Small Membership:** ideally, the group size may be between 15 and 20 that the members are participative in all activities of the SHG. In a smaller group, members get opportunities of the SHG. In a smaller group, members get opportunity to speak openly and freely. However, the membership may not be too small that its financial transactions turn out to be insignificant.
4. **Attendance:** total participation in regular group meeting lends strength to the effectiveness of SHGs. To achieve this, the SHGs should p[lace strong emphasis on regular attendance in the group meetings.
5. **Transparency in functioning:** it is important that all financial and non-financial transactions are transparent in an SHG. This promotes trust, mutual faith and confidence among its members. Maintenance of books of accounts as also other records like the minutes book, attendance register, etc. are important.

6. **Set of Byelaws**: the SHG may discuss and finalize a set of byelaw, indicating rules and regulations for the SHGs functioning and also roles and responsibilities of members. It is better to have a written set of byelaw. The self help promoting institutions and bank may guide the SHGs in this.
7. **Thrift:** the habit of thrift is fundamental of the SHG and helps in building up a strong common fund.
8. **Utilization saving for loaning:** once an SHG has accumulated sizable amount in the form of saving say for a period of about 3-6 months, the members may be allowed to avail loans against their saving for emergent consumption and supplementary income generating credit needs.

Women's Movement Through SHGs

Throughout history women have collectively struggled against direct and indirect barriers to their self-development and their full social, political and economic participation. The history of the women's movement is usually dated to the social reform movements of the 19th century and when campaigns for the betterment of the conditions of women's lives were taken up, initially by men. By the end of the century women had begun to organize themselves. Gradually they took up a number of causes such as education, conditions of women's work and so on. The women's organizations started struggle for women's rights in the early part of the twentieth century. At present women movement has influenced policy and planning of the government for development empowerment. The activism within the movement has influenced policy and planning of the Government for development and empowerment. Women's movement in general are directed by objectives like promote better understanding of the process of social, technological and environmental changes, to contribute to the pursuit of human rights and to develop alternative concept, approach and strategies to bring out necessary with autonomy, freedom and full rights of citizens.

Process of SHGs

It is probably the world's largest and most successful micro-finance programme for the rural poor outstanding for its emphasis on self on self-reliance and local autonomy of the very poor. NABARD proposes to reach 100 million of India's rural poor with saving and credit by 2008. NABARD has brought out a publication on some basic data on SHGs (NABARD, 1999-2000). According to this, the number of SHGs availing credit has increased from 3,841 in 1997 to 81,780 in 2000. The total number of SHGs linked to the banks stand at 1,14,755 in March 2000. Eighty five per cent of them are women groups. The number of financial institutions extending credit to SHGs has increased from 120 in 1997 to 266 in 2000. Out of the 266 financial institutions, 27,13,165 and 61 are public, private, regional, rural and cooperative banks respectively. These SHGs are operating in 362 districts of 24 states and Union Territories. The number of NGOs dealing with the SHGs has increased from 220 in 1997 to 718 in 2000. Bank loan to these groups has increased from Rs.118 millions in 1997 to Rs.1,930 millions in 2000. The number of families assisted increased from 0.15 million in 1997 to 1.90 millions in 2000. Three broad models SHG bank linkages have emerged over the past few years in India.

Impact of SHGs

The formation of SHGs have benefited its members in numerous ways; not only have the assets, incomes and employment opportunities for the women within these SHGs increased considerably over time, but there has also been a significant shift in the use of the loans from personal consumption to their being used for income generating purposes. In addition, members have been able to increase savings and accumulate capital and in so doing, are now more financially stable. This financial security that has been created for SHG members has also improved their risk absorption capacity and has reduced their vulnerability to and dependence on informal money lenders. Furthermore, members capital costs are on the decline and most are now able to finance their household expenditures for primary needs such as food, education and health with ease.

Role of SHGs in Women Empowerment

The Self Help Groups and micro-credit organizations have a long history. In Vietnam, Tontines or Hui with 10-15 members involved in financial activities in cash or in kind have been in existence for generations. In Indonesia, Credit Unions, Fishermen Groups, Village Based Bank like institutions, Irrigation Groups etc. have been in existence since long. In Bangladesh, the success story of Grameen Bank is well known. Other countries like Thailand, Nepal, Srilanka and India have also experienced the role of SHGs in uplifting the socio-economic conditions of rural poor, particularly women. Women are an integral part of every economy. All round development and harmonious growth of a nation would be possible only when women are considered as equal partners in progress with men. However, in most developing countries, women have a low social and economic status. In such countries effective empowerment of women is essential to harness the women labour in the main stream of economic development. Empowerment of women is a holistic concept. It is multi-dimensional in its approach and covers social, political, economic and social aspects. Of all these facets of women's development, economic empowerment is of utmost significance in order to achieve a lasting and sustainable development of society. Self- Help Groups are the voluntary organizations which disburse micro credit to the members and facilitate them to enter into entrepreneurial activities. In India, these Self-Help Groups are promoted by N.G.O.s, banks and co-operatives. The National Bank for Agriculture and Rural Development (NABARD) launched a pilot project for linking SHGs in February, 1992. The Reserve Bank of India advises the commercial banks actively to participate in the linkage Programme. Normally, after six months of existence of SHGs and after collecting a sufficient thrift fund, the Groups approach the link banks (either commercial or co-operative) with its credit plan. The NABARD gives 100 per cent refinance to the Banks on their lending through the SHGs.

Women's Empowerment and Micro Finance: Different Paradigms

Concern with women's access to credit and assumptions about contributions to women's empowerment are not new. From the early 1970s women's movements in a number of countries became increasingly interested in the degree to which women were able to access poverty-focused credit programmes and credit cooperatives. In India organizations like Self- Employed Women's Association (SEWA) among others with origins and affiliations in the Indian labour and women's movements identified credit as a major constraint in their work with informal sector women workers. The problem of women's access to credit was given particular emphasis at the first International Women's Conference in Mexico in 1975 as part of the emerging awareness of the importance of women's productive role both for national economies, and for women's rights. This led to the setting up of the Women's World Banking network and production of manuals for women's credit provision. Other women's organizations world-wide set up credit and savings components both as a way of increasing women's incomes and bringing women together to address wider gender issues. From the mid-1980s there was a mushrooming of donor, government and NGO-sponsored credit programmes in the wake of the 1985 Nairobi women's conference.

The 1980s and 1990s also saw development and rapid expansion of large minimalist poverty-targeted micro-finance institutions and networks like Grameen Bank, ACCION and Finca among others. In these organizations and others evidence of significantly higher female repayment rates led to increasing emphasis on targeting women as an efficiency strategy to increase credit recovery. A number of donors also saw female-targeted financially-sustainable micro-finance as a means of marrying internal demands for increased efficiency because of declining budgets with demands of the increasingly vocal gender lobbies. The trend was further reinforced by the Micro Credit Summit Campaign starting in 1997 which had 'reaching and empowering women' as it's second key goal after poverty reduction. Micro-finance for women has recently been seen as a key strategy in meeting not only Millennium Goal 3 on gender equality, but also poverty Reduction, Health, HIV/AIDS and other goals.

Poverty Reduction Paradigm

The poverty alleviation paradigm underlies many NGO integrated poverty-targeted community development programmes. Poverty alleviation here is defined in broader terms than market incomes to encompass increasing capacities and choices and decreasing the vulnerability of poor people. The main focus of programmes as a whole is on developing sustainable livelihoods, community development and social service provision like literacy, healthcare and infrastructure development. There is not only a concern with reaching the poor, but also the poorest. Policy debates have focused particularly on the importance of small savings and loan provision for consumption as well as production, group formation and the possible justification for some level of subsidy for programmes working with particular client groups or in particular contexts. Some programmes have developed effective methodologies for poverty targeting and/or operating in remote areas. Such strategies have recently become a focus of interest from some donors and also the Micro credit Summit Campaign. Here gender lobbies have argued for targeting women because of higher levels of female poverty and women's responsibility for household well-being. However although gender inequality is recognized as an issue, the focus is on assistance to households and there is a tendency to see gender issues as cultural and hence not subject to outside intervention. Although term 'empowerment' is frequently used in general terms, often synonymous with a multi-dimensional definition of poverty alleviation, the term 'women empowerment' is often considered best avoided as being too controversial and political. The assumption is that increasing women's access to micro-finance will enable women to make a greater contribution to household income and this, together with other interventions to increase household well-being, will translate into improved well-being for women and enable women to bring about wider changes in gender inequality.

Financial Sustainability Paradigm

The financial self-sustainability paradigm (also referred to as the financial systems approach or sustainability approach) underlies the models of microfinance promoted since the mid-1990s by most donor agencies and the Best Practice guidelines promoted in publications by USAID, World Bank, UNDP and CGAP. The ultimate aim is large programmes which are profitable and fully self-supporting in competition with other private sector banking institutions and able to raise funds from international financial markets rather than relying on funds from development agencies. The main target group, despite claims to reach the poorest, is the 'bankable poor': small entrepreneurs and farmers. This emphasis on financial sustainability is seen as necessary to create institutions which reach significant numbers of poor people in the context of declining aid budgets and opposition to welfare and redistribution in macro-economic policy.

Policy discussions have focused particularly on setting of interest rates to cover costs, separation of micro-finance from other interventions to enable separate accounting and Programme expansion to increase outreach and economies of scale, reduction of transaction costs and ways of using groups to decrease costs of delivery. Recent guidelines for CGAP funding and best practice focus on production of a 'financial sustainability index' which charts progress of programmes in covering costs from incomes. Within this paradigm gender lobbies have been able to argue for targeting women on the grounds of high female repayment rates and the need to stimulate women's economic activity as a hitherto underutilized resource for economic growth. They have had some success in ensuring that considerations of female targeting are integrated into conditions of micro-finance delivery and Programme evaluation. Alongside this focus on female targeting, the term 'empowerment' is frequently used in promotional literature. Definitions of empowerment are in individualist terms with the ultimate aim being the expansion of individual choice or capacity for Self-reliance. It is assumed that increasing women's access to micro-finance services will in itself lead to individual economic empowerment through enabling women's decisions about savings and credit use, enabling women to set up micro-enterprise, increasing incomes under their control. It is then assumed that this increased economic empowerment will lead to increased well-being of women and also to social and political empowerment.

These paradigms do not correspond systematically to any one organizational model of micro-finance. Micro-finance providers with the same organizational form e.g. village bank, Grameen model or cooperative model may have very different gender policies and/or emphases and strategies for poverty alleviation. The three paradigms represent different 'discourses' each with its own relatively consistent internal logic in relating aims to policies, based on different underlying understandings of development. They are not only different, but often seen as 'incompatible discourses' in uneasy tension and with continually contested degrees of dominance. In many programmes and donor agencies there is considerable disagreement, lack of communication and/or personal animosity and promoted by different stakeholders within organizations between staff involved in micro-finance (generally firm followers of financial self-sustainability), staff concerned with human development (generally with more sympathy for the poverty alleviation paradigm and emphasizing participation and integrated development) gender lobbies (generally incorporating at least some elements of the feminist empowerment paradigm). What is of concern in current debates is the way in which the use of apparently similar terminology of empowerment, participation and sustainability conceals radical differences in policy priorities.

Although women's empowerment may be a stated aim in the rhetoric of official gender policy and programme promotion, in practice it becomes subsumed in and marginalized by concerns of financial sustainability and/or poverty alleviation.

Micro Finance Instrument for Women's Empowerment

Micro Finance is emerging as a powerful instrument for poverty alleviation in the new economy. In India, micro finance scene is dominated by Self Help Groups (SHGs) – Bank Linkage Programme, aimed at providing a cost effective mechanism for providing financial services to the "unreached poor". Based on the philosophy of peer pressure and group savings as collateral substitute , the SHG programme has been successful in not only in meeting peculiar needs of the rural poor, but also in strengthening collective self-help capacities of the poor at the local level, leading to their empowerment. Micro Finance for the poor and women has received extensive recognition as a strategy for poverty reduction and for economic empowerment. Increasingly in the last five years , there is questioning of whether micro credit is most effective approach to economic empowerment of poorest and, among them, women in particular. Development practitioners in India and developing countries often argue that the exaggerated focus on micro finance as a solution for the poor has led to neglect by the state and public institutions in addressing employment and livelihood needs of the poor. Credit for empowerment is about organizing people, particularly around credit and building capacities to manage money. The focus is on getting the poor to mobilize their own funds, building their capacities and empowering them to leverage external credit. Perception women is that learning to manage money and rotate funds builds women's capacities and confidence to intervene in local governance beyond the limited goals of ensuring access to credit. Further, it combines the goals of financial sustainability with that of creating community owned institutions. Before 1990's, credit schemes for rural women were almost negligible. The concept of women's credit was born on the insistence by women oriented studies that highlighted the discrimination and struggle of women in having the access of credit. However, there is a perceptible gap in financing genuine credit needs of the poor especially women in the rural sector.

There are certain misconception about the poor people that they need loan at subsidized rate of interest on soft terms, they lack education, skill, capacity to save, credit worthiness and therefore are not bankable. Nevertheless the experience of several SHGs reveals that rural poor are actually efficient managers of credit and finance. Availability of timely and adequate credit is essential for them to undertake any economic activity rather than credit subsidy. The Government measures have attempted to help the poor by implementing different poverty alleviation programmes but with little success. Since most of them are target based involving lengthy procedures for loan disbursement, high transaction costs, and lack of supervision and monitoring. Since the credit requirements of the rural poor cannot be adopted on project lending app roach as it is in the case of organized sector, there emerged the need for an informal credit supply through SHGs. The rural poor with the assistance from NGOs have demonstrated their potential for self help to secure economic and financial strength. Various case studies show that there is a positive correlation between credit availability and women's empowerment.

Problem and Challenges

Surveys have shown that many elements contribute to make it more Difficult for women empowerment through micro businesses. These elements are:

1. Lack of knowledge of the market and potential profitability, thus making the choice of business difficult.
2. Inadequate book-keeping.
3. Employment of too many relatives which increases social pressure to share benefits.
4. Setting prices arbitrarily.
5. Lack of capital.

6. High interest rates.
7. Inventory and inflation accounting is never undertaken.
8. Credit policies that can gradually ruin their business (many customers cannot pay cash; on the other hand, suppliers are very harsh towards women).

Other shortcomings includes:

(a) *Burden of meeting:* Time consuming meetings, in particular in programmes based on group lending, and time consuming income generating activities without reduction of traditional responsibilities increase women's work and time burden.

(b) *New Pressures:* By using social capital, in-group lending/group collateral programmes, additional stresses and pressures are introduced, which might increase vulnerability and reflect disempowerment.

(c) *Reinforcement of traditional gender roles:* lack of economic empowerment: Micro finance assists women to perform traditional roles better and women thus remain trapped in low productivity sectors, not moving from the group of survival enterprises to micro-enterprises. There are evidence of men withdrawing their contributions to certain types of household expenditures.

Challenging Economic Empowerment: However impact on incomes is widely variable. Studies which consider income levels find that for the majority of borrowers income increases are small, and in some cases negative. All the evidence suggests that most women invest in existing activities which are low profit and insecure and/or in their husband's activities. In many programmes and contexts it is only in a minority of cases that women can develop lucrative activities of their own through credit and savings alone. It is clear that women's choices about activity and their ability to increase incomes are seriously constrained by gender inequalities in access to other resources for investment, responsibility for household subsistence expenditure, lack of time because of unpaid domestic work and low levels of mobility, constraints on sexuality and sexual violence which limit access to markets in many cultures. These gender constraints are in addition to market constraints on expansion of the informal sector and resource and skill constraints on the ability of poor men as well as women to move up from survival activities to expanding businesses. There are signs, particularly in some urban markets like Harare and Lusaka that the rapid expansion of micro-finance programmes may be contributing to market saturation in 'female' activities and hence declining profits.

Challenging Well Being and Intra Household Relation: There have undoubtedly been women whose status in the household has improved, particularly where they have become successful entrepreneurs. Even where income impacts have been small, or men have used the loan, the fact that micro-finance programmes have thought women worth targeting and women bring an asset into the household may give some women more negotiating power. Savings provide women with a means of building up an asset base. Women themselves also often value the opportunity to be seen to be making a greater contribution to household well-being giving them greater confidence and sense of self-worth. However women's contribution to increased income going into households does not ensure that women necessarily benefit or that there is any challenge to gender inequalities within the household. Women's expenditure patterns may replicate rather than counter gender inequalities and continue to disadvantage girls. Without substitute care for small children, the elderly and disabled, and provision of services to reduce domestic work many programmes reported adverse effects of women's outside work on children and the elderly. Daughters in particular may be withdrawn from school to assist their mothers. Although in some contexts women may be seeking to increase their influence within joint decision-making processes rather than independent control over income, neither of these outcomes can be assumed. Women's perceptions of value and self-worth are not necessarily translated into actual well-being benefits or change in gender relations in the household. Worryingly, in response to women's increased (but still low) incomes evidence indicates that men may be withdrawing more of their own contribution for their own luxury expenditure. Men are often very enthusiastic about women's credit programmes, and other income generation out programmes, for this reason because their wives no longer 'nag' them for money. Small increases in access to income and influence may therefore be at the cost of heavier work loads, increased stress and women's health. Although in many cases women's increased contribution to household well-being has improved domestic relations, in other cases it intensifies tensions.

Challenging Social and Political Empowerment: There have been positive changes in household and community perceptions of women's productive role, as well as changes at the individual level. In societies like Sudan and Bangladesh where women's role has been very circumscribed and women previously had little opportunity to meet women outside their immediate family there have sometimes been significant changes. It is likely that changes at the individual, household and community levels are interlinked and that individual women who gain respect in their households then act as role models for others leading to a wider process of change in community perceptions and male willingness to accept change.

Micro-finance has also been strategically used by some NGOs as an entry point for wider social and political mobilization of women around gender issues. For example SEWA in India, CODEC in Bangladesh and CIPCRE in Cameroon, indicate the potential of micro-finance to form a basis for organization against other issues like domestic violence, male alcohol abuse and dowry. However there is no necessary link between women's individual economic empowerment and/or participation in micro-finance groups and social and political empowerment. These changes are not an automatic consequence of microfinance per se. As noted above, women's increased productive role has also often had it costs. There is no necessary link between women's individual economic empowerment and/or participation in micro-finance groups and social and political empowerment. These changes are not an automatic consequence of microfinance per se. As noted above, women's increased productive role has also often had it costs 21. In most programmes there is little attempt to link micro-finance with wider social and political activity. In the absence of specific measures to encourage this there is little evidence of any significant contribution of micro-finance. Micro-finance groups may put severe strains on women's existing networks if repayment becomes a problem.

There is evidence to the contrary that micro-finance and income-earning may take women away from other social and political activities. The evidence therefore indicates that contributions of micro-finance per se to women's empowerment cannot be assumed and current complacency in this regard is misplaced. In many cases contextual constraints at all levels have prevented women from accessing programmes, increasing or controlling incomes or challenging subordination. Where women are not able to significantly increase incomes under their control or negotiate changes in intra-household and community gender inequalities, women may become dependent on loans to continue in very low-paid occupations with heavier workloads and enjoying little benefit. For some women micro-finance has been positively disempowering, as indicated by some of the cases shown above which are far from isolated examples:

1. Credit (i.e. debt) may lead to severe impoverishment, abandonment and put serious strains on networks with other women.
2. Pressure to save may mean women forgoing their own necessary consumption.
3. The contribution of micro-finance alone appears to be most limited for the poorest and most disadvantaged women.

All the evidence suggests the poorest women are the most likely to be explicitly excluded by programmes and also peer groups where repayment is the prime consideration and/or where the main emphasis of programmes is on existing micro-entrepreneurs. It also suggests that even where they get access to credit they are particularly vulnerable to falling further into debt.

Conclusions and Suggestions

Numerous traditional and informal system of credit that were already in existence before micro finance came into vogue. Viability of micro finance needs to be understood from a dimension that is far broader- in looking at its long-term aspects too .very little attention has been given to empowerment questions or ways in which both empowerment and sustainability aims may be accommodated. Failure to take into account impact on income also has potentially adverse implications for both repayment and outreach, and hence also for financial sustainability. An effort is made here to present some of these aspects to complete the picture.

A conclusion that emerges from this account is that micro finance can contribute to solving the problems of inadequate housing and urban services as an integral part of poverty alleviation programmes. credit requirements of the low income borrower without imposing unbearably high cost of monitoring its The challenge lies in finding the level of flexibility in the credit instrument that could make it match the multiple end use upon the lenders. A promising solution is to provide multipurpose lone or composite credit for income generation, housing improvement and consumption support. Consumption loan is found to be especially important during the gestation period between commencing a new economic activity and deriving positive income. Careful research on demand for financing and savings behavior of the potential borrowers and their participation in determining the mix of multi-purpose loans are essential in making the concept work. The organizations involved in micro credit initiatives should take account of the fact that:

1. Credit is important for development but cannot by itself enable very poor women to overcome their poverty.
2. Making credit available to women does not automatically mean they have control over its use and over any income they might generate from micro enterprises.
3. In situations of chronic poverty it is more important to provide saving services than to offer credit.
4. A useful indicator of the tangible impact of micro credit schemes is the number of additional proposals and demands presented by local villagers to public authorities.

Nevertheless ensuring that the micro-finance sector continues to move forward in relation to gender equality and women's empowerment will require a long-term strategic process of the same order as the one in relation to poverty if gender is not to continue to 'evaporate' in a combination of complacency and resistance within donor agencies and the micro-finance sector. This will involve:

1. Ongoing exchange of experience and innovation between practitioners.
2. Constant awareness and questioning of 'bad practice'.
3. Lobbying donors for sufficient funding for empowerment strategies.
4. Bringing together the different players in the sector to develop coherent policies and for gender advocacy.

India is the country where a collaborative model between banks, NGOs, MFIs and Women's organizations is furthest advanced. It therefore serves as a good starting point to look at what we know so far about 'Best Practice' in relation to micro-finance for women's empowerment and how different institutions can work together.

It is clear that gender strategies in micro finance need to look beyond just increasing women's access to savings and credit and organizing self help groups to look strategically at how programmes can actively promote gender equality and women's empowerment. Moreover the focus should be on developing a diversified micro finance sector where different type of organizations, NGO, MFIs and formal sector banks all should have gender policies adapted to the needs of their particular target groups/institutional roles and capacities and collaborate and work together to make a significant contribution to gender equality and pro-poor development.

Gender Based Violence Against Women
Government Efforts Against Violence

Violence against Women [VAW] is globally pervasive. It exists in every country, cutting across boundaries of culture, class, caste, education, income, ethnicity and age. These trends are also reflected in the status of women in India. Census data shows that while the sex ratio has risen since the last decade, it is still low at 933, the juvenile sex ratio in India has reached an all time low of 927. Census data 2001, official statistics from the National Crimes Record Bureau [NCRB] reveals a trend of rising crimes Record Bureau [NCRB] reveals a trend of rising crimes against women. Cultural practices in India such as dowry, child marriage, sati, the Devadasi tradition and ill treatment of widows enhance girls and women's vulnerability to the experience of violence. Gender differential treatment related to nutrition, health care, education, mobility and other life opportunities places girls and women at a higher risk of gender violation.

Violence against women continues to be unabated. According to present official statistic there are more than 9000 women killed in dowry related crimes in India every year. Thousands of others commit suicide or die accidental deaths, there are 337 cases of Crimes against Women [CAW] are reported in India every day and 42 women are raped daily out of this one-fourth of the rape victims are children. Apart from this every hour 5 women face cruelty at home by husbands and his relatives. Despite stringent laws Justice is a distant dream for most victims. National Crime Records Bureau has indicated that the incidence of rape cases and dowry deaths during 2007 increased by 8.9 per cent. Further statistics reveal that 71 per cent of all rape cases were reported in five states and one Union Territory-Maharashtra, Madhya Pradesh, West Bengal, Andhra Pradesh, Uttar Pradesh and Delhi.

A Global Concern

Gender based violence has emerged as a global issue crossing the regional, social, cultural and economic boundaries of the countries. According to state statistics, about 18 per cent of women are being sexually abused in U.S. as per the U.N. Report the other developed countries like Denmark, Germany, U.K., Switzerland and other could not provide the accurate statistics. In U.S. the Department of Justice reported that every year 3-4 million women are battered by their husbands or partners. Six well designed studies from the U.S. suggest that between one in five and one in seven, U.S. women will be the victims of a completed rape in her lifetime. The U.S. is in consistence with studies of rape in other parts of the World.

Type of Violence Against Women

1. **Drug Related:** drugs and alcohol are positively correlated with crime and VAW. Alcoholism raises violence and consequently family disintegration. Even there are some incidents where the father raped his daughter under the influence of alcohol. The most common form of violence world is wife battering, which is the direct result of alcoholism.

2. **Rape and Custodial Rape:** One of the most heinous crimes against women is that men violate their right not to be subjected to torture or other cruel in human or degrading treatment or punishment. The whole identity

of the women is thus distorted. In most cases the victims are branded as women of loose morals. The life of the victims is also endangered in some of the cases. Custodial rape is extremely heinous, especially since the offender are supposed to be guardians of law. Most often when the abuser is a male member of the family, pressure from other family members or even the community members in the name of "Family Honor" is the main consideration. In such cases there is virtually a conspiracy of silence.

3. **Harassment at workplace/Eve-Teasing:** Harassment at workplace is real. Pervasive jokes with sexual undertones, obscene behavior with sexual overtures and direct sexual harassment all of them combine to make the atmosphere in the work-place unhealthy and discriminator to women. It seriously affects women's psychological and physical well being. Eve-teasing is a crime committed in crowed areas in the cities. The public transport is one of the commonest places of its occurrence, it is also frequent in public parks, places of worship, tourists spots etc. it is not only a legal problem but also a socio-physiological problem. It hampers the freedom of women.
4. **Dowry related violence:** the trends of dowry related violence is on the rise. Earlier, dowry was accepted as a compensation for the girl who would be deprived of a share in her parental property. Now a day it has become a practice to demand dowry and at times it leads to bride burning and harassment to innocent girl.
5. **Domestic Violence:** the most alarming and yet under reported crime against women is domestic violence. It crosses all barriers of class, income, race, culture and religion. It is the great obstacle to gender equality and securing the rights of women. SAHELI, a Delhi based women's organisation has reported that wife-beating is common among all social classes. However, the pattern of violence varies from one class to other. The whole neighbourhood witness when a slum dweller beat his wife while it is extremely of private nature is a middle class professional tortures his wife.

The Life Cycle of Violence Against Women

Women are more likely to be physically assaulted or murdered by someone they know, often a family member or intimate partner. They are also at greater risk of being sexually assaulted or exploited, either in childhood, adolescence, or as adults. Women are vulnerable to different types of violence at different moments in their lives. Following diagram shows the life cycle violence against women.

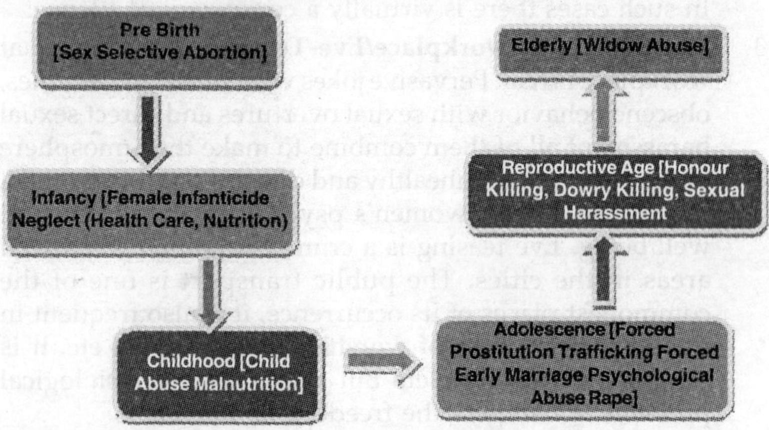

Gender Based and Family Based Violence

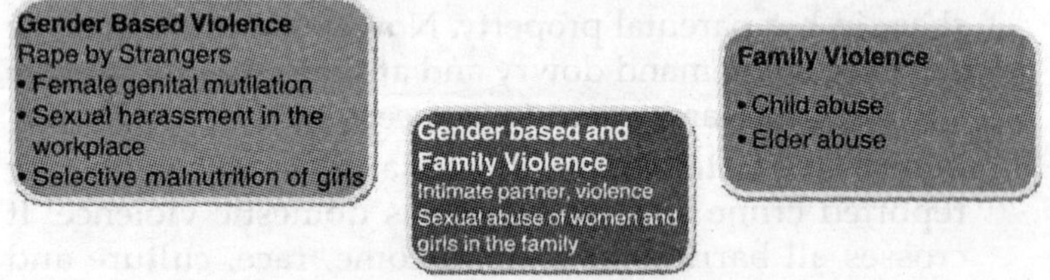

Government Support System Against Domestic Violence

Certain proposed amendments are being considered by the relevant ministries, suggestions are being made on the matter of making penalties for crimes more stringent. Sensitization of law enforcement personnel and policy makers is being carried through initiatives by the Government and Voluntary sectors. Special Police cells and Police Stations managed by Women have been set up in an early 14 states for encouraging women to report cases of violence against them. Helpline services for distressed women have been set up in many states. A national centre for gender training and research has been established in Mussoorie for Gender Sensitization of young administrators and policy makers.

Indian has actively participated in drafting a Regional Convention on Prevention and Combating Trafficking in Women and Children for Prostitution to check cross border trafficking through proper intergovernmental coordination by the SAARC member countries. A plan of action to combat trafficking and commercial sexual exploitation of women and children has been finalized by the Government. The progress of its implementation in the states and Union territories is being monitored by the Central Advisory Committee.

1. **National Commission for Women (NCW) 1992:** NCW which came into being in 1992, has made serious efforts to oversee the working of the constitutional and legal safeguards for women. The commission's mandated role and activities include a review of laws, as well as looking into specific complaints of atrocities, denial of rights and harassment and exploitation of women with a view to taking remedial action and assisting and resorting their legitimate rights. It has undertaken a review of 39 laws relating to women. State Commission for Women have been set up in as many as 16 states and Union territories, the latest being A.P. Several states have been involved in the formulating and implementing respective state policies for women.
2. **Women's Development Bureau:** Department of Women and Child Development (DWCD) is reviewing four laws which it administrators with a view to making their provisions more stringent and removing any loopholes. These laws are The Dowry Prohibition Act [1961], Indecent Representation of Women [Prohibition] Act [1986], The Commission of Sati [Prevention] Act [1987] and The Immoral Traffic [Prevention] Act [1956].

3. **Beijing Platform For Action (PFA):** The Indian Government while presenting its country report in the 4th World Conference on Women at Beijing in 1995 had recognized VAW [Violence against Women] as one of the eleven critical areas of concern. PFA defined the VAW as an act of gender based violence that results in or is likely to result in physical, sexual or psychological harms of suffering to women, including threats of such acts coercion or arbitrary deprivation of liberty whether occurring in public or private life. India will continue to meet the commitments at Beijing. It has ushered in the new millennium by declaring the year 2001 as the year of Women's Empowerment. Six years on the programme of change has taken root, the promise made have been met, though not in full measure. But the struggle for gender justice will continue.
4. **Protection of Women from Domestic Violence Act 2005:** It was brought into force by the Indian government from October 26, 2006. The Act was passed by the Parliament in August 2005 and assented to by the President on 13 September 2005. This act included following rights:
   - *(a)* **Right to obtain assistance and protection**: A woman who is victimized by acts of *domestic violence* will have the right to obtain the services and assistance of Police Officers, Protection Officers, Service Providers, Shelter Homes and medical establishments as well as the right to simultaneously file her own complaint under Section 498 A of the Indian Penal Code for matrimonial cruelty.
   - *(b)* **Right to issuance of Orders**: She can get the following orders issued in her favour through the courts once the offence of *domestic violence* is prima facie established.

Protection Orders: The court can pass a protection order to prevent the accused from aiding or committing an act of *domestic violence*, entering the workplace, school or other places frequented by the aggrieved person, establishing any kind of communication with her, alienating any assets used by both parties, causing violence to her relatives or doing any other act specified in the Protection order.

Residence Orders: This order ensures that the aggrieved person is not dispossessed, her possessions not disturbed, the shared household is not alienated or disposed off, she is provided an alternative accommodation by the Respondent if she so requires, the Respondent is removed from the shared household and he and his relatives are barred from entering the area allotted to her. However, an order to remove oneself from the shared household cannot be passed against any woman.

Monetary Relief: The Respondent can be made accountable for all expenses incurred and losses suffered by the aggrieved person and her child due to the infliction of *domestic violence*. Such relief may include loss of earnings, medical expenses, loss or damage to property, and payments towards maintenance of the aggrieved person and her children.

Custody Orders: This order grants temporary custody of any child or children to the aggrieved person or any person making an application on her behalf. It may make arrangements for visit of such child or children by the Respondent or may disallow such visit if it is harmful to the interests of the child or children.

Compensation Orders: The Respondent may be directed to pay compensation and damages for injuries caused to the aggrieved person as a result of the acts of *domestic violence* by the Respondent. Such injuries may also include mental torture and emotional distressed caused to her.

Interim and Ex parte Orders: Such orders may be passed if it is deemed just and proper upon commission of an act of *domestic violence* or likelihood of such commission by the Respondent. Such orders are passed on the basis of an affidavit of the aggrieved person against the Respondent.

(c) **Right to obtain relief granted by other suits and legal proceedings**: The aggrieved person will be entitled to obtain relief granted by other suits and legal proceedings initiated before a civil court, family court or a criminal court.

5. **Family Courts Act 1984:** The need to establish the Family Courts was first emphasized by the late Smt. Durgabai Deshmukh. A Family Court may receive as evidence any report, statement, documents, information or matter that may, in its opinion, assist it to deal effectually with a dispute, whether or not the same would be otherwise relevant or admissible under the Indian Evidence Act, 1872. These family courts at Delhi are equipped with counselors and psychologists who ensure that the disputes are handled by experts who do not forget that while there may be core legal issues to be dealt with; there is also a human and psychological dimension to be dealt with in these matters. The role of the counselors is not limited to counseling but extends to reconciliation and mutual settlement wherever deemed feasible. family courts was a dynamic step so far as reducing the backlog and disposing of cases while ensuring that there is an effective delivery of justice goes.

6. **Support System:** Support System have been devised to protect and provide rehabilitation to women. Around 80 protective and juvenile homes have been established by the Government. These provide education and vocational training. The Central Special Welfare Board [CSWB] provides financial support to NGOs which run child development and care centers for the children of sex workers. In some state like West Bengal and Tamil Nadu projects have been sanctioned under the ICDS and Non Formal Education [NFE] for the rehabilitation of the children of sex workers under the social defense scheme. Also the Voluntary Action Bureau [VBB] and Family Counseling Centers [FCC] are providing counseling and rehabilitative services to vulnerable women and children

who are victims of family maladjustments and atrocities. Networking, lobbying and Provision of Welfare services to the victims and their children as well as innovative community sensitization programmes are also being conducted by NGOs on the Girls child. For example, in the Sonagachi area of Calcutta, sex workers formed a committee on their own to protect their and also registered a cooperative to create az source of income. The Government has been making concerted efforts to tackle this widespread problem. On one hand through extensive research and review, it is strengthening the existing legislation and developing new institutional machinery to encourage women to report crimes against them. On the other hand, a network of short stay homes and working women's hostels assisted by the Government has been set up. The *National Advisory Council [NAC]* conducted a programme on Domestic Violence coordinated by the International Centre for Research on Women {ICRW] in December 2000. It helped on drawing attention to the scourge of Domestic Violence against women and the need to have comprehensive legislation that provides effective and immediate protection for Women and Children. A few of the recent studies conducted through the ICRW programme have examined Domestic Violence throughout India and made a compelling case for immediate attention and action.

Violence Against Women
An Analysis in Uttarakhand

Women and Girls are born in to social and cultural system steeped in inequality and discrimination. They receive an unfair shape of opportunities, attentions and resources from the moment of their conception. One of the most inequality is Violence against women and Girls [VAWG]. Violence against women [VAW] is globally pervasive. It exists in every country, cutting across boundaries of culture, class, caste, education, income, ethnicity and age. These trends are also reflected in the status of women in India. Census data shows that while the sex ratio has risen since the last decade, it is still low at 933, the juvenile sex ratio in India has reached an all time low of 927. Census data 2001, official statistics from the National Crimes Reckord Bureau [NCRB] reveals a trend of rising crimes Record Bureau [NCRB] reveals a trend of rising crimes against women. Cultural practices in India such as dowry, child marriage, sati, the Devadasi tradition and ill treatment of widows enhance girls and women's vulnerability to the experience of violence. Gender differential treatment related to nutrition, health care, education, mobility and other life opportunities places girls and women at a higher risk of gender violation.

Objectives

1. To understand the nature and type of torture women come across due to domestic violence.
2. To know the type of family responsibilities that they are forced to take up under such circumstances.
3. To explore the view and opinions of the women members about the type of emotional problems.
4. To suggest some possible solutions domination and power game. However, the crux of the present world order is for mitigation the discrimination and violence against women.

Methodology

The research study was carried out in the Rudrapur block of district Udham Singh Nagar by selecting Gokulnagar, Dinespur and Anandpur, Raghavnagar villages as these were the village whereas in all, 120 rural women constituted the sample of the study. An Interview schedule was used to collect data.

Results and Discussion

All the four villages under study are basically inhabited by poor farmers or agricultural daily laborers and a majority of women respondents [80 per cent] are illiterate and a few of them are little bit literate, about 60 per cent of the families are living below the poverty line.

Manifestation of Voilence Against Women

Women are frequently subjected to physical abuse in all the four sample villages. It is around 56 per cent and two villages cross the average level also. A total of 67 women out of 120 sample experience physical torture in their families, followed by mental torture which is 16.6 per cent of the total. Economic and sexual abuse rank third and fourth respectively. Table 8.1 depicts the type of physical torture the women respondents experience in their families.

Table 8.1: Manifestation of Different Types of Domestic Violence

Name of the Village	Physical Abuse	Mental Abuse	Sexual Abuse	Eco. Abuse	Total
Gokulnagar	18 (60)	6 (20)	4 (13)	2 (6.6)	30
Raghavnagar	16 (53.3)	5 (16.6)	4 (13)	5 (16.6)	30
Anandpur	19 (63.3)	4 (13)	2 (6.6)	5 (16.6)	30
Dineshpur	14 (46.6)	5 (16.6)	6 (20)	5 (16.6)	30
Total	67 (55.8)	20 (16.6)	16 (13.3)	17 (14.16)	120

Women were uniformity subjected to one or more of physical torture which is shown in Table 8.1 slapping and beating by stick is quite common either in the in toxicated state i,e. after consuming country liquor [easily available in the rural areas], or for dowry while demanding money from women to gamble [gambling is rampant in the rural area] or to drink more wine. Around 45 per cent of respondents reported kicking as a form of physical assault other forms of physical torture were burning pouring hot water over body, hitting using physical objects to cause injury, threat of murder at knife point etc.

Table 8.2: Physical Torture Experienced by Women Respondents

Sl. No.	Torture	Respondents	Per cent
1.	Beating by stick	42	62.67
2.	Slapping	50	74.62
3.	Kicking	30	44.77
4.	Burning/Pouring hot water over the body	4	5.97
5.	Using Physical objects to cause injury	10	14.92
6.	Threat of murder at knife point	5	7.46
7.	Hitting	8	11.94

1. A good proportion of respondents narrated that despite physical torture their respective drunkard husband spends their hard earned money in the unwanted and undesirable manner.
2. Majority of the women are psychologically frustrated on account of shame, fear, grief and guilt.
3. With the husband's addition to drinking, majority of women reported grief over loss of prestige, personal dignity, long friendship and finance and the like.
4. In most of the cases the wives are turned to be the case takers of the male counterpart on top of it, while bringing the drunkard husband in very awkward conditions back to the home from public places they had to apologies to others.
5. It is observed that most of the women are not aware of their rights, but very captions about their duties.
6. Housewives reported regarding their fear and nervousness during sexual relationship because they were compelled to it by their drunkard husbands. This nervousness upset the drunkard husband and his sexual pleasure. The agitated husband's in such cases were reported to opt for extra martial for satisfy their urge.

Suggestions

Against this backdrop, it is suggested that the existing legislations for the protection of women should be stringent. Severe punishment should be imposed on those who use the women as the "Disposable commodity". New legislations must be introduced. Improving adult education in the rural areas can sensitize both men and women relating to gender bias.

Conclusion

The problem of women is neither personal nor limited to the community of women but part of a larger socio-economic and political context. Therefore, strategies to curb violence against women must be addressed with in overall framework of reducing violence in society. Violence needs to be confronted at its roots. Reduction of violence against women means righting the economies, cultural, social, educational, legal and political and other bases of inequality. Social institutions, attitudes and practices that perpetuate inequality and reinforce violence against women must change relationship built on equitable balance of power and mutual respect between genders must be fostered.

Empowerment of Rural Women
Concern and Commitment

Empowerment is the act of bestowing power and authority on someone. Women empowerment thus refers to the conferring of leverage to women who are otherwise deprived. This includes granting to women effectual decision-making power, the power to influence others decisions along with economic, social and civil freedom. Women in India have been disadvantaged for ages mainly because they were believed to be and treated as inferior to men. Sadly, a pseudo-empowerment process has been undertaken each time women's welfare was given consideration to. There has been a failure in detecting where the problem is and what empowerment means. In short, female empowerment processes in India are moving at a staggering pace contrary to what the popular belief is. The women, in order to be empowered, firstly need authority at home, which they don't. This doesn't necessitate arresting women empowerment schemes beyond domestic affairs. The process should be carried out concurrently at home and outside. Within the family, they must have equal say as men, so should be the case at work. There are five major components which if ensured would lead to appropriate women empowerment and those are: proper education, social equity and status, improved health, economic or financial stability and political participation. In India, a whopping 56 per cent of the women are illiterate as against a considerably lower 24 per cent in case of men, evincing the palpable inequity. This should be done away with by ensuring increased enrolment of girls in schools initially and then colleges. Educating the girl child is now an order of the government, with the Right to Education act in force which will address the cause of literacy dramatically. This apart adult literacy programmes should be initiated in villages to contribute to the escalation in female literacy.

Elements of Women Empowerment

The most extensive element of women empowerment is providing them with social rank, status and justice. Even today the media flashes reports of dowry deaths, child marriages, and female infanticides. Various forms of women centric crimes constitute a big problem which can be mended with stringent laws in place. Certainly there isn't any dearth of law that protects a woman in India, but the cases of justice being ultimately handed out are limited. India records about 7000 dowry deaths per year. 38 per cent women face torture, 22 per cent molestation and 12 per cent rape in their lifetime. Shockingly, 33 per cent of all crimes against women are committed by family members including husbands. This brings us to domestic violence, an ignominious phenomenon in India that haunts several women in villages, towns and metropolises. A law has however been constituted to tackle this menace which is called 'The prevention of domestic violence act'. The IT-BPO industry, which propelled India's economic surge, boasts of 60 per cent women employees verifying that a rich number of women today get along with computers better than cookery. A good proportion of women in urban India are financially independent. However, financial independence alone does not signify empowerment. Working women who can earn their own living aren't spared of domestic violence; instead this phenomenon is quite prevalent in cities. Surveys conducted by UNICEF show that 45 per cent of men in India have admitted to have physically abused their wives. In NE India, 20 per cent young girls are forced into prostitution, sold to brothels and yet others are trafficked to neighboring nations. Health, they say, is the biggest wealth. UNICEF recently revealed that married women from India are the most anaemic in the world and this has been attributed to low social rank of women and bad quality of food. To talk of the health oriented repercussions of trafficking, there has been a rise in the AIDS count as well.

Gender Inequality

Women have been subject to inequality, gender bias, sexual abuse and much more oppression since many centuries. Women have also been ostracized in the name of 'Family Honour' when we wanted to do things our way. Recently there was a flare on the honour killings that took place in the states of Punjab and Harayana, where the girl of the family was killed if she married against her parents' wishes. The Khap Panchayats justify the killings too! What can justify such a heinous crime? Women have always learnt to keep quiet and be puppets in the hands of men.

But this is just one side of the story. The other side has experienced 'Women Power' in almost all fields. The biggest example that we have in front of us is that of Sudha Narayan Murthy, the Head of Infosys. Then we have Sonia Gandhi, President of the Indian National Congress. We have a very famous activist Medha Patkar who started the '*Narmada Bachao Aandolan*' which was also supported by Aamir Khan. It's not only these big stars that have shined. Just to bring to light again the Jessica Lal murder case which was closed and denied justice; her sister Sabrina Lal had the courage to approach a newspaper like Tehelka and get her sister justice with the help of a journalist. All this shows how women are strong and capable enough to get out of any tough situation themselves. But in our country we still have women and girls bound to the age-old customs and traditions like child marriage and female infanticide. Most of all this happens in the rural interiors of our country where education for girls is forbidden once they reach puberty or sometimes even before that. I think the first step that we should take, collectively, is to start educating ourselves and people around us.

Education

Education is the key factor to the solution to all the problems of women. It gives us the strength to distinguish between what is right and what is wrong and also to stand for ourselves. It's the duty of the mother to teach her sons to respect women, only then will they respect the opposite sex in the future. A strong civic sense comes from what children view around them. If they see their father beating their mother they will definitely feel that women are the weaker sex and so it's okay to oppress them but if they sees that their father is treating the mother equally at all times they will know that women are not weak in any field. So basically portrayal of women in a right way is absolutely essential not only for boys to respect them but also for girls so that they can build a sufficiently good self confidence.

Women in India enjoy the right to elect and get elected. A bill seeking women's reservation in Parliament and State Legislative Assemblies to strengthen the foundation of democracy and governance has yet to see the light of the day. In this context, there is need for concern, commitment and accountability of publicly elected women representatives to empower rural women in particular in the background of international women's movement, Government of India's initiatives to guarantee and protect women's rights and status and ineffective and inefficient law enforcement machinery in India.

Political Participation of Women

The political participation of women is an important facet. Sadly, the representation of women in national politics is only 11 per cent. The parliament has passed a bill that reserves 33 per cent of seats for women in Lok Sabha and all state assemblies in what is termed as a historic bill. This has been perceived by some as vote bank politics as well. Although many nations have taken this route to empower the fairer sex, this is not the best way. In India, where political dynasties are a big thing, there is high possibility that wives and daughters of existent politicians make their way into the parliament. Proxy representation, which the bill allows, deifies a major tenet of empowerment – decision making. Female members of the kin who are likely to gain political seats would be, in most cases, dictated by the male politician whose relative she is, something which has got nothing to do with empowerment of women. While this could be one of the cases, it is believed that the bill is elitist, something that does not befit empowerment of women either, given that India is a nation where the poor and the middle class form the majority of population. The proposed law also insinuates that women are too incapable too progress without reservation, which is very much anti-empowerment in nature since a crucial aspect of empowerment is to instill a strong sense of self confidence in a woman's mind. The impact of suitable female empowerment can be recognized by a statement issued by UNDP which says: India's GDP rate could escalate further if the female employment rate is bolstered.

Women's Rights

It was 1869, when a British MP John Stuart Mill in Parliament emphatically pleaded for women's right to vote and it was the New Zealand, the first country in the world, to give women the right to vote on 19 September 1893. Women in other countries continued to campaign for their equality for years till they got it. In 1910 Ms Clara Zetkin of Germany, in the Copenhagen International Conference of Working Women, proposed celebration of Women's Day every year in every country to press for their demands. The conference of over 100 women from 17 countries resolved to celebrate the International Women's Day [IWD]. While the news for the celebration of the first IWD on 19 March 1911 in Germany was spread throughout the world, two journals viz *"The Vote for Women"* in Germany and *"Women's Day"* in Austria carried articles, *"Women and Parliament"*, *"The Working Women and Municipal Affairs"*, *"What has the housewife got to do with politics"*?, etc which analyzed the question of the equality of women in the Government and society and concluded the absolute necessity to make parliament more democratic by extending the franchise to women. From 1913, the IWD is celebrated on 8 March and the United Nations during the International Women's Year in 1975, officially recognized the IWD to sharply focus on this day serious concerns and achievements of women in fields of Politics, social, economic etc and reflect local and global gender issues. Subsequently women in many countries got the right to get elected too to specifically voice the concern of women.

Women in India

According to studies, women in ancient India enjoyed equal status and rights with men in all fields of life; they were educated; they married at a mature age and were probably free to choose their husbands. European scholars observed in the 19th century Hindu women as *"naturally chaste"* and *"more virtuous"* than other women. During the medieval period, the Indian woman's position in the society deteriorated however. During the British rule many reformers fought for the social and economic upliftment of the women. Traditions such as Sati, Jauhar and Devadasis have been banned. In 1917, the first women's delegation, supported by the Indian National Congress, presented the Secretary of State the charter of demand of women's political rights. The All India Women's Education Conference was held in Pune in 1927. Women played an important part in India's struggle for independence. Women now freely participate in all activities of politics, education, art, culture, media, entertainment, service sector, science and technology etc.

Women-farmer and Agriculture

India has been an agrarian country. Women constitute about 66 per cent of the agricultural work force. Around 48 per cent self-employed farmers are women and 64 per cent of the informal sector work force depending on agriculture is women. Rural women have, since many centuries, been putting in unfathomable, unbearable and inadequately paid joyless drudgery to earn for their families' livelihood and provide food security to country's 1.13 billion people. The plight of most rural women has been pathetic since they have to collect firewood, fetch drinking water, search fodder to feed cattle, work on their meager land to raise crops and as laborers on other farms, take care of children etc. Hunger and deprivation affect about 260 million people in the country. India is a home to 40 per cent of the world's underweight children and ranks 126 out of 177 countries in the UNDP Human Development Index. The country is also the home of the largest number of poor and malnourished people in the world and finding difficult to reduce hunger and poverty by half by 2015 as expected under U.N. MDGs. As many as 40 per cent of the farmers interviewed by the National Sample Survey Organisation said *"they wanted to quit farming if there was another option"*. The average total income of farm households with up to two hectares was less than 80 per cent of their consumption expenditure. Annual average farmer suicides increased from 15,747 [1997-2001] to 17,366 [2002-07]. A report on UN World Food Day released on 16 October 2009 praised China for reducing the number of hungry by 58 million in 10 years through strong State support for small holder farmers but criticized economically liberal India where 30 million people have been added to the ranks of the hungry since mid-1990s. Agricultural policies failed to build capacity among small farmers to grow more and respond to market needs, as a result of which hard hit and sufferers are women-farmer and their children.

Self-Help-Groups

It was only after mid 1990s that most rural women slowly and steadily found opportunity to access credit through efforts of NGOs to form and nurture Self-Help-Groups and then link them to financing banks. Self-Help-Group Linkage Bank programme has covered 3.47 million SHGs and 45.1 million households. More than 90 per cent SHGs comprised women borrowers. Women, despite their unbearable hardships and commitments to their children for food, health and education, have beyond doubt demonstrated their loyalty to financing banks through above 95 per cent repayment of loans. Despite this they have difficulties to get long-term loans and adequate loan of high value.

Savings by SHGs

As many as 41,60,584 SHGs saved sum of Rs. 35.127 billion with banks, showing Rs. 8,443 per SHG. In fact, the actual savings of the groups would be higher as the amounts saved with banks do not reflect the amount of savings of members of SHGs used for internal lending within groups as per the practice currently in vogue. Government and banks should gratefully acknowledge their hard earned savings deposited for nation's economic development.

Elected Women-Representatives

The developed economies of USA and Europe have already demonstrated strict compliance with laws concerning women's rights and status through most effective Law and Order enforcing machinery and efficient judicial system. Since India is expected to emerge as a super economic power the publicly elected women representatives [existing and future] in PRIs, State Legislative Assemblies, Parliament and Rajya Sabha may need to demonstrate serious concern and commitment to strengthen Law and Order enforcing machinery at all levels, make it effective and accountable specifically in respect of following aspects in which cases it has proved to be grossly ineffective.

Weak Enforcement

Although child marriage has been banned since 1860 and the Child Marriage Restraint Act was passed in 1929, it is still a common practice. The worst feature of the child marriage has been the child widows are condemned to a life of great agony, shaving heads, living in isolation and shunned by the society. According to UNICEF's "State of World Children,

2009" report 47 per cent of India's women aged 20 to 24 were married before the prescribed legal age of 18 years, with 56 per cent in rural areas. About 40 per cent of world's child marriages occur in India. The Immoral Traffic [Prevention] Act was passed in 1956, yet cases of immoral trafficking of young girls and women have been increasing. In 1961, Government of India passed the Dowry Prohibition Act. According to a 1997 report, at least 5000 women die each year because of dowry demand. Though all medical tests determining the sex of the child have been banned, India has a high masculine sex ratio. The chief reason is that many girls die before being born or reaching to adulthood. This is attributed to the female infanticide and sex selective abortions. The dowry tradition has been one of the main reasons for sex selective abortion and female infanticide. The Indecent Representation of Women [Prohibition] Act was passed in 1987. However, several incidences of its violation do occur off and on. The Protection of Women Domestic Violence Act [2005] came into force on 26, October 2006. Yet the incidence of domestic violence is higher in lower socio-economic classes. Police records show high incidence of crimes against women. The National Crime Research Bureau in 1998 reported that the growth rate of crimes against women would be higher than population growth rate by 2010. Many cases are not registered with police due to the social stigma attached to rape and molestation cases or inaction on the part of police. Official statistics [1990] showed a dramatic increase in the number of crimes against women related to molestation and sexual harassment at work place. The Supreme Court in 1997 while delivering a landmark judgment against sexual harassment of women in the work place laid down detailed guidelines for prevention and redressal of grievances. The National Commission for Women subsequently elaborated them in to a code of conduct for employers.

Areas of Serious Concern: Women's elected representatives must accord priority to following issues, which have yet not been resolved.

Female-headed Households: According to 1992-93 year data, while only 9.2 per cent of households in India were female-headed, about 35 per cent of the households below poverty line were female-headed.

Land and Property Rights: In most Indian families, women do not own any property in their own names and do not get a share of parental property. Some of the laws discriminate against women, when it comes to land and property rights. Married daughters, when faced with marital harassment, have no residential rights in the ancestral home. Christian women have yet not received equal rights of divorce and succession.

Education: Studies confirm that female literacy has a significant influence in improving social and economic status of women. The female literacy rate is woefully lower than that of male. Compared to boys, far fewer girls are enrolled in schools and many of them are drop out. According to the National Sample Survey data of 1997, only Kerala and Mizoram have approached universal female literacy rate. According to the U.S. Department of Commerce, the chief barriers to female education in India are inadequate school and sanitary facilities, shortage of female teachers and gender bias in curriculum.

Health and Family planning: The average female life expectancy in India is low compared to many countries. In many families, particularly in rural areas the girls and women and mothers face nutritional discrimination within the family and are anaemic and malnourished. The maternal mortality in India is the second highest in the world. The health professionals supervise only 42 per cent of births in the country. Most women deliver with the help from woman in the family who often lack the skills and resources to save mother's life if she is in danger. According to UNDP Human Development Report 1997, 88 per cent of pregnant women [age 15-49 years] were suffering from anaemia. The average woman in rural areas has little or no control over her potential for reproductivity. Women do not have access to safe and self-controlled methods of contraception. The public health system emphasizes permanent methods like sterilization or long-term methods like IUD that do not need follow-up. Sterilization accounts for over 75 per cent of total contraception, with female sterilization accounting for 95 per cent of sterilizations.

Work participation: Though the country has a large percentage of women workers, there is a serious underestimation of women's contribution as workers to nation's economy. There are, however, fewer women in the paid work force than those of men. In rural areas, agriculture and allied sector employed as many as 89.5 per cent of total female labor. Women's average contribution, in overall farm output, is estimated at 55 per cent to 66 per cent of the total labor. According to 1991 World Bank report, women accounted for 94 per cent of total employment in dairy sector. Women contributed 51 per cent of total employment in forest-based small-scale enterprises.

Talaq System: Many Muslim women have questioned the Fundamentalist Leaders' interpretation of women's rights under the Shariat Law and have criticized the Triple Talaq System.

Enabling environment: Enabling environment should be created in rural areas that can facilitate all rural women easy access to fuel, safe drinking water, sanitation, education, insurance, health care, public distribution system. While women-farmers should be enabled to have hassle-free access to credit, inputs, technology and marketing and their non-institutional debt should be redeemed by institutional credit, rural women need to be relieved from joyless drudgery of agricultural task through adequate and planned mechanization of agriculture and assisted to take up non-farm sector income generating activities under the purview of K&VIC, handloom, handicraft, sericulture, coir boards, NABARD, SIDBI, lead bank, DRDA, DIC and service-oriented micro enterprises for which a plethora of schemes and financial assistance are available. What is required is creating awareness among women, improving their technical, managerial and financial skill, capacity building, knowledge management through required training and provision of modern tools and equipment and easy access to credit, technology and marketing services.

Decision-making Process and Position: As per 73rd and 74th Constitution Amendment Acts, all local bodies should reserve one-third of their seats for women. Through PRIs over a million women have enrolled in political life. Women are still under represented in governance as well as decision-making process and positions. Elected women representatives in PRIs need to be intensively trained to develop skill, capacity building and knowledge management that can help them generate adequate confidence to participate effectively in decision-making process as well as occupy decision-making positions.

Nodal Office of NCW: The nodal office of National Commission for Women should be established in each block and district to protect the rights of women, girls and children, voice their issues and concerns and pay undivided attention to monitor the compliance with the existing Laws and establish effective coordination with other related offices.

Women Role as a Entrepreneur: Women Entrepreneurs may be defined as the women or group of women who initiate, organise and co-operate a business enterprise. Government of India has defined women entrepreneurs as an enterprise owned and controlled by a woman having a minimum financial interest of 51 per cent of the capital and giving at least 51 per cent of employment generated in the enterprise to women. The Indian women are no longer treated as show pieces to be kept at home. They are also enjoying the impact of globalisation and making an influence not only on domestic but also on international sphere. Women are doing a wonderful job striking a balance between their house and career. Here are a few: *(The lists consists of no political figure and concentrates only on business leaders and organisational heads).*

1. **Dr. Kiran Mazumdar-Shaw, Chairman & Managing Director of Biocon Ltd.**, who became India's richest woman in 2004, was educated at the Bishop Cotton Girls School and Mount Carmel College in Bangalore. She

founded Biocon India with a capital of Rs. 10,000 in her garage in 1978 – the initial operation was to extract an enzyme from papaya. Her application for loans were turned down by banks then – on three counts – biotechnology was then a new word, thecompany lacked assets, women entrepreneurs were still a rarity. Today, her company is the bigget biopharmaceutical firm in the country.

2. **Ekta Kapoor, creative head of Balaji Telefilms,** is the daughter of Jeetendra and sister of Tushar Kapoor. She has been synonymous with the rage of soap operas in Indian TV, after her most famous venture *'Kyunki Saas Bhi Kabhi Bahu Thi'* which was aired in 2000 on Star plus. Ekta dominates Indian Television.At the 6th Indian Telly Awards 2006,she bagged the Hall Of Fame award for her contributions.
3. **Neelam Dhawan, Managing Director, Microsoft India,** leads Microsoft India. She is a graduate from St. Stephens College in 1980,and also passed out from Delhis Faculty Of Management studies in 1982. Then she was keen on joining FMCG majors like Hindustan Lever and Asian Paints, both companies rejected Dhawan, as they didnot wish to appoint women for marketing and sales.
4. **Naina Lal Kidwai,** was the first Indian woman to graduate from Harvard Business School. Fortune magazine listed Kidwai among the worlds top 50 Corporate Women from 2000 to 2003. According to the Economic times, she is the first woman to head the operations of a foreign bank in India. (HSBC)
5. **Indu Jain,** the multi-faceted lady used to be the Chairman of the Times Group-The most powerful and largest Media house India has known. Indu Jain is known by many different identities such as that of spiritualist, humanist, entrepreneur, an educationalist but most prominently she played the role of the Chairman of Times Group. Indu Jain is the perfect picture of the successful Indian Woman entrepreneur.

6. **Priya Paul**, she has a bachelor's degree specialising in Economics from Wellesley College, USA. She entered her family business and is currently the Chairperson of Park Hotels.
7. **Simone Tata, has been instrumental in changing a small subsidary of Tata Oil Mills** into the largest cosmetic brand in India – LAKME, synonymous today with Indian Fashion. She became a part of Lakme during 1961 and has been responsible for turning the company into one of the biggest brands of fashion in India. At present she is the Chairperson of Trent Limited, a subsidary of Tata Group.
8. **Mallika Srinivasan, currently the Director of TAFE-Tractors and Farm Equipment**, India , was honoured with the title of Businesswoman of the Year during 2006 by the Economic Times. She joined the company in 1986 and has since been responsible for accelerating turnover from 85 crores to 2900 crores within a span of 2 decades.
9. **Preetha Reddy, Managing Director of Apollo Hospitals**, Chennai, one of the largest healthcare conglomerates of India, is one of the pioneer businesswoman of India in the segment of Health Care Industry.
10. **Ranjana Kumar, currently Vigilance Commissioner in Central Vigilance Commission**, after her retirement as the Chairperson of NABARD- National Bank For Agricultural and Rural Development, is a prominent Indian Banker. When the Government of India appointed her as the Chairperson and Managing Director of The Indian Bank, she became the first woman to become head of a public sector bank in India. At that time of her appointment, The Indian Bank was saddled with huge losses and during her tenure she ensured the turn around of The Indian Bank.

Women like these are an inspiration for all other women who strive to achieve great heights in their lives. Taking them as our role models each one of us can be there where they are right now. All we need have is faith in ourselves, confidence and above all a fixed aim that we need work towards.

Women Empowerment and Sustainable Agriculture Development

In a stratified society like ours access and empowerment of different section of the societies are becoming serious concerns and to address it planners, managers, social scientist all over the world have started deliberating and devising way out like anything. In this direction genders issues are dominating over other vulnerable issues like poverty, class conflicts, communities, ethnic issues etc. In ensuring an egalitarian development gender equity still remains as a pertinent question as it has been for the thousands of years of human civilization. Gender issues beyond its epistemological meaning certainly imbibe other components like production relation, access to education, geographical distribution, occupational imperatives, marital system and even physical and physiological weaknesses. The present deliberation will go contextual with the realm of women empowerment in sustainable agriculture development. The sustainability of agriculture development has become a prerogatives to the women's participation moving across the caste, Creed and economic echelons. Our need is to ascertain and assure the areas where women are still far from enjoying the minimum privileges and question of empowerment has been thrown to a very complex, integrated situation the access to resources, institution, decision making process and information etc. are the pertinent question in making the women empowered, confident, and accorded to the mainstream social processes. So, a stepwise discussion will unveil the areas of concerns and the expected redressals therewith: Following are some of the major handicaps in overall development of women and the suggestions to overcome with special reference to agriculture.

Limited Access to Input and Credit

Though women make substantial contributors to agriculture development, their access to the most crucial input credit is limited. Since they are not land owners, the credit flow generally goes in the name of male members (i.e. owners). For promoting women access to farm input & credit, following measures may be taken:

1. Credit flow to rural women could be channeled through credit & thrift societies.
2. Voluntary agencies in each district may be identified which could help in developing women organizations.
3. Credit organizations should simplify the procedures & modalities to suit the educational level of rural women & also organize credit camps in village exclusively for women.
4. Farm women should also be recipient of credit for which possession of assets may not be insisted upon.
5. Existing loaning policies of NABARD need orientation towards women credit eligibility by granting them the status of a producer.

Inadequate Technical Competency

Though women are involved in almost all agricultural operations, yet, they have inadequate technical competency due to their limited exposure to outside world. This has compelled them to follow the age old practices which in turn result in poor work efficiency and drudgery. Training is an important component of HRD which enhances knowledge, skill and attitude. For building technical competency among farm women, specialized need based and skill oriented training should be organized preferably at village level. Some of the priority areas in which women need training are:

1. Conservation and management of natural resources.
2. IPM and INM.
3. Renewable energy sources.
4. Seed production technology.
5. Use of fertilizer.
6. Post-harvest management.

Looking into the importance of conservation and management of natural resources for sustainable development, due emphasis should be given on this aspect and it should be included as an essential feature in all the training programmes organized for farm women. For effective training programmes, following points should be considered:

1. Extension agencies should pursue the family approach to training.
2. Training should be organized at appropriate time specially the preseasonal training.
3. There should be proper followed-up of the programmes and there should be synchronization in time between knowledge and skill transfer and the supply credit and other inputs needed to apply the knowledge.
5. During training, the training institute should identify the active participants and intensive training should be imparted to them so that they can be used as a para-extension workers for dissemination of technical information.

Poor Participation in Decision making

Generally, decision regarding the activities requiring technical competency and money related matters were taken by male members. Since knowledge and economic independence are the parameters of women empowerment enhancing the technical knowledge, skills and building greater involvement in various farm activities.

1. **Poor gender consideration:** Though several technological breakthrough have been observed in the recent past the technologies by the researchers are not tailored to the specific needs of the farm women. With the result, most of the agricultural operations are performed manually and in an unskilled manner which results into greater drudgery on the part of farm women. In order to cater to the technological needs of the farm women, there is need to re-orient the entire research system for which following measures may be taken.:
   (i) In order to make scientific information in agriculture and skill areas more useful, it should be tested and refined keeping in view the different farming situations in socio-cultural milieu. It would lead to women specific technologies.
   (ii) Some of the tasks and operations which women are specifically involved and which are drudgery prone include transplanting, weeding, harvesting, threshing, winnowing etc. Therefore, these require special attention of the farm scientist for evolving relevant technologies or modifying the existing ones.
   (iii) The design, development and testing of agricultural implements and machinery should be undertaken with the active participation of rural women. In this regard with local artisans will be helpful. In essence machinery should be a blessing rather than become a curse.
   (iv) While evolving agricultural technologies; indigenous practices used by women should be paid due attention for blending with the frontier ones for greater adoption. Like research, existing extension systems are also not much oriented towards women folk as reflected by the fact out of the total 88,000 VEWs only about 10 per cent (9000) are female. This has adversely affected the transfer of technology. Most of the extension programmes

are target oriented rather than need based which are formulated without analysing and documenting needs of the farm women. Farm women in India have to be tackled with different kind of extension models because of the fact that they differ with men on various counts, viz. Innovativeness educational level, intellectual ability, flexibility, decision making etc. with this assumption a separate extension strategy needs to be developed for all developmental programmes intended to benefit farm women. Some of the suggestions in this regard are:

(a) Women farmers should be included as the direct clientele in the existing extension systems.

(b) Women development projects should use participatory approach at all stages i.e. in identification of needs, implementation, monitoring and evaluation.

(c) Under T&V system like Kisan Mandal, Mahila Kisan Mandals should be constituted or at least 50 per cent of the women participation in such groups should be assured.

(d) In order to provide effective base for access to services and facilities, women agriculturist should be organised into autonomous groups.

(e) With a view to abreast women with latest agricultural innovations state govt. should initiate: Advance Information Centre for Women at village level.

(f) In order to develop and disseminate appropriate technologies for farm women, there is need to strengthen linkage between various research and extension organisations engaged in transfer of technology.

(g) Female extension personnel should be recruited at various hierarchical levels.

2. **Limited exposure to mass media:** The transfer of technology approach which mainly includes mass media are also not paying due attention towards dissemination of adequate and timely agricultural information to the farm women. Some of the important points in this regards are:
   (i) At present coverage of agricultural programmes on Doordarshan is only 12 per cent of the total telecast time (in Hindi), out of which, the programmes related to women are negligible. Therefore there is utmost need to provide adequate coverage to the programmes related to women, the authorities of mass media may apportion at least 25-30 per cent time to farm technologies/information pin pointed to farm women.
   (ii) A few programmes which are meant for women are telecast at a time, which is not suitable for them. Therefore, the media personnel are required to pay due attention towards timings of the programmes.
   (iii) Though the broadcast of agricultural programmes on AIR is a regular feature, the programmes are monotonous in nature and stereotype. Therefore authorities of AIR should have effective linkage with communication personnel for bringing about the programmes in a variety of ways, viz. use of success stories, experience features etc. that would be more interesting to the listeners.
   (iv) Looking at the low literacy rate of rural women, technical literature developed for them should be in a simple language (preferably in local dialect) with due emphasis on illustrations so that even the neo-literates can make use of it.
   (v) There should be state level co-ordination committee in order to review, monitor and evaluate various programmes being telecast, broadcast and published by the different print media. Feed back and suggestions of the audience/listeners/readers would improve the quality of programmes.

3. **Untapped women potential:** Though women have many inherent capacities like high determination, sense of responsibility, better managerial ability, yet their potential has not been identified by the extension personnel. For example, women are considered as reservoirs of rich traditional wisdom with respect to various agricultural practices. This potential could be explored by the extension scientists and be communicated to the researches for proper moulding of traditional technologies with modern ones. This could certainly help in agricultural production on sustainable basis. Looking to the present status of women in agriculture and their limited access to research and extension services, it is utmost needed to revamp the entire approach towards women farmers to cater to their existing needs emphasizing the future challenges which the country has to face in the coming years. For this, there is no way but to develop the human resources. Hence, empowerment of women is the need of the day, as it is only the surest way of making women as partner's in development and bringing them in the mainstream of development, not only as mere. "Beneficiaries" but also "Contributors". If women are empowered the day is not far away when "Feminization of Agriculture" will be in the offing and the theme "Women Feed the World" will be true in its actual sense. Strategies are the designed and directed actions following a stipulated pathway to accomplish goals. So on the assessed and identified problems following strategic intervention can be suggested.

4. **Short term strategies:** Emphasis in this phase is to fulfill their basic needs through welfare programmes like:
   - *(i)* Literacy programme
   - *(ii)* Family planning programme and health education
   - *(iii)* Nutrition programme for mothers and children
   - *(iv)* Portable water and appropriate fuel for cooking and heating the house

(v) Access to household technology

(vi) Home economic programme

5. **Mid term strategies:** Emphasis is on facilitating their involvement in economic activities and strengthening their economic base for entering in social and political mainstream of the society. Some strategies at this phase are:

   (i) Access to appropriate technology and financial resources

   (ii) Ownership of productive assets

   (iii) Attaining income security through income generating projects

   (iv) Access to communication media to improve their communication and mediation skills

   (v) Access to and prospering of all types of non-formal education like extension and vocational education in order to improve their entrepreneurial skills.

6. **Long term strategies:** Social and political mainstream are important components of empowerment at high level. Some strategies which can be applied at this phase are:

   (i) Enhancing organizational and social leadership skill in community action

   (ii) Building their capacity through collectivization and social political participation.

   (iii) Increasing their negotiation power in action for entailment rights.

   (iv) Increasing their access to political power, policy formulation and strategic gender training programme.

   (v) Establishing organisation or self help groups for their own networking and empowerment through group-building.

   (vi) Providing distance education and correspondence courses.

   (vii) Encouraging socio-cultural changes by exploring gender issues.

7. **Literacy:** Literacy programme is very important in the process of women's empowerment. It is a base for any educational programme. It enables rural women to acquire new knowledge and technology required for improving and developing their tasks in all fields. Literacy helps rural women to bring up their children and carry out the responsibility of motherhood.
8. **Family Planning and Welfare Programme:** Family planning programme and health education are two very important basic needs for empowerment of rural women. In most of the developing countries, rural women suffer from the strain and burden of frequent pregnancies, lack of access to new methods and suitable contraceptives. This is one factor which affect their lives by with drawing them from participating in the process of development.
9. **Non-Formal Education:** Non-Formal Education (NFE) is an effective method of women's empowerment in rural areas. Due to some constrains like lack of sufficient time and higher level of age, it is very difficult to provide formal education to rural women. Therefore, non-formal education is the best vehicle in transferring new knowledge and technology to them NFE for empowerment means people gaining an understanding of and control over social, economic and/ or political forces to improve their standing in society. Some indication of the effect of NFE for empowerment are:
   (i) Increase access to resources
   (ii) Increase collective bargaining power
   (iii) Improved status, self-esteem and cultured identity.
   (iv) Ability to reflect critically and solve problems
   (v) Ability to make choices.
   (vi) Legitimisation of people's demands by officials
   (vii) Self-discipline and ability to work with others.
10. **Extension Programme:** Rural Women would benefit immensely from modern scientific knowledge, technology and skills. Till recent times, agricultural policies and

programmes in most developing countries have generally ignored women's need and concerns as farmers. Only over the last decade, there has been increasing awareness of the extent and significance of women's activities in agriculture. Most developing countries have now started training rural women in new technologies. In spite of recent consideration on launching extension programmes for rural women, some impediments hinder them from reaching extension facilities like:

(i) Illiteracy.

(ii) Financial barriers of govt. and families to invest on women's education.

(iii) Lack of time due to heavy households responsibilities.

(iv) Lack of valid statistics and data about the roles needs and problems of rural women.

(v) Giving less attention to women enterprises by extension and research centres.

(vi) Less number of educated women to take the responsibilities of extension activities (Female, extension workers).

(vii) Social and cultural barriers in some societies in which contact between women with male extension workers is prohibited. There are some appropriate and effective extension educational methods for rural women like.

(viii) Mobile courses instead of farmer's training centre.

(ix) Utilisation of educated girls and widows as female extension workers.

(x) Education of women through negotiation between husband and wife or inter spouse communication.

(xi) Tours and visits organized by women's group or organization (cooperatives etc.).

(xii) Set up extension organisation for rural women like Pakistan, Sri Lanka and Bangladesh.

(xiii) Encourage make extension agents to work with women's group.

(xiv) Post female extensionists in their local areas or close to their husband's workplace.

(xv) Working women extensionists in pairs (husband and wife as extension workers).

(xvi) Encourage and support the establishment of women local groups and organisations to take up responsibility of communicating new science and technology to rural women.

11. **Community Education:** Community education is an integral part of community development and community empowerment is a way by which people involve in-group efforts to identify their problems, analyse their cultural and socio-economic roots of problems, and develop strategies bringing positive change in their lives and in their communities. It is an ongoing process that demands time and continued commitment towards better quality life and justice for community. Community education can uphold there effective involvement of rural women in building community through collective action. This type of education gives them the power to participate in all aspects of community development and be active citizens. This education will also tackle social and cultural barriers which restrict the participation of rural women in social activities.

12. **Adult Education:** Adult education is another type of non-formal education which is an effective strategies intervention for empowerment of women. This will lead the community to have same impression about the necessity of women's empowerment and pay attention to their gender specific needs. Older people have a lifetime experience, knowledge and wisdom to offer to others in their community. In view point, girl's education in some countries where there are social and cultural barriers for educating females, community level work

may help parents understand the value of educating girls. Adults' education classes provide one such opportunity for influencing the thinking of parents.

13. **Access to communication Media:** Access to communication media prepares women for improving their communication and mediation skills to strengthen their capacity to contact and mediate with external world. Consequently, the employment of this skill will prepare the way for transaction of their own experiences, knowledge and work skills with other persons and increase their awareness about the women's rights, allocated facilities, and resources by government or other organisations.
14. **Access to appropriate Technology:** Experience show that the technology can be appropriate for rural women when it has the following characteristics:
    - *(i)* Based on their needs and problems.
    - *(ii)* Cheap, simple and small scale.
    - *(iii)* Harmonise and compatible with local materials, resources and cultures.
    - *(iv)* Locally available skills and knowledge.
    - *(v)* Labour and time saving.
    - *(vi)* Access and control of rural women.

    Due to some implements like, lack of access to land, credit, education, lack of recognition and their contributions to village life, rural women don't have suitable access to and control over new technology.
15. **Access to credit:** One factor hindering rural women's empowerment is their limited access to credit and saving schemes. This problem restricts their access to technology, income generating projects, land possession and allotment of resources required for development. In order to have access to credit setting up self help group local banking system by women, non governmental organisation and provision of facilities by govt. need to be established. SEWA as a women's banking founded by

Mrs. Ela Bhat in Ahmedabad and Indira Mahila Jojna are two successful examples in this direction.

16. **Participation:** Women can be integrated into development process in two ways. Firstly as participants and secondly as beneficiaries of development. Women can be beneficiaries of development, if they are active participants in the development process. They also benefit through greater access to education, employment, improved social services such as health, housing, sanitation and improved technology. Within the development projects, instrumental participation is viewed as a way of achieving certain specific targets; and transformations participation is viewed as an objective itself, and as a means of achieving some higher objective such as self help and or sustainability. Since the goal of empowerment is to meet strategic gender needs proving opportunity for rural women to participate in development programme is not only a way to help community and family but also an occasion for their empowerment.

17. **Work and Empowerment:**
    - *(i)* Farming in a small piece of land
    - *(ii)* Raising livestock
    - *(iii)* Collection of forest produce
    - *(iv)* manufacturing at home or in sheds
    - *(v)* Hawking, vending, trading
    - *(vi)* Providing services
    - *(vii)* Selling manual labour.

    One of the important means of achieving empowerment in the status of women is to promote additional avenues for employment.

18. **Ownership and Control over Resources:** They need to have control over limited resources, like land and livestock, so that they could take away decisions and implement them in any way that is required ownership and control over productive assets will create a sense of

belonging and owning. It will thus help to take responsibility in family and local group activities. Other impact of control is to enhance their decision making ability to meet some physiological needs like self esteem and confidence.

19. **Access to co-operatives and local women's organisation:** Collectivisation has been recognized as a tenant of women's empowerment. It has been defined as a process of bringing a group of women together at a base to become an integral part of an economic activity. Some impact of collectivization on rural women are:
    - *(i)* Bring about new identities inside the group.
    - *(ii)* Facilitating their responsibilities through sharing their information, knowledge, experience-skills, time frames, spaces and other resources like money etc.

Some Suggestions on Empowerment of Rural Women

1. Increasing their access to new information, credit labour, markets and growing sector of economy.
2. Furthering their social and political participation at all levels and overcoming structural barriers to women's full productivity.
3. Increasing govt. assistance for the family unit (child care, health care, F.P.P.)
4. Facilitating the establishment of organizational structures like farmer's group and organizing them gender sensitivity at all level of planning and implementation of development programmes.
5. Increase the economic self-sufficiency of women through self employment.
6. Increase their power of negotiation about redistribution of power resources within households, civil society and the state.
7. Strengthening educational and training programmes for them.

8. Increasing their access to and over appropriate technology that affect on reducing work burden.

Conclusion

Gender sensitivity and systematic approach are two factors important for rural development programme targeted either at women or both women and men. Empowerment is a complicated process, which comprises of short-term and long-term strategy. Under each strategy, several projects need to be formulated and carried out. The process of women empowerment is conceptualized in terms of personal assertions and confidence, ability to project themselves as women, attaining economic independence, ownership of productive assets, ability to handle capital and assets and provide leadership in both women and community related issues at all levels.

Recent ICT Innovations Based Mahatma Gandhi National Rural Employment Guarantee Act

The Mahatma Gandhi National Rural Employment Guarantee Act aims at enhancing the livelihood security of people in rural areas by guaranteeing hundred days of wage-employment in a financial year to a rural household whose adult members volunteer to do unskilled manual work. MGNREGA has a Right based framework, unlike earlier employment generation programmes. Its demand based entitlements stem from the fundamental right "to live with dignity" and sets it apart from other cash conditional transfers, as well as a social safety net, dependent on Government benefaction.

The basic objective of the Act is to enhance livelihood security in rural areas by providing at least 100 days of guaranteed wage employment in a financial year to every household whose adult members volunteer to do unskilled manual labour. It has a bifocal lens as the instrumentality of works generates employment and productive assets. The process of implementation seeks to strengthen decentralized democratic governance, promote equity and empower rural communities. MGNREGA was notified on 2nd February 2006 in 200 districts, extended to additional 130 districts in April

2007 and thereafter notified in the remaining rural areas of the country in April 2008. The Act spans 619 districts, 6400 Blocks, 6 lakh villages and around 2.35 lakh village Panchayats.

Over the last four years, the performance of the Scheme compares favourably with other antipoverty initiatives that India has undertaken. Since its inception, Rs. 101387.6 Crore has been released to States/UTs. The total expenditure was Rs. 98486.46 Crore of which Rs. 66976.91 Crore was given as wages (i.e. 68%). 800 Crore person-days have been generated and the number of works undertaken exceed 45.5.lakhs. More than 50 per cent of the works taken up are related to water conservation.

Measures for Governance Reform and Transparency

A number of measures towards governance reform have been imitated as summarized below:

1. Strengthening administrative systems through additional dedicated personnel.
2. Strengthening the Gram Panchayat (GP) through funds and functionaries.
3. Streamlining financial systems.
4. Opening workers' accounts in banks and Post Offices (About 90 million such accounts have been opened)
5. Intensive monitoring
6. Imitating district Ombudsman
7. Attempting to make social audits more inclusive
8. Setting up a web-based MIS.

The large scale of operations, the limitations of outreach of various services and the need to handle large volumes of information in a transparent manner necessitated the use of ICT in programme delivery. ICT facilities both to support Gram Panchayat and block officer of Programme Officer (PO) as well as public access to information and online transactions are being promoted.

Management Information System

Successful implementation of MGNREGA seriously depends on the establishment and operationalization of a proper computer based Management Information System (MIS) that interconnects all the Gram Panchayats, Blocks, Districts, States and the Union Ministry through an ICT network. A web enabled MIS www.nrega.nic.in has been developed. This makes data transparent and available in the public domain to be equally accessed by all. The village level household data base has internal checks for ensuring consistency and conformity to normative processes. It includes separate pages for approximately 2.5 lakh Gram Panchayats, 6465 Blocks, 619 Districts and 34 States & UTs. The portal places complete transaction level data in public domain for example - Job cards, Demand for work and Muster rolls which is attendance cum payment sheet for worker. All critical parameters get monitored in public domain:

1. Workers' entitlement data and documents such as Registration, job cards, muster rolls Work selection and execution data including, shelf of approved and sanctioned works, work estimates, works under execution, measurement.
2. Employment demanded and provided.
3. Financial indicators such as funds available, funds used, and the disaggregated structure of fund utilizations to assess the amount paid as wages, materials and administrative expenses.

Since the MIS places all critical data on the web and this data is software engineered, it has significant advantages in terms of transparency as it allows cross verification of records and generation of reports on any parameter of the Act. Various stake holders of the project are:

1. Citizen
2. Gram Panchayats, Block Panchayats, Zilla Panchayats
3. Workers
4. Programme officers
5. District Programme Co-ordinators

6. Implementing agencies other than PRIs
7. State RD Departments
8. Ministry of Rural development and administrators in Government of India.

Vision and Objective of the Project

1. NREGA soft envisions implementing e-Governance across State, District and three tiers of Panchayati Raj Institutions.
2. It empowers the common man using the information technology as a facilitator.
3. NREGA soft provides information to citizen in compliance with the right to information Act (RTI Act). It makes available all the documents like Muster Rolls, registration application register, job card/employment register/ muster roll issue register, muster roll receipt register which are hidden from public otherwise.
4. Facilitate faster information exchange between the various stakeholders through the network.

Project Description: Various modules of the software are:

1. Worker Management Module of the software captures Registration, demand for work, work allocation and Muster rolls on which a person worked, the software has the provision of payment of wages through bank/ post office as it captures the bank/post office account number , bank/post office name, branch name for a ll the person who demanded job and their account number are shown in muster toll against their name and calculate unemployment allowance, if any and also keep tracks of number of days of employment of a family.
2. Fund Management Module captures the funds transferred from MoRD/States to Districts and then to Programme officers/Panchayats and expenditure incurred by various implementing agencies on labour, material and contingency. Hence it keeps track of each and every paisa spent under the scheme.

3. Works Management Module captures information about the various works under taken under the scheme at various level (GP, BP, ZP).It facilitates online approval of projects and keeps track of time taken for approval of project. Each project is provided a unique ID and status of work is maintained in the system.
4. Labour Budget allows planning and preparing the labour budget for each Gram Panchayat. The module is so designed that it enables each GP to upload its labour budget which gets consolidated at every level from Block upto the State Level. It captures the details of the works to be taken up in next financial year along with the estimation of the household demanding the works and the persondays. The module is so designed that it is drillable from State to the level of the Gram Panchayat for better monitoring.
5. Social Audit module allows the Gram Panchayat to plan for the social audit and prepare social audit calendar. It has the feature to upload all the issues and minutes of meeting.
6. Workers module (People's Information System) allows the Job card holder to access their information and demand for the work.
7. Grievance redressal system allows a worker/Citizen to lodge complaint and trace the subsequent response.
8. Staffing Position module captures name, telephone numbers etc. of all the officials, planning and implementing agencies from Gram Panchayat to Ministry of Rural Development involved in NREGA, thus strengthening communication and co-ordination among them.
9. Cost Estimation Module makes detailed estimation for the works taken up under NREGA e.g. construction of Tank, Well, Sluice Gate, Earthen road, Cement concrete road etc. This module calculate quantity of work to be done and calculate the per unit rate as per Schedule of

Rates (SOR) for each sub activity of a work. This further helps engineers to fill the Measurement book and calculate wage per day for a particular muster roll.

10. *Alerts:* The software also gives alerts to implementing agencies about the various irregularities, important activities, and messages for funds to be received by the agencies.
11. Knowledge network/ Solution exchange provides a common platform to all stakeholders to exchange their views, pose queries to other stakeholder/Experts and get responses, exhibit their best practices.

Benefits Availed Through NREGA MIS: E-Governance for Masses

1. Computerisation of all NREGA activities
2. All information available for public access
3. Accuracy ensured in payment of wages to workers
4. Lodging of complaints through Grievance Redressal System
5. Facilitation of Social Audit.

Assists Gram Panchayats in NREGA Implementation

1. Tracking of 100 days of employment to a household
2. Generates documents as per NREGA guidelines
3. Tracking of funds from the Ministry to the worker
4. Provides status of available funds in accounts of Panchayats/Blocks/Districts
5. Provides details of unfulfilled demand, works which can be taken up and the unemployment allowance.

Assists Programme Officers and Administrators: Provides strong analysis about programme implementation like:

1. Locations with no registration, no demand for work, no allocation of work, no work in shelf, no on-going work etc.
2. Funds transferred, availability of funds at each level and expenditure on work.

3. Generates Monthly Progress Report (MPR) at Gram Panchayat/Block/District and State level.

MIS Utilizes Information Technology to Meet Challenges

1. NREGAsoft is available in both online and offline mode to meet connectivity barriers.
2. It is unicode enabled and supports all local languages overcoming the language barrier.
3. Software is available in both Microsoft technologies as well as open source technologies.

Mechanism of Data Collection, Compilation and Data Verification

1. All the activities of NREGA are happening at the village level. Panchayat Secretary/Gram Rojgar Sahayak at the Gram Panchayat level are responsible for the record maintenance and account keeping.
2. Stationary like Blank Muster Roll, Cash book, Measurement Book is made available to the Gram Panchayat from the Programme Officer. Blank MR forms goes to the work site where workers mark the attendance. Engineers visit the worksite after the closure of muster roll and do the measurement and fill the Measurement Book. Panchayat secretary maintains the cash book which has details of the amount received and expenditure made on labour and material component.
3. Gram Panchayats where computers are available like West Bengal, Karnataka, Kerala, Himachal Pradesh, Gujarat; the data get entered into the computer which will then be sent by offline/online mechanism to the central server at New Delhi.
4. The Gram Panchayats where computers are not available; the physical records move to Programme Officer office at Block Level where they get digitized and sent to by offline/online mechanism to the central server at New Delhi.
5. The movement of records from Gram Panchayat to Block takes place at a regular interval of 2-3 days.

6. NREGASoft MIS developed for NREGA is a work flow based system. Data entered for any activity cross check/ freezes for the previous activity. Proper checks have been introduced to validate the data entered and stop the wrong entries. For Example:
   (a) For validating the persons on the job card a loose coupling is provided with the Rural Household Survey BPL Census 2002.
   (b) Expenditure cannot be made unless the funds are available with the authority.
   (c) The work can be allocated to a person for a period if he has made a demand in the same period and can appear on the Muster Roll if he/she has been allocated the work within the period of the Muster Roll and his family has not completed 100 days.
   (d) The Job Cards and the Muster Roll are tightly linked that means that every entry in the Muster Roll will have corresponding entry in the Measurement Book.
   (e) Alerts have been raised to indicate the concerned areas so that corrective action can be taken for better implementation of the NREGA.

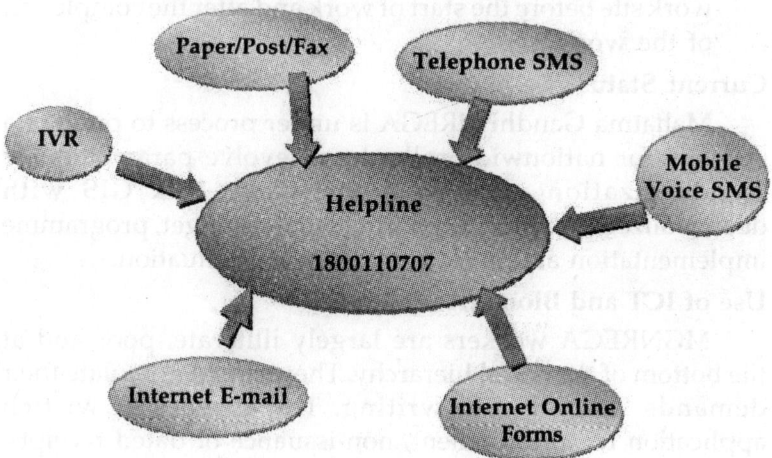

Geographic Information System (GIS), Remote Sensing

The Ministry of Rural Development is planning to take up a GIS project under its ICT Pilot Project initiative. The project is under conceptualization stage. For effective management and assessment of Natural Resources A GIS-based Asset Management System to:

1. Maintain up-to-date inventory of permissible created assets
2. Perform periodic asset assessments & summarize the results using measurement scales
3. Identify soil layers and fertility levels
4. Keep ahead of the maintenance curve

GIS - help to Evolve

1. Appropriate methodology for collection, collation, storage and processing of data on natural resources in a given region and in totality.
2. Standardized formats for natural resources and socio-economic data in an integrated manner to establish linkage among various hierarchical units.
3. To utilize information for planning and development a pilot to be started which will use the remote sensing technology which will be able to capture the status of work site before the start of work and after the completion of the work.

Current Status

Mahatma Gandhi NREGA is under process to prepare a strategy for nationwide rollout and evolve parameters for standardization with an objective to link GIS with decentralized planning, preparing labour budget, programme implementation and asset monitoring & evaluation.

Use of ICT and Biometric Project

MGNREGA workers are largely illiterate, poor and at the bottom of the social hierarchy. They cannot articulate their demands 'formally' in writing. The absence of written application for employment, non-issuance of dated receipts, non-payment of unemployment allowances or compensation for delay in wages are not on account of administrative lapses in record keeping, but reflect the social undercurrents and dynamics that prevent workers from exercising their rights in demanding work from the Gram Panchayat in an equitable manner. The large scale of operations, the limitations of outreach of various services and the need to handle large volumes of information in a transparent manner necessitates the use of ICT in programme delivery. The use of ICT devices and biometrics for authentication will bring in transparency and efficiency. Geared towards real time capture of the processes involved in MGNREGS such as registration, demand of work, issue of dated receipt, allocation of work, attendance at worksite with GPS coordinates, measurement of work, wage payments, etc. it would be instrumental in ensuring transparency and accountability, strengthening MIS reporting and tracking and reducing delays in measurement and payments. The Biometric data will be UIDAI and core banking compliant which may be used by UIDAI to issue the 'Aadhaar' number or by financial institutions for the wage payment in a more transparent manner.

MGNREGA Help Line

1. Department of Rural Development (DRD), Government of India proposes to establish a network of Helplines under MGNREGA at the National, State, District and Block levels for facilitating the redressal of grievances in relation to the implementation of the MGNREGA Scheme. The Helpline consists of a toll free MTNL number (1800110707) that will be used by the MGNREGA households and other individuals and groups to raise their questions, submit their grievances and complaints and seek guidance from the Department of Rural Development.
2. On receipt of the calls, Department of Rural Development intends to resolve the grievances by requesting the field level MGNREGA Authorities to take suitable remedial action and obtain feed-back. Action on each complaint

needs to be ensured and pending complaints need to be closely monitored. The operations will run with the use of latest information and communication technology to provide solutions to complainants on a real time basis.

3. The Helpline consists of a toll free MTNL number (1800110707). The operations will run with the use of latest information and communication technology (ICT) to provide solutions to queries and/or complainants on a real time basis.

Smart Cards, Biometric Scanning For Signatures and Handheld Devices

In view of enormous size of the MGNREGA programme it is necessary to make best use of latest Information and Communication Technologies (ICT). This will not only help in ensuring effective implementation and proper management of the Programme but will also bring transparency and thereby credibility. Since it is a right based programme, Smart Cards / Hand held devices can be used as IT tool to ensure rights and entitlements. Smart Cards have the potential to capture details of the Workers, Work and Wages (WWW) including the muster rolls and the job cards. Many states have started use of smart cards and hand held devices for the wage disbursement like: Tamil Nadu, Karnataka, Andhra Pradesh, Bihar, Orissa, UP, Kerala, etc. To extend the current use of smart cards and hand held devices from wage disbursement to make it operate like a Job card so that all transactions of MGNREGA programme be captured, like: registration, Job card, demand for work, issue of dated receipt, allotment of work, entry into muster roll like attendance from the field through hand held devices which will be able to record latitude and longitude of the area, ensuring presence of worker at the worksite and payment either through 'branch-less banking' by adopting the Business Correspondent Model and using biometric based technology or through low cost ATMs. Smart card and hand held devices will have additional advantage of capturing delays. All transactions will be updated instantly in the MIS and accessible to the beneficiaries as well as the public. It will also enhance the management and monitoring of the Programme. The pilot project is initiated in States like Andhra Pradesh, Kerala, Uttar Pradesh, Bihar and Orissa.

Low cost ATM for Wage Disbursement with Finger Print Authentication and Local Language Interface

ICTs can be fruitfully deployed to ensure that the Scheme is implemented in a transparent manner. The Ministry of Rural Development and UNDP are supporting any IT based applications to assist in the effective implementation of the MGNREGA. In this context, the Ministry of Rural Development (MoRD) and the UNDP are seeking the expertise of the IITM's Rural Technology and Business Incubator (RTBI) to pilot and field test the technology for low-cost ATMs with finger print authentication and local language interface in 5 villages in Tamil Nadu.

National Social Assistance Programme (NSAP)

The National Social Assistance Programme (NSAP) is a welfare programme being administered by the Ministry of Rural Development. This programme is being implemented in rural areas as well as urban areas. NSAP represents a significant step towards the fulfilment of the Directive Principles of State Policy enshrined in the Constitution of India which enjoin upon the State to undertake within its means a number of welfare measures. These are intended to secure for the citizens adequate means of livelihood, raise the standard of living, improve public health, provide free and compulsory education for children etc. In particular, Article 41 of the Constitution of India directs the State to provide public assistance to its citizens in case of unemployment, old age, sickness and disablement and in other cases of undeserved want within the limit of its economic capacity and development. It is in accordance with these noble principles that the Government of India on 15th August 1995 included the National Social Assistance Programme in the Central Budget for 1995-96. The Prime Minister in his broadcast to the Nation on 28th July 1995 announced that the programme will come into effect from 15th August 1995.

Accordingly the Govt. of India launched NSAP as a Centrally Sponsored Scheme w.e.f 15th August 1995 towards fulfilment of these principles.

The National Social Assistance Programme (NSAP) then comprised of National Old Age Pension Scheme (NOAPS), National Family Benefit Scheme (NFBS) and National Maternity Benefit Scheme (NMBS). These programmes were meant for providing social assistance benefit to the aged, the BPL households in the case of death of the primary breadwinner and for maternity. These programmes were aimed to ensure minimum national standards in addition to the benefits that the States were then providing or would provide in future. The scale of benefit and eligibility for various schemes of NSAP when first started were as follows:

1. **National Old Age Pension Scheme (NOAPS):** Rs. 75 per month is provided per beneficiary for destitute above 65 years. The scheme covered destitute having little or no regular means of subsistence from his/her own sources of income or through financial support from family members or other sources. In order to determine destitution, the criteria, if any, currently in force in the State/UT Governments were adapted. The Government of India reserved the right to review these criteria and suggest appropriate revised criteria.
2. **National Family Benefit Scheme (NFBS):** A grant of Rs. 5000 in case of death due to natural causes and Rs. 10,000 in case of accidental death of the "primary breadwinner" is provided to the bereaved household under this scheme. The primary breadwinner as specified in the scheme, whether male or female, had to be a member of the household whose earning contributed substantially to the total household income. The death of such a primary breadwinner occurring whilst he or she is in the age group of 18 to 64 years i.e., more than 18 years of age and less than 65 years of age, makes the family eligible to receive grants under the scheme.

3. **National Maternity Benefit Scheme (NMBS):** Under the scheme, Rs. 300 per pregnancy upto the first two live births is provided. The beneficiary should belong to a household Below the Poverty Line (BPL) according to the criteria prescribed by Government of India. In 1998, the amount of benefit under NFBS was raised to Rs. 10,000 in case of death due to natural causes as well as accidental causes. The assistance under the National Maternity Benefit Scheme which was at Rs. 300/-, was increased to Rs. 500/- per pregnancy.

Transfer of National Maternity Benefit Scheme to D/o Family Welfare

During the course of deliberations to consider National Population Policy in the second meeting held on 15th June,1999, the Group of Ministers observed that National Maternity Benefit Scheme being implemented by the Ministry of Rural Development could be assigned to the Department of Family Welfare to become part and parcel of the Population Stabilization Programme. On receipt of a communication in this regard from the Planning Commission, the Ministry of Rural Development agreed to transfer NMBS to the Department of Family Welfare from the Financial Year 2001-2002 and thus the Scheme was transferred to that Ministry w.e.f. 1st April, 2001.

Annapurna Scheme

On 1st April, 2000 a new Scheme known as Annapurna Scheme was launched. This Scheme aimed at providing food security to meet the requirement of those senior citizens who, though eligible, have remained uncovered under the NOAPS. Under the Annapurna Scheme 10 kgs of food grains per month are provided free of cost to the beneficiary. The number of persons to be benefited from the Scheme are, in the first instance, 20 per cent of the persons eligible to receive pension under NOAPS in States/UTs.

Transfer of NSAP and Annapurna Scheme to State Plan

In the National Development Council Meeting held in January 1997 to discuss the Draft Approach to the Ninth Plan, several Chief Ministers of States suggested for transfer of the Centrally Sponsored Schemes to States. As per the Approach Paper to the Ninth Five Year Plan, it was emphasized that in principle Centrally Sponsored Schemes should be confined to schemes of an inter-state character, matters impinging on national security, selected national priorities where central supervision is essential for effective implementation. As a result of the review of the Centrally Sponsored Schemes by the Planning Commission in consultation with the Mo RD, it was decided to transfer NSAP and Annapurna to the State Plan from the year 2002-03.

With this change, the funds for the operation of these schemes are now being released as Additional Central Assistance (ACA) to the States by the Ministry of Finance. The ACA to be provided to the States/UTs for the NSAP and Annapurna Scheme is decided by the Planning Commission, while the State-wise allocation of ACA is made by the Ministry of Rural Development and Planning Commission. The ACA provided to the States/UTs under NSAP and Annapurna are to be utilized by the States/UTs as Welfare Schemes of NOAPS, NFBS or free food grains to the aged by taking one or two or all of the three schemes or in any another combination in accordance with their own priorities and needs. The Additional Central Assistance to the States constitute a general additionality over and above the normal allocation of the States for such welfare schemes as reflected in the States Budget, both under Plan and Non-Plan. The States have to therefore, provide the Mandatory Minimum Provision (MMP) for these schemes under their own budget. The MoRD has a role in monitoring the expenditure against the ACA and the MMP.

Features of the Schemes

Some of the other important features of the schemes are as follows:

1. *Selection:* The Gram Panchayat / Municipalities are expected to play an active role in the identification of the

beneficiaries under the three schemes.

2. *Disbursement:* Apart from the disbursal of benefits through the accounts of the beneficiaries in Banks or in Post Office Savings Banks or through Postal Money Order the assistance under NOAPS, may also be disbursed in public meetings such as Gram Sabha meetings in rural areas and by neighbourhood/mohalla committees in urban areas.
3. *Monitoring:* The States/UTs have the flexibility to implement the schemes through any State Govt. Department. They have to however, designate a Nodal Secretary at the State level to report the progress of implementation by coordinating with different departments concerned with the implementation of the schemes. The progress of implementation of the schemes is to be reported through quarterly reports in a given monitoring format by the 15th of month of the following quarter. Non reporting of the physical and financial progress reports is construed as lack of progress and therefore, may result in the non-release of additional central assistance for the last quarter of the financial year. Since the ACA allocations for the schemes lapse at the end of the financial year, the instalments cannot be released during the next financial year, even if a State Govt. reports progress subsequent to the cut-off dates fixed as above. The NSAP is included in the schemes to be reviewed by the Vigilance & Monitoring Committee (V&MC) constituted at the District Level, along with other Rural Development Schemes. MPs re represented in the V&MC in the District.
4. *Guidelines of the Programme:* Guidelines were issued by the MoRD to all the States and UTs when NSAP was a Centrally Sponsored Programme. The State Governments may now issue their own guidelines for more effective implementation of the schemes. The State Governments have been given the requisite flexibility in the choice and implementation of the schemes. It is expected that State Governments will streamline disbursements so that the

payments are made timely, will also have a mechanism for a more transparent system of sanction especially in the event of death of beneficiaries under NOAPS, adopt a system of annual verification and will also actively involve the Gram Panchayats.

5. *State-run Schemes:* Several States supplement the old age scheme with their own budgets. Most States are giving more than the amount made available under NOAPS while some States cover additional beneficiaries and others have reduced the age for eligibility. Presently the work on a state-wise compilation of all the pension schemes run by each state, including the pension schemes under NSAP, is underway.

Enhancement of Pension Amount Under NOAPS during 2006-07

Finance Minister in his Budget Speech for the year 2006-07 had announced as follows:

National Social Assistance Programme: " *Old age pensions are granted under the National Social Assistance Programme(NSAP) to destitute persons above the age of 65 years at Rs.75 per month. I propose to increase the pension to Rs.200 per month. I would urge State Governments to make an equal contribution from their resources so that a destitute pensioner would get at least Rs.400 per month.*" Accordingly the rate of pension under NOAPS was revised to Rs.200/- per month per beneficiary.

Revision of the Eligibility Criteria Under NOAPS in 2007

Government of India on 13.9.2007 modified the eligibility criteria for grant of old age pension to persons aged 65 years or higher and belonging to a household below the poverty line according to the criteria prescribed by the Government of India, from the erstwhile criteria of the beneficiary being a destitute of 65 years of age or above. Thus the pension was universalized.

Introduction of Two New Pension Schemes in 2009: Indira Gandhi National Widow Pension Scheme (IGNWPS): In February

2009, GOI has approved pension to BPL widows in the age group of 40-64 years @ Rs. 200 p.m. per beneficiary.

Indira Gandhi National Disability Pension Scheme (IGNDPS): In February 2009, GOI has also approved pension under Indira Gandhi National Disability Pension Scheme (IGNDPS) for BPL persons with severe or multiple disabilities between the age group of 18-64 years @ Rs. 200 p.m. per beneficiary.

Enhancement of Pension Amount Under IGNOAPS in 2011

The Hon'ble Finance Minister while presenting the Union Budget 2011-12 in the Parliament on 28th February 2011 announced that 'under the on-going Indira Gandhi National Old Age Pension Scheme for BPL beneficiaries, the eligibility for pension is proposed to be reduced from 65 years at present to 60 years. Further, for those who are 80 years and above, the pension amount is being raised from Rs. 200 at present to Rs. 500 per month.' Accordingly the eligibility age for pension under IGNOAPS has been reduced to 60 years w.e.f. 1st April, 2011. The rate of pension under IGNOAPS was increased to Rs. 500/- per month per beneficiary for those beneficiaries of age 80 years and above w.e.f. 1st April, 2011. Accordingly the upper age limit for receipt of pension under Indira Gandhi National Widow Pension Scheme (IGNWPS) and Indira Gandhi National Disability Pension Scheme (IGNDPS) was reduced to 59 years beyond which they stand migrated to IGNOAPS.

Present status of NSAP

Thus, presently NSAP now comprises of the following five schemes:

1. **Indira Gandhi National Old Age Pension Scheme (IGNOAPS):** Under the scheme, BPL persons aged 60 years or above are entitled to a monthly pension of Rs. 200/- up to 79 years of age and Rs. 500/- thereafter.
2. **Indira Gandhi National Widow Pension Scheme (IGNWPS):** BPL widows aged 40-59 years are entitled to a monthly pension of Rs. 200/-.

3. **Indira Gandhi National Disability Pension Scheme (IGNDPS):** BPL persons aged 18-59 years with severe and multiple disabilities are entitled to a monthly pension of Rs. 200/-.
4. **National Family Benefit Scheme (NFBS):** Under the scheme a BPL household is entitled to lump sum amount of money on the death of primary breadwinner aged between 18 and 64 years. The amount of assistance is Rs. 10.000/-.
5. **Annapurna:** Under the scheme, 10 kg of food grains per month are provided free of cost to those senior citizens who, though eligible, have remained uncovered under NOAPS.

Implementation of NSAP Schemes

The NSAP is implemented in the States/UTs in accordance with the general conditions applicable to all components of the NSAP as well as specific condition applicable to each component. The NSAP Schemes are mainly implemented by the Social Welfare Departments in the States. But NSAP is implemented by Rural Development Department in the States of Andhra Pradesh, Assam, Goa, Meghalaya and West Bengal; by the Department of Women & Child Development in Orissa and Puducherry; by the Revenue Department in Karnataka and Tamil Nadu and by the Department of Labour Employment & Training in Jharkhand. The NSAP extends to both the rural as well as urban areas. Though the implementation of various schemes under NSAP is not uniform across the country, the issues of implementation are regularly being discussed with the State Government officials in the Nodal Officers' meetings and quarterly PRC meetings.

Computerisation of Database and Operationalisation of NSAP-MIS

On the occasion of the launching of the Indira Gandhi National Old Age Pension Scheme (IGNOAPS), Hon'ble Finance Minister in his speech indicated that all out efforts should be made to include details of every beneficiary in a computerized data base. A system should be devised so as to credit the amount of pension payable to each beneficiary directly into his account either in a Post Office or in a scheduled commercial bank. In compliance of the said directions and also in order to increase the transparency and accountability in the implementation, it had been decided to computerize the data base of the beneficiaries under various schemes of NSAP. NIC has been accordingly entrusted with the project and the software development. The software captures all the essential processes from identification till termination of the pension. The legacy date of more than 1 crore beneficiaries has been placed on the NSAP website. States have been asked to start operationalising the software for the districts for which data has been uploaded.

Monitoring of the Scheme

Annual verification and Social Audit has been introduced under NSAP. All the States are to complete the Annual verification by 30th June and the Social Audit by 30th September, each year. A checklist for the schemes under NSAP is provided to the National Level Monitors (NLMs) during their field visits. Each NLM is advised to visit the district, block and village level offices and meet the government functionaries, public representatives and the beneficiaries to get feedback on the implementation of the schemes under NSAP. Monthly meeting of the Divisional Head with the Nodal Officers of each State/UT is held in Delhi. Also a quarterly Performance Review Committee meeting is also held.

Financial and Physical Achievements

Summary of the combined allocations, total releases under the three Schemes and the coverage of beneficiaries in respect of each of the Schemes after these were transferred to the State Plan are as in Table 12.1 and Table 12.2 respectively.

Table 12.1: Financial Progress (Rs. in lakhs)

Year	Combined Allocation	Total Releases
2002-03	68000.00	65709.86
2003-04	67987.00	60226.79
2004-05	118987.00	103201.74
2005-06	119000.00	118971.00
2006-07	248097.00	248961.44
2007- 08	289148.20	288973.21
2008-09	450000.00	450000.00
2009-10	520000.00	515549.72
2010-11	516200.00	516200.00
2011-12	615757.00	* 210059.98

* Releases up to July, 2011.

Table 12.2: Physical Progress Reported by the States/Union Territories

Year	Coverage of Beneficiaries				
	IGNOAPS	IGNWPS	IGNDPS	NFBS	Annapurna
2002-03	7471509	**	**	85209	796682
2003-04	6534000	**	**	209456	958669
2004-05	8079386	**	**	261981	850768
2005-06	8002561	**	**	272828	857079
2006-07	8645371	**	**	171232	750319
2007-08	11514026	**	**	334168	1076210
2008-09	15483836	**	**	395460	883232
2009-10	16333578	3213467	699680	343726	1015655
2010-11	17059756	3425390	1328310	334924	963689
2011-12 #	9116385	2134256	471205	77052	466286

** IGNWPS and IGNDPS were introduced in February 2009

Figures as on 24.08.2011

Provision of Urban Amenities in Rural Areas (PURA) and Twelfth Five-Year Plan

Lack of livelihood opportunities, modern amenities, and services necessary for decent living in rural areas results in a sense of deprivation and dissatisfaction amongst a large percentage of population and leads to migration of people to urban areas. This is primarily due to the big differences in the availability of physical and social infrastructure in rural and urban areas. In order to address these issues, the Government has, in the past, launched various schemes at different points of time. However, due to several reasons, the impact has not been very visible. The deliveries of these schemes were not simultaneous and although huge sum were earmarked for capital expenditure, very little resources were spent on the operation and maintenance of the assets. Also, each of these schemes operated autonomously and the standards set for infrastructure services delivery in the rural areas were far below those set for the urban population.

Hence, in spite of several schemes, there continued to be a substantial flow of migration from the rural to urban areas. In order to catalyze the convergence between different infrastructure schemes and create a new model for management of urban services in the rural areas, the Provision for Urban Amenities in Rural Areas ("PURA") Scheme has been developed.

PURA aims to achieve *"holistic and accelerated development of compact areas around a potential growth centre in a Panchayat (or group of Panchayats) through PPP by providing livelihood opportunities and urban amenities to improve the quality of life in rural areas."* The PURA Scheme (provision of Urban Amenities in Rural Areas) envisages rapid growth of rural India given enhanced connectivity and infrastructure, the rural population would be empowered and enabled to create opportunities and livelihoods for themselves on a sustainable and growing basis. The key characteristics of the scheme are:

1. Simultaneous delivery of key infrastructure in villages leading to optimal use of resources.
2. Provision of funds for O&M of assets for 10 years post-construction, along with capital investment for creation of assets.
3. Transformation of several schemes into a single project, to be implemented as per set standards in a defined timeframe, with the requirements of each scheme being kept intact.
4. Combining livelihoods creation with infrastructure development.
5. Enforcement of standards of service delivery in rural areas almost at par with those obtaining in urban areas.
6. Enforcement of service standards through a legally binding arrangement.

The speed of urbanization poses an unprecedented policy change yet India has barely engaged in a national discussion about how to handle this seismic shift in the make-up of the nation. The population of India residing in urban areas will increase from 340 million to 590 million by 2030. Urbanization is expected to speed up across India, impacting almost every state. As India expands, India's economic make-up will also change. In 1995, India's GDP split almost evenly between its rural and urban economies. In 2008, its urban GDP is accounting for 58 per cent of its overall GDP and if the current trend continues it is expected that urban India will generate 70 per cent of India's GDP by 2030. The challenge for India will be to ramp up investment in line with economic growth.

Indian cities are failing to provide a basic standard of living to their urban residents, and life could become tougher as cities expand. As the urban population and its incomes increase, demand for every key service will increase five to sevenfold in cities of every size and type. If India continues to invest in urban infrastructure at its current rate very low by international comparison gridlock and urban decay will result. India urgently needs to adopt a new approach to manage urbanization. Urban India today is distributed in shape with a diverse range of large and small cities, spread widely around the nation. To address the issue of urbanization, India should continue to aim at a distributed model of urbanization because this suits its federal structure and also helps to ensure that migration flows are not balanced towards any particular city or cities. To control the migration from rural to urban areas, it is necessary to provide basic amenities and facilities in rural areas which are similar to those in urban areas. Schemes like PURA attempt to bridge these gaps in order to ensure that the rural areas have amenities which are at par with those in urban India. This would help in whittling down the migration from rural to urban areas.

The objective of the scheme is to provide urban amenities and livelihood opportunities in rural areas to bridge the rural-urban divide, thereby reducing migration from rural to urban areas.

The mission of the restructured PURA Scheme is holistic and accelerated development of compact areas around a potential growth centre in a Gram Panchayat (or cluster of contiguous Gram Panchayats) through the Public-Private Partnership (PPP) framework, to provide urban amenities and livelihood opportunities and improve the quality of life in rural areas. The scheme aims to provide urban amenities and livelihood opportunities in rural areas to bridge the rural-urban divide.

This aim of the PURA Scheme is proposed to be achieved under the framework of PPP between the Gram Panchayats and their private sector partner. Core funding shall be sourced from the convergence of Central Government schemes and complemented by additional support through the PURA Scheme. The private sector shall also bring on board its share of investment besides operational expertise. The PURA Scheme would be implemented and managed by the private sector on considerations of economic viability, but designed in a manner whereby it would be fully aligned with the overall objective of rural development. To attract the private sector, the scheme has a "project-based" design with well-defined risks and identified measures for risk mitigation and risk-sharing among the sponsoring authority (Gram Panchayat), Government, the State Government, and the selected bidder. The scheme is designed to ensure that private sector shall bring in efficiency in construction, skill enhancement and operation and maintenance of the project.

PURA Cluster in Markham Grant, Uttarakhand

PURA Cluster is proposed in Markham Grant which is the largest panchayat in the state of Uttarakhand, comprise of 23 villages and a population of around 20,000 as per Census 2001. The Panchayat has agriculture as its main economic activity. In spite of its location proximity to urban nodes such as Doiwala block and Dehradun District head quarters, the cluster lacks in key urban provisions result in migration of village population and reduction of sustainable agriculture activities. The proposed PURA project covers the mandatory MoRD schemes and integrate some of the Non MoRD Schemes like Village street lighting (Ministry of New and Renewable Energy), Gramin Bhandhar Yojana (Ministry of Animal Husbandry). The key economic activities proposed under the project includes agricultural warehouse with modern trading terminal, fodder manufacturing plant and mobile health clinic.

It is proposed that the organic wastes shall be subjected to vermin composting the output from which can help the local community improve soil fertility to sustain their main economic activity of agriculture. The project also aims at providing a rural health clinic which will offer all primary diagnostic services under one roof. A mobile health clinic is also proposed to extend the health and diagnostic services to nearby rural areas and remote hilly areas in this region. The Project has proposed to cover 100 per cent population covered with potable quality piped water supply as per specifications, 100 per cent coverage of sanitation services with measures undertaken for qualifying under Nirmal Gram Puraskar.

PURA Cluster in Mallapuram District, Kerala

The PURA Cluster is proposed in Thirurangadi Gram Panchayat of Malappuram district which is one of the old habitations of Kerala. The Gram Panchayat has an area of 17.73 sq.km and Population of 59612 (2010). PURA Project integrate the mandatory MoRD schemes and several other Non MoRD schemes. The Non-MoRD schemes covered include Solar Photovoltaic Programme by Ministry of New and Renewable Energy (MNRE), Rajiv Gandhi Gramin Vidhyutikaran Yojana by Ministry of Power, Renewable Energy Park Scheme by MNRE, Rashtriya Krishi Vikas Yojana by Ministry of Agriculture, Common Service Centres and State Date Centres, by Department of IT and Scheme of financial assistance to the Polytechnic Institutes, Ministry of Information Technology. The key economic activities proposed in the project are coconut cluster development for increasing the production and productivity of coconut. It is also proposed to develop a rural business hub comprising of modern rural slaughter house; meat processing; cold storage for preservation of value added products; fish processing and preservation; and, market infrastructure, warehousing and auction centre. Add on project comprises of development of allied water based tourism activities on Kadalundi River. To sustain the economic activities it is proposed to develop a bus stand cum multipurpose complex and to develop a resort. The project is proposed to Impact on standard of living for 25,000 population. It is envisaged that after the implementation of PURA Project, 92 per cent population shall be covered with potable quality piped water supply as per specifications, 100 per cent of unpaved roads will be paved and local employment shall be generated for 2740 people/day.

Way Forward: Strategies for The 12th Plan

The basic objective for the 12th Plan is aimed at faster, more inclusive, and sustainable growth. The infrastructure investments have seen significant improvement during the 11th Plan, but the pace of infrastructure development needs further acceleration if the infrastructure gaps are to be bridged within a reasonable time frame. *"Although PPPs have been successful in a number of infrastructure sectors, and efforts will need to be continued in further encouraging private sector involvement, it is felt that public investment in infrastructure, particularly irrigation, watershed development and urban infrastructure, will need an additional 0.7 percentage points of GDP increase over the next five years. As per the approach paper, skill development needs a major focus at all levels. We must involve PPP to ensure that the skills developed also lead to employability."* Underlying this reason it shall be imperative for the government to upscale the PURA Scheme to cover several new towns and villages.

Perspective/Outlook for the 12th Plan

MoRD is in the process of initiating additional 10-12 projects with a budget of approximately Rs. 550 crores (based on the present requirement of PURA Grant suggested by the bidders). These projects would be undertaken with the modifications and improvements based on the learning's from the first batch of pilot projects. Significant interest has been shown in the PURA projects that are implemented through the PPP route. However, as mentioned above, there are several issues relating to the projects, which need to be addressed to aid the successful implementation of the projects. Further, in order to ensure the up scaling of the scheme, an active role has to be envisaged for the State Governments and Gram

Panchayats. Besides, it is recommended that the Scheme be converted from a Central Sector Scheme to a Centrally Sponsored Scheme. In order to ensure effective implementation, replication of the experience in the pilot phase has to be undertaken before up scaling the Scheme. In order to achieve a visible impact, locations witnessing higher migration of the rural youth may be considered as priority areas for the implementation of the scheme. In addition, the scale of the PURA projects should be increased and focus should be on linking infrastructure development to the prevalent rural occupation.

The PURA Scheme has moved further after undertaking the exercise for pilot PURA projects and MoRD intends to expand the coverage of the scheme to ensure that more and more potential areas are benefitted from the scheme. Based on the discussion held with the Planning

Commission, it was suggested that PURA could focus on 3000 new census towns. A census town is one which has:

1. a minimum population of 5,000;
2. at least 75 per cent of male working population engaged in non-agricultural pursuits; and
3. a density of population of at least 400 persons per sq km.

Further consultations were undertaken with the Planning Commission and it was decided that the focus of the scheme should remain on rural areas in addition to census towns. With the objective of preserving the rural character of the scheme, the working group recommends that cluster formation during the 12th five year plan should be based any of the following three types of growth centres:

1. 3000 odd new census towns.
2. Non-municipal block headquarters.
3. Any other rural cluster with a potential growth centre.

Poverty Alleviation Programmes for Rural Development

India's anti-poverty strategy for urban and rural areas has three broad strands; promotion of economic growth; human development and targeted programmes to address the multi-dimensional nature of poverty. The monitorable targets for the Tenth Five Year Plan included quantitative targets for reduction in the incidence of poverty, according to which poverty was projected to be reduced by 5 percentage points by the end of the Tenth Plan period, by which time new estimates for poverty would be available. While there is a consensus that there has been a decline in the incidence of poverty during 1990s, it is difficult to assess the extent of this decline as there has been considerable debate regarding comparability of data due to changes in the methodology adopted by the National Sample Survey Organisation (NSSO) between 1993-94 and 1999-2000.

The targeted anti-poverty programmes have been rationalised, restructured and revamped in the Tenth Plan with a view to enhancing their efficacy and impact. In November 2004, National Food for Work Programme (NFFWP) was launched in 150 backward districts to enhance the wage employment opportunities for the poor. The government also tabled the National Rural Employment Guarantee Bill in Parliament in December 2004. There are two systems for poverty allivation given as following:

1. Public Distribution System

The public distribution system (PDS), as it was introduced originally was not an antipoverty scheme but a mechanism for the management of a buffer stock in foodgrain in order to ensure price stablisation. However, providing food to the poor at prices they can afford must be an integral part of the strategy of poverty reduction. The PDS attracted the following major criticisms:

1. It did not really target states with a large number of poor.
2. It was biased in favour of certain states as well as urban areas, although the latter was much less clear if only households purchasing foodgrains were considered.
3. It is not particularly effective in providing subsidised foodgrains to the poorer groups in low income/high poverty regions.
4. The fiscal burden due to food subsidy needed to be controlled which could be done by targeting the food subsidy to poor consumers.

In June 1997, the Government of India introduced the Targeted Public Distribution System (TPDS) with appropriate focus on the poor. Under TPDS, above the poverty line (APL) families are provided foodgrains at nearly the full economic cost and BPL families at about half this rate. The scale of issue under TPDS began with 10 kg per family per month for BPL families, but has been progressively increased over the years and is now 35 kg per family per month with effect from 1st April 2002. The scale of issue for the APL families has also been determined at 35 kg per family per month from the same date. The Antyodaya Anna Yojana (AAY) was launched in December 2000 and involved the identification of 1 crore poorest of the poor families who would be provided 25 kg foodgrains a month at a highly subsidised price of

Rs. 2 per kg for wheat and Rs. 3 per kg for rice. The scale of issue has since been increased from 25 kg per family per month to 35 kg per family per month with effect from 1 April 2002. The scheme has been expanded to cover 2.5 crore families.

The main objective of the TPDS was to improve the PDS consumption of the poor by offering them cereals at highly subsidised prices (and simultaneously wean away the non-poor from the PDS). Since 2000, the introduction of the AAY was further expected to improve the PDS offtake and consumption by the poorest. One would, therefore, expect PDS offtake to become more aligned with the total number of poor in each state. Among the medium/high income states, Kerala.s share in offtake has been declining along with that of Gujarat and West Bengal. Among the poor states, Madhya Pradesh and Uttar Pradesh show an increasing share in total offtake. Overall, the correlation between the total offtake of cereals and number of poor in each state, has been improving and was statistically significant in 2003-04. Thus, at least at the level of offtake, the TPDS has now been better able to target the states with higher number of poor than in the past.

2. District Rural Development Agency (DRDA)

The District Rural Development Agency (DRDA) has traditionally been the principal organ at the district level to oversee the implementation of different anti poverty programmes. Since its inception in 1980, the administrative costs of the DRDAs were met by way of setting apart a share of the allocation for each programme. However, there was no uniformity amongst the programmes with reference to administrative costs. Therefore, keeping in view the need for an effective agency at the district level to coordinate the anti poverty efforts, a new CSS 'Strengthening of DRDA Administration' was launched with effect from April 1, 1999 with funding on a 75:25 basis between the Centre and States. Since the salary structure in different States is varied, the States can follow their own salary structure under the programme, but the ceiling of administrative cost per district applicable from 1999-2000 has been fixed as given below.

However, the ceiling can be raised every year up to 5 per cent to meet cost increases due to inflation, etc. Category A District (less than 6 blocks) Rs.46.00 lakhs, Category B District (6-10 blocks) Rs. 57.00 lakhs, Category C District (11-15 blocks) Rs. 65.00 lakhs, Category D District (more than 15 blocks) Rs. 67.00 lakhs. The DRDA is visualized as a specialized and a professional agency capable of managing the anti poverty programmes of the Ministry of Rural Development (MORD) and to effectively relate these to the overall effort of poverty eradication in the district. While the DRDAs are not the implementing agencies, they are effective in enhancing the quality of implementation through overseeing the implementation of different programmes and ensuring that necessary linkages are provided. To this extent, the DRDA is a supporting and a facilitating organisation and plays a very effective role as a catalyst in development process.

The role of the DRDA is in terms of planning for effective implementation of antipoverty programmes; coordinating with other agencies – Governmental, non-Governmental, technical and financial for successful programme implementation, enabling the community and the rural poor to participate in the decision making process, overseeing the implementation to ensure adherence to guidelines, quality, equity and efficiency; reporting to the prescribed authorities on the implementation; and promoting transparency in decision making and implementation. The DRDAs coordinate with the line departments, the Panchayati Raj Institutions (PRIs), the banks and other financial institutions, the NGOs as well as technical institutions with a view to bring about convergence of approach among different agencies for poverty alleviation. The DRDAs while maintaining their separate identity function under the Chairmanship of the Chairman of the Zilla Parishad. They are a facilitating and supporting organisation to the Zilla Parishad, providing necessary executive and technical support in respect of poverty reduction efforts. Wherever the Zilla Parishads are not in existence or are not functional, the DRDAs function under the Collector/ District Magistrate/Deputy Commissioner, as the case may be. During 2000-01, a total allocation of Rs. 322.26 crores was made under the programme and an expenditure of Rs. 165.50 crores was incurred. For 2001-02, a Central outlay of Rs. 220.00 crores has been earmarked for the programme.

While there has been a decline in the rural poverty from 244 million (37% of the rural population) in the country in 1993-94 to 193 million (27% of the rural population) as per latest estimates of 1999-2000, eradication of poverty remains a challenging task for the Government. Given the enormity and complexity of the problem, a multi-pronged approach has been adopted. While high economic growth with a focus on sectors which are employment intensive facilitates removal of poverty in the long run, this strategy has been complemented with a focus on building of capabilities through provision of basic services like education, health, housing, etc. for improving the quality of life of the people. In addition, direct State intervention through targeted anti poverty programmes (self and wage employment schemes and social security schemes) also form a part of the strategy. While growth is the prime mover, anti-poverty programmes supplement the growth effort and protect the poor from destitution, sharp fluctuations in employment and incomes, and social insecurity.

Further, with regard to governance, it has been recognized that ensuring greater participation of Panchayati Raj Institutions (PRIs) is the most effective mechanism for poverty reduction. The specifically designed anti-poverty programmes for generation of both self employment and wage employment in rural areas have been redesigned and restructured in 1999-2000 in order to enhance their efficacy/ impact on the poor and improve their sustainability. These schemes are briefly discussed below:

1. Swarnjayanti Gram Swarozgar Yojana (SGSY)

The Swaranjayanti Gram Swarozgar Yojana (SGSY) was launched with effect from 1.4.1999, keeping in view the strengths and weaknesses of the earlier schemes of Integrated Rural Development Programme (IRDP) and allied programmes along with Million Wells Scheme (MWS) which ceased to be in operation. The objective of restructuring was to make the programme more effective in providing sustainable incomes through micro enterprises while providing for flexibility of design to suit local needs. Funds under the SGSY are shared by the Centre and the States in the ratio of 75:25. In the case of UTs, the scheme is fully funded by the Centre. SGSY is conceived as a holistic programme of micro enterprises covering all aspects of self employment and establishing effective linkages between the components viz; organisation of the rural poor into self help groups (SHGs) and their capacity building, planning of activity clusters, infrastructure build up, technology, credit and marketing. Micro enterprises in the rural areas are sought to be established by building on the potential of the rural poor. The objective of the programme is to bring the existing poor families above the poverty line. The list of BPL households, identified through BPL census, duly approved by the Gram Sabha forms the basis for assistance to families under SGSY. Under the programme, the focus is on vulnerable sections among the rural poor with SCs/STs accounting for 50 per cent, women 40 per cent and the disabled 3 per cent of the beneficiaries. Group/individual beneficiaries (also called Swarozgaris) are assisted under the programme. While the identification of individual beneficiaries is made through a participatory approach, the programme lays emphasis on organisation of poor into Self Help Groups (SHGs) and their capacity building. The SHG may consist of 10 to 20 persons. In case of minor irrigation or the disabled, the minimum is 5 persons. Under the scheme, progressively, majority of the funding would be for SHGs. Group activities stand a better chance of success because it is easier to provide back up support and marketing linkages for group activities. Involvement of women members in each SHG is encouraged and at the block level it is stipulated that, at least half of the groups will be exclusively women's groups. For providing a revolving fund to the SHGs, the DRDAs could use ten per cent of the allocation under SGSY.

2. Jawahar Gram Samridhi Yojana (JGSY)

With the view to lay thrust on creation of rural infrastructure as per the felt needs of the village community the Jawahar Rozgar Yojana (JRY) was restructured as the Jawahar Gram Samridhi Yojana (JGSY) with effect from 1.4.1999. While the JRY resulted in creation of durable assets the overriding priority of the programme was the creation of wage employment, therefore, it was felt that in order to make the programme effective and meaningful focus needed to be laid on rural infrastructure in a planned manner. The programme is being implemented by the Gram Panchayats as they can effectively determine their infrastructure needs. For this purpose, the funds are directly released to the Gram Panchayats by the DRDAs/Zilla Parishads. The JGSY is implemented as a CSS with funding in the ratio of 75:25 between the Centre and the States. In the case of UTs, all funds are provided by the Centre. JGSY has the primary objective of creation of demand driven community village infrastructure including durable assets at the village level and assets to enable the rural poor to increase the opportunities for sustained employment. The secondary objective is generation of supplementary employment for the unemployed poor in the rural areas. The wage employment under the programme is given to Below Poverty Lines (BPL) families. The wages under the programme are either the minimum wages notified by the States or higher wages as fixed by the States through the prescribed procedure. All works that result in the creation of durable productive community assets can be taken up under the programme as per the felt need of the area/people by the village panchayat. These include creation of infrastructure for SCs/STs habitations, infrastructure support for SGSY, infrastructure required for supporting agricultural activities in the village, community infrastructure for education and health, roads and other social, economic and physical infrastructure. The wage material ratio of 60:40 can be suitably relaxed so as to enable the building up of demand driven rural infrastructure. Efforts to ensure that labour intensive works are taken up with sustainable low cost technology are also made. While there is no sectoral earmarking of resources under JGSY, 22.5 per cent of the annual allocation must be spent on individual beneficiary schemes for SCs/STs and 3 per cent is to be utilized for creation of barrier free infrastructure for the disabled. Further the State Government is given Rs. 10 lakh or 1 per cent of the annual allocation, whichever is less, for expenses incurred on training of officials/non-officials (Panchayat functionaries) involved in implementation of JGSY under the condition that atleast 50 per cent of the expenses be incurred on non-officials (Panchayat functionaries).

3. Sampoorna Grameen Rozgar Yojana

The Sampoorna Grameen Rozgar Yojana (SGRY) is a wage employment scheme launched in September 2001, and the Jawahar Gram Samridhi Yojana (JGSY) and Employment Assurance Scheme (EAS) were merged under this programme from Ist April 2002. The primary objective of the scheme is to provide additional wage employment in all rural areas and thereby provide food security and improve nutritional levels. The secondary objective is the creation of durable community, social and economic assets and infrastructure development in rural areas. A special component under SGRY provides foodgrains to calamity stricken states for undertaking relief activities. The SGRY is open to all rural persons who are in need of wage employment and desire to do manual and unskilled work in and around the village/habitat. The programme is self-targeting in nature. Thirty per cent of employment opportunities under the programme are reserved for women. The programme is implemented through the panchayati raj institutions (PRIs).

Till 2003-04, the programme was implemented in two streams, the first implemented by the district panchayats and panchayat samitis and the second by the village panchayats. Since 2004-05, the programme is being implemented as an integrated scheme by all the three tiers of the PRIs and the funds are shared by the district, intermediate and village panchayats in the ratio 20:30:50. A minimum of Rs. 50,000 per year is provided to each Gram Panchayat. Wages under the programme are paid partly in the form of foodgrains and partly in cash. Minimum wages fixed by the states are paid under the scheme. The minimum amount of foodgrains to be given as part of wages are 5 kg per manday and a minimum of 25 per cent of the wages are to be paid in cash. Contractors/ middlemen or any other intermediate agency are not permitted to be engaged for the execution of any of the works under the programme. The programme is implemented as a Centrally sponsored scheme on cost-sharing basis between the Centre and the states in the ratio of 75:25 of the cash component of the programme. Foodgrains under the programme are provided to the states/Union Territories free of cost. Each zilla parishad/DRDA, intermediate level and village panchayat prepares an annual action plan to include the works to be undertaken under the scheme. Completion of incomplete works is given priority and emphasis is laid on labour-intensive works. Priority is to be given to soil and moisture conservation, minor irrigation, rejuvenation of drinking water sources, augmentation of ground water, traditional water harvesting structures, desiltation of village tanks/ponds, construction of rural link roads, drainage works, afforestation, schools, kitchen sheds for schools, dispensaries, community centres, panchayat ghars, development of haats (markets), etc. However, the nature of works should be such that they could be completed in one or two years. Up to a maximum of 15 per cent of the funds can be spent on maintenance of assets created under the programme by the zilla parishads/DRDAs/ intermediate panchayats/village panchayats.

4. Employment Assurance Scheme (EAS)

On 2nd October, 1993 the EAS was launched in 1778 identified backward blocks of 257 districts situated in drought prone, desert, tribal and hill areas where the Revamped Public Distribution System (RPDS) was in operation. Subsequently the programme was extended to more blocks and thereafter was universalized and implemented in all the 5448 rural blocks. The EAS was recast w.e.f. 1999-2000 as the single wage employment programme. While the basic parameters have been retained, the scheme has become allocative scheme instead of demand driven scheme and a fixed annual outlay is to be provided to the States/UTs. In keeping with the spirit of democratic decentralization the Zilla Parishads have been designed as the 'Implementing Authority' for the scheme. The programme is implemented as a CSS on a cost sharing ratio of 75:25 between the Centre and States and is fully funded by the Centre in case of UTs. The primary objective of the EAS is creation of additional wage employment opportunities during the period of acute shortage of wage employment through manual work for the rural poor living below the poverty line. The secondary objective is the creation of durable community, social and economic assets for sustained employment and development.EAS is open to all the needy rural persons who require wage employment. A maximum of two adults per family are provided wage employment. While providing employment, preference is given to SCs/STs and parents of child labour withdrawn from hazardous occupations who are below the poverty line. The programme is implemented through the Zilla Parishads (DRDAs in those States where Zilla Parishads do not exist). The list of works is finalized by the Zilla Parishads in consultation with the Members of Parliament. Where Zilla Parishads are not in existence, a Committee consisting of MLAs, MPs and other public representatives is constituted for selection of works. Gram Sabhas are informed about the details of works taken up under the scheme. Seventy per cent of the funds allocated for each district are released to the Panchayat Samitis while thirty per cent is reserved at the district level to be utilized in the areas suffering from endemic labour exodus/areas of distress. Diversion of funds from one district to another and from one Panchayat to another is not permitted. Eighty per cent of the funds are released to the district as per normal procedure and the remaining twenty per cent are to be released as an incentive only if the States have put in place elected and empowered Panchayati Raj Institutions (PRIs).

5. Food for Work Programme

The Food for Work Programme, aims at augmenting food security through wage employment in the drought affected rural areas in Eight States viz., Chattisgarh, Gujarat, Himachal Pradesh, Madhya Pradesh, Maharashtra, Orissa, Rajasthan and Uttaranchal after due notification. The programme was launched w.e.f. February, 2001 for 5 months to be extended at the discretion of the Government of India. The scheme is in operation in rural areas that are notified by the State Governments as drought affected. The Programme may be extended to the other areas as may be affected by the Natural Calamities such as Flood, Cyclone or Earthquake by the Central Government. The Centre makes available appropriate quantity of food grains free of cost to each of the drought affected States as an additionality under the programme. Wages by the State Government can be paid partly in kind (up to 5 kgs. of food grains per manday) and partly in cash. The State Government is free to calculate the cost of food grains paid in wages, at BPL rates or APL rates or any where between these two rates. The workers are paid the balance of wages in cash, such that they are assured of the notified Minimum wages. Since the objective of the Food for Work Programme is to provide wage employment, preference is given to labour-intensive works that help in drought-proofing and can be completed within 90 days.

6. Annapurna

The Annapurna Scheme came into effect from 1.4.2000 as a 100 per cent Centrally Sponsored Scheme. The programme aims at providing food security to meet the requirement of those senior citizens who though eligible have remained uncovered under the under the National Old Age Pension Scheme(NOAPS). Free foodgrains @ 10 kgs per month per beneficiary are provided under this Scheme. The eligibility criteria for claiming benefit under the Scheme are:

(*a*) The age of the applicant (male or female) should be 65 years or above;

(*b*) The applicant must be a destitute in the sense of having little or no regular means of subsistence from his/her own sources of income or through financial support from family members or other sources; and

(*c*) The applicant should not be in receipt of pension under NOAPS or State pension schemes.

The State Food & Civil Supplies Departments have been made the nodal Department for implementing the Scheme in view of their access to the existing infrastructure for distribution of foodgrains through the Targeted Public Distribution System(TPDS). The Food Corporation of India ensures availability of foodgrains as per the requirement of the States. At District level, the Collector/CEO is responsible for co-ordination to ensure adequate supply of foodgrains. The identification of beneficiaries is done by the Panchayats and Municipalities and they are also responsible for publicity of the scheme in their respective areas. The funds allocated to the States are released in one installment. As against the B.E. of Rs. 100.00 crores for the scheme in 2000-01, an expenditure of Rs. 99.80 crores is anticipated. During 2001-02, a Central allocation of Rs. 300.00 crores has been provided under the programme.

7. Antyodaya Anna Yojana

Antyodaya Anna Yojana has been launched by the Hon'ble Prime Minister of India on the 25th December, 2000. This scheme reflects the commitments of the Government of India to ensure food security for all, create a hunger free India in the next five years and to reform and improve the Public Distribution System so as to serve the poorest of the poor in rural and urban areas. It contemplates identification of one crore poorest of the poor families and providing them with food grains @ 25 kg. per family per month at highly subsidized rates of Rs. 2 a kg. for wheat and Rs. 3 a kg. for rice. The basis of this estimation of one crore household is the 50th Round of the NSSO survey held during 1993-94. In its report titled, "Reported Adequacy of Food Intake in India", the NSSO observed that 5 per cent of rural household and 2 per cent of urban households reported that they did not have "two square meals a day" during all parts of the year. While according to NSSO, the respondents understood very clearly the implications of the question asked, the NSSO has been criticized on the ground that the answer does not make it clear how big or small the "meal" was meant to be. The real problem lies in excess stock of food grains. The Government is faced with a total food stock of about 60 million tonnes. While the buffer norm may veer around 20 million tonnes, the normal off take under TPDS for BPL househlds has been expected to be 15 million tonnes at the enhanced allocation of 20 kgs. of food grains per month and those for APL households in the range of 5-10 million tonnes. Somehow, on account of lower market price the off take of both these groups under the Public Distribution System has not been as expected. Adding on the existing APL-BPL group of households, yet another category of "poorest of the poor household" and distribution of food grains at further reduced price, would at the most help increase off take of food grains by 3 million tones. This would not be addressing the problem of excess food stocks. The food subsidy which has already touched Rs.13,675 will only go up by another Rs.1000-1500 crores. The surplus stock of food grains (over and above the buffer norms) could best be utilized for launching massive Food for Work Programme, creating in the process useful assets like school buildings, rural roads, ponds and tanks and also encouraging female literacy through inducing the girl child to go to school through allocating them additional amount of food grains. This is easily a better option to utilize food grains in place of exporting it at a subsidy which in all probability would be fed to the cattle abroad. The Finance Minister in his Budget Speech for the year 1999-2000 had announced the launching of a new scheme "Annapurna" to provide food security to those indigent senior citizens who though eligible are not covered under the National Old Age Pension Scheme. The Ministry of Rural Development, Government of India, which was chosen as the nodal Ministry for implementing this programme, accordingly grounded the scheme on 1st April, 2000.

8. National Rural Employment Guarantee Bill

The National Rural Employment Guarantee Bill was tabled in Parliament on 21st December 2004. The Bill provides that state governments shall provide 100 days of unskilled manual work in a financial year to every poor household in the rural areas whose adult members volunteer to do such work. In order to make the programme result-oriented, it has been proposed that the scheme should be implemented in phases. Accordingly, in the first phase, the proposed legislation would be implemented in the 150 districts where the NFFWP is being implemented. The legislation would be implemented in the other districts, based on the experience gained from the first phase.

9. National Social Assistance Programme

The National Social Assistance Programme (NSAP) was launched as a Centrally sponsored scheme (CSS) on 15 August 1995, with the aim of providing social assistance benefit to poor households in the case of old age, death of primary breadwinner and maternity. The programme supplements the efforts of the state governments with the objective of ensuring minimum national levels of well-being and the Central assistance is an addition to the benefit that the states are already providing on social protection schemes. With a view to ensuring better linkage with nutrition and national population control programmes, the maternity benefit component of the NSAP was transferred to the Department of Family Welfare in 2001-02. Since then NSAP has only the following two components:

1. **National Old Age Pension Scheme (NOAPS):** Old age pension of Rs.75 per beneficiary per month is provided to aged destitute persons with little or no regular means

of subsistence from their own sources of income or through support from family members or other sources.

2. **National Family Benefit Scheme (NFBS):** A lump sum benefit of Rs.10,000 is provided in the case death of primary breadwinner of a BPL family due to natural or accidental causes. The family benefit is paid to a surviving member of the household of deceased who is determined to be the head of the household.

10. Urban Poverty Alleviation Programmes

Trends in urban poverty in percentage and numerical terms show some encouraging signs, though at the urban poor still face certain persistent problems at the ground level. One encouraging fact is that along with a fall in the proportion of the urban poor, there is also a reduction in terms of absolute numbers. Though, at the national level, the percentage of the poor in rural areas is significantly higher than in urban areas, states such as Andhra Pradesh, Goa, Gujarat, Haryana, Karnataka, Kerala, Madhya Pradesh, Maharashtra, Rajasthan, Tamil Nadu, Delhi and the Union Territory of Pondicherry have higher levels of urban poverty. While income levels are rising to meet the basic nutritional needs, the other equally basic needs of shelter, civic amenities, health care, educational and social needs, etc. are not being met adequately. Urban poverty, thus, emerges as a more complex phenomenon than rural poverty, as can be seen from these aspects:

1. **Level of basic amenities:** There are serious deficiencies in urban infrastructure as a result of the rapid growth of urban population and low investment in urban development. The percentage of households having flush toilets exhibits a strong positive correlation with economic development, much more than any other indicator of amenities. The coverage of civic amenities, specifically electricity, drinking water and toilets, is uneven and the .urban poor. Generally receive low priority.
2. **Town or city size and poverty:** The incidence of poverty in a town, as measured by head count ratio (HCR), declines steadily with increasing size. A larger incidence

of secondary and high-value tertiary activities in large cities gives people residing there a higher level of income. In contrast, the income levels of people in small and medium towns tend to be low because of the poor economic base and lack of employment opportunities in the organised sector.

3. **Household size:** The fact that household size affects the poverty status of a household is well known. Larger households tend to have a higher probability of being poor.

Housing Schemes

Housing is one of the components considered to be vital for human survival and, therefore, essential for socio-economic development. As part of the efforts to meet the housing needs of the rural poor, Government of India, is implementing Indira Awaas Yojana (IAY) since 1985. Earlier, it was a sub scheme of Jawahar Rozgar Yojana (JRY), however, from April 1996, IAY is being implemented as an independent Centrally Sponsored Scheme (CSS). In the Ninth Five Year Plan Government has identified housing as one of the priority areas under 'Special Action Plan for Social Infrastructure' which aims at 'Housing for All'. Towards this end, the construction of 20 lakh additional housing units annually have been proposed, of which 13 lakh houses have to be constructed in rural areas in addition to the houses constructed under existing programmes. To achieve this, Special Action Plan for Rural Housing was prepared under which a composite housing strategy was adopted. The multi pronged strategy includes modification in the existing housing scheme and certain new initiatives, which are listed below:

1. Indira Awaas Yojana (IAY)

The IAY continues to be the most important Centrally Sponsored housing scheme for providing dwelling units free of cost to the rural poor living below the poverty line at the unit cost of Rs. 20,000/- in plain areas and Rs. 22,000/- in the hilly/difficult areas. It is funded on cost sharing ratio of 75:25 between Central Government and States. The objective of

IAY is to provide dwelling units free of cost to the Scheduled Castes (SCs) and Scheduled Tribes (STs) and freed bonded labourers and non - SCs/STs living below poverty line in rural areas. From 1995-96, the IAY benefits have been extended to the widows or next of kin of defence personnel killed in action. Benefits have also been extended to ex-servicemen and retired members of para military forces as long as they fulfill the normal eligibility condition of IAY. 3 per cent of funds are reserved for benefit of disabled below the poverty line in rural areas. However, the benefit to non - SCs and STs shall not be more than 40 per cent of IAY allocation. As the IAY has a limited format i.e. construction of new houses, it has been decided to modify to implement it in two parts viz:

(a) construction of new houses (at an average weighted cost of Rs. 20,900); and

(b) upgradation of kutcha and unserviceable houses (at a unit cost of Rs. 10,000).

From 1999-2000, the criteria for allocation of funds to States/UTs under IAY has been changed from poverty ratio to 50 per cent poverty ratio and 50 per cent housing shortage in the State. Similarly, the criteria for allocation of funds to a district in a State has been changed to the SC/ST population and housing shortage, with equal weightage to each of them. The Central allocation under the IAY for 2001-02 is Rs. 1527.00 crore.

2. Credit-cum-Subsidy Scheme

The Credit-cum-Subsidy Scheme for Rural Housing was launched with effect from 1.4.1999. The scheme targets rural families having annual income up to Rs. 32,000/-. However, preference should be given to rural households belonging to Below Poverty Line category. While subsidy is restricted to Rs. 10,000/-, the maximum loan amount that can be availed is Rs. 40,000/- The subsidy portion is shared by the Centre and the State in 75:25 ratio. The loan portion is to be disbursed by the commercial banks, housing finance institutions etc. The scheme is being implemented through State Housing Board,

State Housing Corporation, Specified Scheduled Commercial Bank, Housing Finance Institution or the District Rural Development Agencies (DRDAs) /Zilla Parishads (ZPs).

3. Innovative Stream for Rural Housing and Habitat Development

This scheme has been launched with effect from 1.4.1999, to encourage innovative, cost effective and environment friendly solutions in building/housing sectors in rural areas. The objective is to promote/propagate innovative housing technologies, designs and materials in the rural areas. It is being implemented on project basis. All recognized Government organisations/institutions and reputed NGOs well experienced in the technology promotion and propagation of cost effective and environmental friendly housing technologies, designs and material may apply for funding to the Ministry of Rural Development.

4. Equity Support to Housing and Urban Development Corporation (HUDCO)

To meet the housing requirement of Economically Weaker Sections and Low Income Groups in rural areas and to improve the outreach of housing finance in rural areas, the equity support by Ministry of Rural Development (MORD) to HUDCO has been increased from Rs. 5.00 crore to Rs. 355 crore during Ninth Five Year Plan period. It facilitates HUDCO to leverage eight times the amount provided by MORD as equity from the market for construction of additional houses in the rural areas. So far, an amount of Rs. 305.00 crore has been released to HUDCO. Balance amount of Rs. 50.00 crore is likely to be released during 2001-02.

5. National Mission for Rural Housing and Habitat

A National Mission for Rural Housing and Habitat has been set up by the MORD to facilitate the science and technology inputs, on a continuous basis, in the sector and to provide convergence of technology, habitat and energy related issues in order to provide affordable shelter for all in the rural areas, within a specified time frame and through community participation.

6. Samagra Awaas Yojana (SAY)

The basic objective of SAY is to improve the quality of life of the people as well as over all habitat. The scheme attempts to breach the limited shelter concern of 'four walls and a roof' by providing convergence of housing, sanitation and drinking water schemes and ensure their effective implementation by suitable and sustainable induction of technology, Information, Education and Communication (IEC) and innovative ideas. The scheme was launched in 1999-2000 on pilot basis in one Block each of 25 districts of 24 States and one UT selected from the 58 Pilot Districts, which have been identified for implementing a participatory approach under the AcceleratedRural Water Supply Programme (ARWSP). A special Central assistance of Rs. 25 lakh is being provided for each Block for undertaking overall habitat development and IEC work with 10 per cent contribution coming from the people.

7. Pradhan Mantri's Gramodaya Yojana: Gramin Awaas

Pradhan Mantri Gramodaya Yojana: Gramin Awaas (PMGY:GA) has been launched only from 2000-01. The Ministry of Rural Development (MORD) is the nodal Ministry responsible for the implementation and monitoring of the rural housing (gramin awaas) component of the programme, whose guidelines have been circulated to all States/UTs. The scheme is based on Indira Awaas Yojana. States/UTs are required to send project proposals to the MORD for release of funds under PMGY:GA. Releases are being made by the Ministry of Finance on the recommendation of the MORD. An amount of Rs. 286.84 crore was released by Ministry of Finance during 2000-01. An outlay of Rs. 280.00 crore has been allocated Additional Central Assistance (ACA) for Rural Shelter component of PMGY during 2001-02.

8. Valmiki Ambedkar Awas Yojana

The Valmiki Ambedkar Awas Yojana (VAMBAY) was introduced in 2001-02 to provide shelters or upgrading existing shelters of the BPL population living in urban slums. The

Government of India provides 50 per cent Central subsidy while the states have the option of mobilising their matching portion of 50 per cent from other sources, such as their own budget provision, resources of local bodies, loans from other agencies, contributions from beneficiaries or NGOs etc. Under this scheme, 20 per cent of the total allocation is provided for sanitation and community toilets. During the first three years of the Tenth Plan, Rs. 727.58 crore, accounting for 36 per cent of the Tenth Plan allocation of Rs. 2,043 crore has been utilised. Against the target of 1 lakh, 1.06 lakh and 1.12 lakh dwelling units for the first three years of the Tenth Plan, 1,10,388 houses were constructed in the first year 1,08,376 dwelling units were constructed in the second year and 1,13,004 dwelling units were covered in the third respectively.

9. Night Shelter For Urban Shelterless

The Night Shelter for Urban Shelterless scheme is a CSS which is funded on the basis of 50:50 between Centre and the states or implementing agencies or through the Housing and Urban Development Corporation (HUDCO) as loan. The scheme facilitates the construction of composite night shelters with community toilets and baths for urban shelterless. During the first three years of the Tenth Plan, Rs. 8 crore, or 26 per cent (assuming full utilisation of 2004-05 allocations) of Tenth Plan allocation of Rs. 30.97 crore, is expected to be utilised. The scheme is a demand-driven one and the Ministry of Urban Employment and Poverty Alleviation is not receiving adequate number of proposals from the states.

Other programmes

1. Drought Prone Area Programme (DPAP)

DPAP aims at to minimize the adverse effects of drought on production of crops and livestock and productivity of land, water and human resources ultimately leading to the drought proofing of the affected areas. It also aims at promoting overall economic development and improving the socio-economic conditions of the resource poor and disadvantaged sections inhabiting the programme areas. During the Ninth

Five Year Plan, the programme covers 961 blocks of 180 districts in 16 States namely Andhra Pradesh, Bihar, Chattisgarh, Gujarat, Himachal Pradesh, Jammu & Kashmir, Jharkhand, Karnataka, Madhya Pradesh, Maharashtra, Orissa, Rajasthan, Tamil Nadu, Uttar Pradesh, Uttranchal and West Bengal. Since 1995-96, 11738 watershed projects of 500 hectare each have been sanctioned for development on watershed basis till end of March, 2001. In the first four years of the Ninth Plan, an area of 19.35 lakh hectare has been covered with Central releases of Rs. 448.29 crore to the programme States. During 2001-02, an outlay of Rs. 210 crore has been provided to cover an area of 7.90 lakh hectare under DPAP.

2. Desert Development Programme (DDP)

DDP has been envisaged as an essentially land based activity and conceived as a long term measure for restoration of ecological balance by conserving, developing and harnessing land, water, livestock and human resources. The main objectives of this programme are:

(i) combating drought and desertification;

(ii) encouraging restoration of ecological balance;

(iii) mitigating the adverse effects of drought and adverse edapho-climatic conditions on crops and livestock and productivity of land, water and human resources;

(iv) promoting economic development of village community; and

(v) improving socio economic conditions of the resource poor and disadvantaged sections of village community viz; assetless and women.

Presently, this programme covers 232 blocks of 40 districts in seven States viz; Andhra Pradesh, Gujarat, Haryana, Himachal Pradesh, Jammu and Kashmir, Karnataka and Rajasthan. Since 1995-96, 5353 projects costing about Rs. 1338.25 crore have been sanctioned till end of March 2001. In the first four years of the Ninth Plan, an area of 8.48 lakh hectare approximately has been covered with total Central release of Rs. 369.79 crore. During 2001-02, an outlay of Rs. 160 crores was provided to cover an area of 4.04 lakh ha. (approximately). Under DPAP and DDP, funds are directly released to DRDAs/Zilla Parishads for implementation of the programme. From 1999-2000, the funding pattern under these programmes have been changed to 75:25 cost sharing basis between the Centre and the States for the projects sanctioned after 1.4.1999.

3. Integrated Wastelands Development Programme (IWDP)

IWDP was started in 1988-89 by Ministry of Environment & Forests with an objective of development of wasteland based on village/micro watershed plan. However, the scheme was transferred to the Department of Wastelands Development (now called Department of Land Resources) during 1992-93. The stakeholders prepare these plan after taking into consideration the capability of land, site conditions and local needs. Promoting the overall economic development and improvement of economic condition of the resources poor and disadvantaged section of inhabitants. The projects under IWDP are being implemented in districts of the country. IWDP is a 100 per cent Centrally Sponsored Scheme. The cost norm is Rs. 4000 per hectare. The basic objective of this scheme is to take up integrated wastelands development based on village/micro watershed plan. The stakeholders prepare these plan after taking into consideration land capability, site conditions and local needs. The scheme also helps in generation of employment in rural areas besides enhancing people's participation in the waste lands development programmes at all stages. This leads to equitable sharing of benefits and sustainable development. The major activities taken up under the scheme are:

(i) soil and moisture conservation measures like terracing, bunding, trenching, vegetative barriers etc.;

(ii) planting and sowing of multi purpose trees, shrubs, grasses, legumes and pasture land development;

(iii) encouraging natural regeneration;

(iv) promotion of agro-forestry and horticulture;

(v) wood substitution and fuel wood conservation measures;

(vi) measures needed to disseminate technology; training, extension and creation of greater degree of awareness among the participants; and

(vii) encouraging people's participation.

The programme is being implemented in 222 districts in 25 States of the country. Since 1995-96, 298 projects have been sanctioned for treatment of an area of 29.24 lakh hectares at a total cost of Rs.1134.00 crore till the end of March, 2001. In the first four years of the Ninth Plan, an area of 6.51 lakh hectare has been covered with an expenditure of Rs.326.80 crore. During 2001-02, an outlay of Rs.430.00 crore provided to cover an area of 4.00 lakh hectare.

Centrally Sponsored Schemes

1. Integrated Rural Housing Programme

(a) New Houses

Under this scheme free houses are constructed for the houseless families living below the poverty line in rural areas. The scheme is funded by the Centre and the State in the ratio of 75:25. Unit cost has been fixed as Rs. 20,000 for ordinary soil and Rs. 22,000 for difficult soil. Besides this, the State Government provides a sum of Rs. 12,000 per house for laying RCC roof. Beneficiaries are selected through Grama Sabha. Houses are allotted in the name of women head of the family. During 2002-03, 37,686 houses were taken up at a cost of Rs. 121.78 crores which includes Central release of Rs. 57.42 crores and State release of 64.36 crores including roof cost.

(b) Upgradation of unserviceable Kutcha Houses

This is a sub component of Integrated Rural Housing Programme of which 20 per cent of the allocation is ear marked for upgradation of kutcha houses of the families living below the poverty line in rural areas. Unit cost has been fixed as Rs.

10000/, which is shared by the centre and the state in the ratio of 75:25. Beneficiaries are selected by the Grama Sabha. During 2002-2003, 19,142 Kutcha house were taken up for upgradation, at a cost of Rs. 19.14 crores which includes Central release of Rs. 14.36 crores and State release of Rs. 4.78 crores.

*(c) **Innovative Stream for Rural Housing and Habitant Development***

This scheme intends to popularise low cost building technology and materials in rural areas. Under this scheme, houses are constructed free of cost to the rural poor. Infrastructure facilities such as drinking water, drainage, streets etc., are provided by dovetailing other ongoing schemes. This scheme is fully funded by the Government of India. Two projects can be taken up for each district. Cost of each Project would vary from Rs. 20 lakhs to Rs. 50 lakhs. Since the inception of the scheme, proposals in respect of 20 districts had been sent to Government of India for a total project cost of Rs. 7.06 crores. Out of this 14 projects were sanctioned at a cost of Rs. 4.33 crores. The balance projects are under the scrutiny of Government of India.

4. Pradhan Mantri Gramodaya Yojana (PMGY – Rural Shelter)

Under this scheme Government of India provides additional assistance, for shelter, primary education, primary health, nutrition, water supply and electrification in rural areas. Rural Shelter Component alone is implemented by the Rural Development Department, During 2002-2003, 5818 units were taken up for the allotment of Rs. 18.78 crores.

5. Pradhan Mantri Gram Sadak Yojana (PMGSY)

This scheme aims to provide all weather roads to all rural habitations with population of more than 1000 by 2003 and all habitations of more than 500 population by the year 2007. So far, works covering 2291.150 Kms of roads at a cost of Rs. 267.192 crores have been taken up. The National Quality Monitors of GOI have rated the quality of works, the best in the country. The performance of the State in terms of fund utilisation has been appreciated by Government of India and the Center has enhanced the allotment of 2001-02 by Rs. 35.00 crores which is an increase of 43.75 per cent over the original allotment of Rs. 80 crores.

6. Member of Parliament Local Area Development Programme (MPLADP)

A sum of Rs. 2.00 crores is allotted per MP (Lok Sabha and Rajya Sabha) for taking up developmental works identified by the concerned MP. With regard to Members of the Lok Sabha the scheme is implemented in the districts falling within the constituency of the concerned Members of Parliament. In the case of Rajya Sabha, the M.P can choose any district within the state that the M.P. belongs to. As far as the nominated members are concerned, they can choose any district in India for the implementation of the Programme. The District Collector gives administrative sanction for the works and the works are executed through open tender system, During 2002-03, a sum of Rs. 98.00 crores was released by the Government of India with which 5086 works have been taken up.

8. Restructured Central Rural Sanitation Programme (RCRSP)

The objective of the programme is to improve sanitary conditions in rural areas. It is a project based programme focusing on Total Sanitation Campaign. The projects envisage demand driven approach with greater public participation. The project period will cover 24 months, spread over 3 years. Cost of the project is shared between the Government of India, State Government and beneficiaries. It is implemented in 16 districts at a total project cost of Rs. 184.80 crores. Totally, 12,29,999 individual household latrines, 12,686 school toilets, 12,083 Anganwadi toilets, 1,076 Sanitary Complexes for Women and 142 Rural Sanitary Marts have been taken up. During 2002-03 projects have been sanctioned for Salem, Sivagangai, Dindigul, Thoothukudi, Thanjavur and Tiruvallur Districts.

9. National Programme of Improved Chulahs

The objectives of the programme are to prevent deforestation for fuel, to eliminate health hazard faced by women in cooking and to reduce drudgery in collection of fuel materials in rural areas. This programme is fully funded by the Government of India.Under the programme semi permanent chulahs with a life span of minimum 5 years are provided to the beneficiaries. Subsidy of Rs. 80/- per chulah is provided. During 2002-2003 a sum of Rs. 15 lakhs was released, benefiting 15,000 beneficiaries.

10. National Project on Biogas Development

This programme aims at promoting eco-friendly non conventional energy sources with multiple benefits. Prevention of deforestation, production of enriched manure and improvement of sanitation and hygiene by linking sanitary toilets with bio-gas plants are the major thrust areas of this programme. This programme is fully funded by the Government of India with a subsidy component of Rs. 1,800/- for general category and Rs. 2,300/- for scheduled category in the plains. An uniform rate of Rs. 3,500/- is provided for hilly areas. An amount of Rs. 700/- is provided for installation and maintenance of every plant to the Turnkey agent.

Social Sector Programmes

1. Conversion of Unserviceable Houses into Pucca/Semi-Pucca

As the need for upgradation is acutely felt, 20 percent of the IAY allocation has been earmarked for conversion of unserviceable kutcha houses into pucca/semipucca houses with effect from April 1, 1999. A maximum assistance of Rs. 10,000/- per unit is provided for conversion of unserviceable kutcha houses into pucca/semipucca.

2. Samagra Awas Yojana

Samagra Awas Yojana is a comprehensive housing scheme launched recently with a view to ensuring integrated provision of shelter, sanitation and drinking water. It has been decided to take up Samagra Awas Yojana on pilot basis in one block each of 25 districts of 24 States and one Union Territory which have been identified for implementing the participatory approach under the Accelerated Rural Water Supply Programme. The existing schemes of contribution coming from the people. So far an amount of Rs. 145 lakh has been released, i.e. Rs. 25 lakh each to Himachal Pradesh, Karnataka, Kerala, Tamil Nadu and Madhya Pradesh, and Rs. 20 lakh to West Bengal.

3. Rural Water Supply Programme

As the provision of safe drinking water in the rural areas is the responsibility of the States, funds are being provided for the provision of this facility in the State's budgets right from the First Five Year Plan period. The Accelerated Rural Water Supply Programme (ARWSP) was introduced in 1972-73 by the Government of India, with a view to assisting the States and Union Territories (UTs) to accelerate the pace of drinking water supply.

Aadhar Number
Providing Identification Number to Rural People

India has taken up the huge task of providing Unique Identification Number known as *Aadhar* to all citizens of the country. As the word connotes *foundation*, the 12 digit identification number aims to be the foundation of our rights and claims to a wide range of facilities. It also stands to be the very basis of one's identity. The responsibility of issuing the number rests on the Unique Identification Authority of India (UIDAI). The very purpose of the UID project is to give every Indian resident a unique number thereby preventing all kinds of duplication that currently exist. The targeted time for completing this Himalayan task will be the end of 2015.

Understanding Aadhar

The requirement of a unique identification number was felt even before. Though such a number was created for BPL families, it was felt that the number could be highly beneficial if issued to all citizens of the country. Consequently, the Unique Identification Authority was constituted in 2008 and Mr. Nandan Nilkeni was appointed as its chairman from 2nd July 2009 onwards for five years initial period. The project aims to collect the biometrics of all ten fingers, face and also the iris image of both eyes of an individual. Then the number will be stored in a centralized database and linked to the basic demographics and biometric information such as the already collected photograph, fingerprints and iris of the individual. All these ensure the uniqueness of the number and thereby reduce the chances of errors. The most important advantage of Aadhar is that the card will provide a simple solution to various kinds of documentary proof. As it contains all kinds of personal details, it will check efforts to create fake identity for individual benefits so that various types of duplication of data can be easily and effectively blocked. The card will ensure wide usage such as income tax purposes, banking transactions, checking black money transfer, using the card as license, credit cum debit cum ATM card and the like. Aadhar will also enable mobility of people across different parts of the country for search of job and so on. Thus, Aadhar will be highly beneficial for both the individuals as well as the government for carrying out a lot of day to day activities smoothly and transparently.

Unique Identification Numbers Around the World

Unique Identification Authority of India (UIDAI) has been created by the Government of India as an as an attached office under the Planning Commission. Its role is to develop and implement the necessary institutional, technical and legal infrastructure to issue Unique Identity numbers to Indian residents. UIDAI has adopted the name Aadhaar for the 12-digit unique number which it will issue for all residents. The number will be stored in a centralized database and will be linked to the basic demographics and biometric information – photograph, ten fingerprints and iris – of each individual. The features of the Aadhaar will be that this number will only provide identity and prove identity not citizenship, and facilitate enrolment of residents with proper verification and adoption of a partnership model. The UIDAI will be the regulatory authority managing a Central ID Repository (CIDR), which will issue UID numbers, update resident information and authenticate the identity of the residents as required.

Technology systems will have a major role across the UDIAI infrastructure. The UID database will be stored on a central server. Enrolment of the resident will be computerized, and information exchange between Registrars and the CIDR will be over a network. Authentication of the residents will be online. The Authority will put systems in place for the security and safety of information. The UID Technology Solution encompasses application software, system software, infrastructure, including IT systems, Private Cloud of Data Centres. It also encompasses all the processes required to architect, design develop, release, deploy and manage the solution and manage the cloud & data center operations. The UID Software system consists of the enrolment client application, enrolment and authentication server applications, and AADHAAR Unified portal, Business Intelligence Module, Fraud Detection Module and the entire supporting software platform. The CIDR refers to the infrastructure including NOC, Cloud of Data Centres, Network, Servers and Storage, for production, staging and testing. The CIDR operations refer to the managed services required to operate the cloud of data centers and associated infrastructure (Network, Servers, Storage, Power, and HVAC).

Of course India is not the first country to link identity with biometrics on a national scale. Attempts have been made before by several countries around the world and many of them are using biometrics as basis for identification of citizens in some form. With Aadhar therefore, India joins a club of more than fifty nations around the world that already have some form of national identity cards. The list includes most of the European Union countries, United States, Brazil, Indonesia, Israel, Hong Kong, Chile, Sri Lanka and many more. We shall now try to identify those identification numbers of countries around the world.

Denmark has a ten digit *Personal Identification Number* called 'CPR' used widely for several purposes like health care, tax payments, banking and insurance etc. This number is a part of the personal information stored in the Civil

Registration System which was established in 1968. CPR is in the format of DDMMYY-SSSS where DDMMYY is the date of birth and SSSS is a sequence of number. The first digit shows the century of birth and the last digit is odd for males and even for females. In Ireland, there exists the *Personal Public Service Number* (PPS No) which is widely used for a widening variety of public services. The basic format of PPS No is 1234567A and it is unique to each individual.

The United States right from 1936 with the establishment of Social Security Administration was issuing a *Social Security Number* (SSN) to its citizens. Though SSN was used for social security purposes initially, it is now being used widely for a number of non-social security needs and for services such as child support collections, low enforcement etc. In Canada, a *Social Insurance Number* (SIN) is used for various government programmes. SIN is a nine digit number created in 1964 to serve as an account number for pension and employment insurance programmes. Later, the number was used for tax reporting and many other administrative purposes

Chile's *National Identification Number* is called RUN. This number is used as multi-purpose number such as tax payer number, passport number, social insurance number, driving license number etc. Brazil, another Latin American country had been providing unique ID cards to its citizens since the beginning of 20th century. The card called the *National Identity/ Insurance Card Number* is the national identity document in Brazil. The Card contains the name, the birth date, the names of parents, the signature and the thumb print of the citizens. Argentina's national identity number is known as *National Identity Document* – DNI - assigned at the time of birth of individuals. It is noted that most of the poor people in Argentina do not have DNI card.

Sri Lanka also provides a *National Identity Card* (NIC) to all citizens above 16 years of age. NIC is a 10 digit number in the format of 00000000A where 0 is a digit and A is a letter. NIC is strictly required in Sri Lanka for identity proof and is used while applying for passport, driving license and appearing to vote. In Indonesia, all citizens are provided a 16 digit unique identification number known as *Nomor Induk Kependudukan.*

The number is in the format of PPRRSSDDMMYY where, PP stands for province, RR stands for regency or city, SS stands for sub district code, DDMMYY denote the date of birth and finally XXXX is the computerized number. A *Hong Kong Identity Card* (HKID) mandatory for all citizens above 11 years of age and its long term residents is being used in Hong Kong.

While we recognize the attempts made by countries around the world in providing a unique identification number to their citizens, we would be fully justified in feeling proud of our own project, which is perhaps the largest of its kind given India's huge population and her demographic complexities.

Applications of UID

UID Technology solution has three main parts, namely UID Technology Solution (UID-TS) , Partner Systems interacting with the UID-TS and the UID Stakeholder Ecosystem . The three components are described briefly as below.

The application hosted by CIDR can be broadly categorized under the core applications and supporting applications. In the core category are the enrolment and authentication applications services, while the supporting category consists of applications required for administration, analytics, reporting, fraud detection interfaces to Logistics Provider and Contact Centre and the portal. The Enrolment Application services comprises of the client enrolment request for providing a UID. The enrolment application orchestrates the enrolment workflow by integrating various sub-systems such as demographic data validation, biometric de-duplication, and UID generation. Lifecycle updates (not only initial enrolment) such as correction, on-going updates, child re-enrolments, death reporting, etc. are also possible through the application. Manual Exception Workflow is required to resolve Enrolment requests that cannot be resolved automatically. Basic Letter Printing and Delivery functionality is also available.

The Authentication Application provides the identity authentication services. Various authentication request types such demographic, biometric, simple or advanced authentications are supported. The UID number submitted is used for 1:1 match for the resident's record. The inputs would be then matched against the resident information stored in CIDR databases to authenticate the resident.

The Fraud Detection Application is deployed to detect and reduce identity fraud. For example identify fraud scenarios that the application needs to handle are: misrepresentation of information, multiple registrations by same resident, registration for non-existent residents, or authentication as someone else. Multiple approaches are used for detecting fraud. The Administrative Application takes care of user management, roles and access control, business process automation, and status reporting. It ensures a trust network across both internal and external entities. The external entities could be registrars, enrolment agencies, field agencies, introducers, authentication user agencies, and other partners within the eco system.

UIDAI has selected biometrics as the primary method to check for duplicate identity records, in order to ensure that an individual can establish their identity uniquely in an easy and cost-effective manner. Hence, one of the key component of the UID Technology is the Biometric Solution. Three have been selected by UIDAI to operate simultaneously in CIDR. The biometric solution is intended to perform the following functions:

(a) Biometric image capture, segmentation & quality check during the enrolment process.

(b) Matching of biometrics to enable provision of identity verification by UIDAI.

(c) 1:N biometric de-duplication to enable issuance of Unique ID to every resident of India.

Biometric Enrollment: the Biometric Solution is able to provide components to capture, segment and perform quality check of biometric images as part of enrollment client software. These components are capture device independent and provide consistent and compliant images for the enrollment server. The biometric data captured is as per data formats laid out in Biometric Design Standards for UID Applications, Biometric Committee Report.

Biometric De-duplication (multi-modal de-duplication solution): The other core component of UID enrolment is biometric duplicate check. The duplicate check function of the proposed Biometric Solution receives incoming multi-modal biometric data and performs biometric duplicate check against the gallery. UIDAI at present captures multi-modal biometric features (Fingerprints, Face and Iris) of every resident for 1:N biometric de-duplication. It is expected that with the implementation of Aadhaar technology and ecosystem the residents who enroll for Aadhaar will no longer face the problem of performing repeated Know Your Customer (KYC) checks. Residents would also be spared the trouble of repeatedly proving identity through documents each time they wish to access services such as obtaining a bank account, passport, or driving license etc. By providing a clear proof of identity, Aadhaar is expected to empower poor and underprivileged residents in accessing services such as the formal banking system and give them the opportunity to easily avail various other services provided by the Government. The centralized technology infrastructure of the UIDAI will enable 'anytime, anywhere' authentication. Aadhaar will thus give migrants mobility of identity. Aadhaar authentication can be done both offline and online. Online authentication through a cell phone or land line connection will allow residents to verify their identity remotely. Remotely, online Aadhaar-linked identity verification will give poor and rural residents the same flexibility that urban non-poor residents presently have in verifying their identity and accessing services such as banking and retail. Besides the social benefits, the technology benefits to the Government sector could be manifold. The UID Technology would enable creation of an e-governance cloud platform to be shared by central and state governments, ready to use platforms, easy to build applications with reusable technology elements and components, processes and skills , provide a boost to relevant technology, including biometrics. It is thus seen that the UID Technology Solution (UID-TS) will be the core technology solution enabling Unique ID implementation. This technology solution will have three key roles to play:

1. Capture and store biographic, photographic and biometric information of residents of India.
2. Generate and assign a Unique, 12-digit ID number for each resident.
3. Act as a means for identity and address verification for various user agencies with a certain level of assurance.

The core technology challenges related to the UID Technology Solution flow from the biometric matching system. At the heart of the challenge is the enrollment process that would require the UID Technology Solution to perform the biometric de-duplication on a population of India's size with acceptable degrees of accuracy and turnaround time. Surrounding the challenge are issues of 'nearly difficult to predict' workloads on the system and security.

Community Radio
Unraveling Its Potential to Rural Women

> *"Just as a bird cannot fly with one wing only, a nation would not march further if women are left behind."*
>
> **–Ranjit Singh**

Women are the base for all round development venture. No Nation can develop without the development of women. Women, the reservoir of productive human resource constitutes almost half of the country's total population. Women have strong potential role in many aspects of economic development, in relation to their family responsibility as well as their Agriculture production activity. Women status is pure indicator of progress of any Nation. Women are the laps in which a new seed of life grows up, but in the country like India, condition of women is not so good. Women are weaker sections of the society suffering from various problems. According to World Bank (2003) about one third of the total disease burden in developing country of women is linked to health problems related to pregnancy, child birth, abortion and reproduction tract infection due to lack of awareness about many aspects. Previous researches have confirmed that women are suffering from various problems due to lack of knowledge, awareness on the many aspects. *Information is like a deep well, fed by perennial spring and our mind is the little bucket that we drop in to it"*. We will get as much as we can assimilate. Thus information is power. Right Information given the right time can empower the rural women. Empowerment is the One of the key factors in determining the success of development.

> *"Empowering women is prerequisite for creating nation, when women are empowered, society with stability is assured. Empowerment of women is essential as their value system lead to the development of good family, good society and good nation"*
>
> **–Dr. APJ Abdul Kalam**

There are various Information Communication Technologies as radio, television, mobile, internet are used to aware the rural women for many aspects. Among all these technologies Community Radio is powerful medium for disseminating the message effectively among the rural people. It is only medium having maximum coverage as compared to any other media in developing countries. It serves a recognizable community. The community can be territorial or geographical - a township, village, district or island. It can also be a group of people with common interests, who are not necessarily living in one defined territory. Consequently, community radio can be managed or controlled by one group, by combined groups, or of people such as women, children, farmers, fisher folk, ethnic groups, or senior citizens. Studies have shown that the most relevant information - educational and developmental – is disseminated and exchanged. Important local issues are aired. A free market place of ideas and opinions is opened up and people are given the opportunity to express themselves socially, politically and culturally. Community radio helps to put the community members in charge of their own affairs. Community radio is one medium for the women Empowerment. 64 community radio are working in India. Anna FM is India's first campus 'community' radio, launched on 1 Feb. 2004, which is run by Education and Multimedia Research Centre (EM²RC), and all programmes are produced by the students of Media Sciences at Anna University. Presently Gyan Vani, Radio Active, Jamia, Holy cross, DU, KONGUE, Sagarmatha and Kumaon Vani etc. Community radio are working in India. These CRS broadcasted various programmes related to many aspects as health, hygiene, and women right and environment issues. Various research studies have confirmed that Community radio is powerful communication medium to empower the rural women.

India is the second most populous country having crossed the population of one billion. The population of women in India is 496,514,346. The most glaring evidence of gender bias in India is the low sex ratio. According to Census 2001, Sex ratio is 927 females per 1000 males and this ratio is 990 females per 1000 males worldwide. India's adverse sex ratio reflects relative neglect of women's health and their social subordination. Out of that number, 120 million women live in poverty. Over 70 per cent of India's population currently derives its livelihood from land resources, which includes 84 per cent of the economically-active women. Ours is male dominated society where women are described as the "Second Sex" and the "Second Creature" who live on surplus. Their very existence has been considered as parasite on the men who rule them. Female subordination has been an essential feature of human life in all contemporary societies, although with a varying degree and expression male dominance. One of the important manifestations of this women subordination lies in the division of lab our which provides a cheap and ready source of labour. Division of labour between sexes is culturally imposed and this segregated role pattern has led to a structural subordination of women to man. However structural subordination of women to men has been able to prevent them from playing a vital role in the overall development of the society. Especially, their active participation in economic activities has become common in all countries, developed and developing.

Participation of women in socio-economic activities is a global issue. Women play a very crucial part in the socio-economic activities and have now become an integral part of global market. The developed countries, many of which are now characterized by full employment still there is room for more women in the work force. On the other hand, the developing countries which are marked by labour surplus, the income of the families by and large is low and the economic vulnerability of the family compels their women members to go for work, supplementing the increase of income of their respective families.

Community radio is a type of radio service that caters to the interests of a certain area, broadcasting content that is popular to a local audience but which may often be overlooked by commercial or mass-media broadcasters. (UNESCO 2002) Community radio is an effective tool in protecting and promoting local culture. It is the best way to meet the needs of communication at local level because it helps to create a place where various people in the community including seniors, youths, mothers with small children, students, religious leaders, people with disabilities meet. The community radio is a form of local radio which defines itself as an autonomous entity and relies on the community for its survival without any commercial aims or objects. It is a medium that gives voice to the voiceless, that serves as the mouthpiece of the marginalised and is at the heart of communication and democratic processes within societies.

So Community radio is a local radio and participatory in nature, owned and run by the community, to serve the needs of the people. Community radio aims to change social conditions and improve the quality of cultural life through meaningful and relevant programme. People actively take part in formulating the station's policy, strategy and programme content.

Concept of Community radio: Community radio is confined to a small geographical area. It depends on low power transmission covering not more than 20-30 km. radius.

It serves a community which uses common resources for livelihood, has common development issues and concerns, which are relatively localized, nevertheless connected to national and regional development goals.

Evolution of Community radio: The concept of community radio developed in the West as an alternative to or a critique of the mainstream broadcast media. Tracing its origins in Europe in the 1960s and 1970s, McCain and Lowe (1990) found "Swashbuckling entrepreneurs boarded the airwaves illegally and seized as much of the audiences as they could carry away from the treasure chest monopolies controlled by the State with its public service model of broadcasting." Thus, pirate stations have been a major factor in motivating governments and national broadcasting systems to introduce legitimate local radio in Europe. In Latin American countries, community radio came into being as a critique of, and alternative to, predominantly commercial oriented radio broadcasting networks. There, the thrust was to use radio as a medium to support education of the marginalised populations.

Rules and Laws for Community Radio Stations in India

Community radio has grown since the New Order Era was over (1998). Since then, there are hundreds community radio exist but none of them affiliated or gather in one big association which has a clear division of community empowerment. Many of community radio exist because of hobby, specific interest, and only run temporary. Even so, the government has recognized their existence through defined community radio in the new Broadcasting Law. According to Broadcasting Law No. 32 year 2002, Article 21-249:

Section 6 [Community Broadcasting Institutions]

Article 21: (1) Community Broadcasting Institutions as referred to in Article 13 clause (2) point c, are broadcasting institutions in the form of Indonesian legal entities that are founded by certain communities. The Community Broadcasting Institutions are independent and non-commercial for they provide services to their community. The transmitters are low in power. (2) The Community Broadcasting Institutions as referred to in clause (1) operate on the following bases: a. Non profit oriented and not a part of a profit oriented company; and b. To educate and teach the community to increase welfare by promoting programmes in the field of culture, education and information that reflect national identity. (3) The Community Broadcasting Institution is a non partisan community organization that: *(a)* is neither a representative of a foreign organization or institution nor a member of international community; *(b)* is not related to illegal organizations; and *(c)* is not a tool for the propaganda of certain groups or factions.

Article 22: (1) A Community Broadcasting Institution is established by the fund contributed by a certain community and belongs to the community. (2) A Community Broadcasting Institution receives funding from donation, grants, sponsors and other legal sources with no string attached.

Article 23: (1) Community Broadcasting Institutions are not allowed to receive foreign initial fund to establish the stations and operational fund. (2) Community Broadcasting Institutions are not allowed to run advertisings and/or other commercials except the PSA's.

Article 24: (1) A Community Broadcasting Institution is obliged to develop codes of ethics and regulations that must be known widely by the community and other members of the society. (2) In the case of the existence grievance from the community or other members of the society on the violation of code of ethics and/or regulations, the Community Broadcasting Institution is obliged to take actions in accordance to guidelines and prevailing provisions.

There are three unique points clear from the above articles:

1. The community radio should educate and teach the community to increase welfare by promoting programmes in the field of culture, education and information that reflect national identity.

2. A Community Broadcasting Institution is established by the fund contributed by a certain community and belongs to the community.
3. Community Broadcasting Institutions are not allowed to run advertisings and/or other commercials except the PSA's.

From these three points we can conclude that the strength of a community radio is coming within the community and have more intimate relationship with its listener.

Model of Community Radio

Ensuring Participation-SEHJOG Model [SINGH, 2009]

The fundamental principle of Community radio for the farmers' community should be that the farmers can help in identifying the appropriate path to agricultural development. Farmers' participation at all stages relates in one way or the other to the selection, design, presentation, testing and adoption of appropriate technologies. Together with the farmers the constraints are ranked according to their severity and potential solution are identified after determining what flexibilities exists in the farming systems currently practiced.

Objective

To improve the well being of farm families by increasing the overall productivity of the farming system in the context of both, the private and societal goals, given the constraints and potentials imposed by the factors that determine the existing farming system.

SEHJOG Model

According to Singh (2009) Community radio for farmers can not fulfill its objective of being a community radio without the active and genuine participation of the farmers. Participation can be at two levels, sharing personal experiences and demonstration of the same to the community. Preference should be given to the common farmers especially small and marginal farmers doing well, invented own techniques and tools must be selected. They should be motivated to come to the radio station for recording. Some monetary incentives can be given to help the selected farmers to prepare for their participation. Rehearsals can be done.

1. Selection for participation
2. Ensuring participation
3. Helping participants to prepare
4. Joint programme planning
5. Organising training
6. Genuine participation

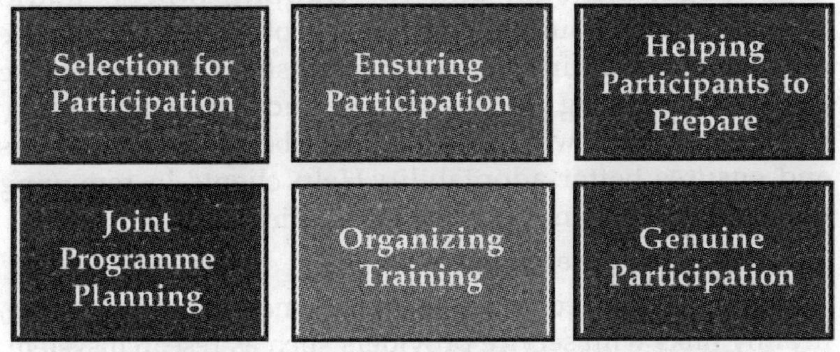

Three functional components

1. Technical input
2. Facilities
3. Participation

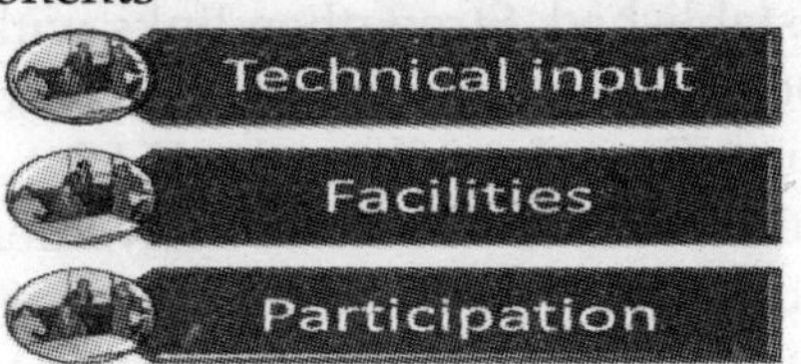

Technical Input

The success of community radio for agriculture will depends upon the selection delivery, acceptability and adoption of the transmitted information. Three elements have been identified.

1. Promotion of tested and recommended practices

Deliver only evidence based and most up to date practices which can improve the farm efficiency and income of the client farmers. Avoid unproven practices to reduce risk.

Remove unnecessary barriers that hinder adoption. Avoid unproven practices, which waste resources and faith of the listeners. Promote only those which has an visible impact.

2. Adoptability

Responsibility of community radio does not end with technology of communication. The objective is to encourage the adoption of the technology. To enhance conviction, modify approaches as needed. Provide training to the selected farmers, regarding the various modes of presentation. The people trained can then become responsible for sharing their knowledge and skill and for training others. Radio administration should ask clients and other key progranme constituents for their opinion and suggestions on hoe to make their functioning better and effective. Community participation empower community members to solve problems and ensures better adoptability.Help clients in removing unnecessary barriers that hinder adoption.

3. Link with other services

In order to select message and promote their acceptance, healthy links with service providers such as research system, extension system, services and supplies agencies have to be established. Strengthen links with services which give clients better and quicker access to required advice, services and supplies. An effort should be made to provide required services and advice at convenient locations throughout the community to minimize the distance and repeated visits to farmers must go to meet providers. Listeners' training camps can act as venues for providing services and supplies. Encourage exchange of information, collaboration and team work with in listeners; groups.

Facilities

Basic facilities are essential for success an deficiency of the radio. Akashvani usually complains of shortage of resources. This should not affect community radio, as it is going a serve a limited number of people of a specific area. Resourcefully organisation do nit let common constraints

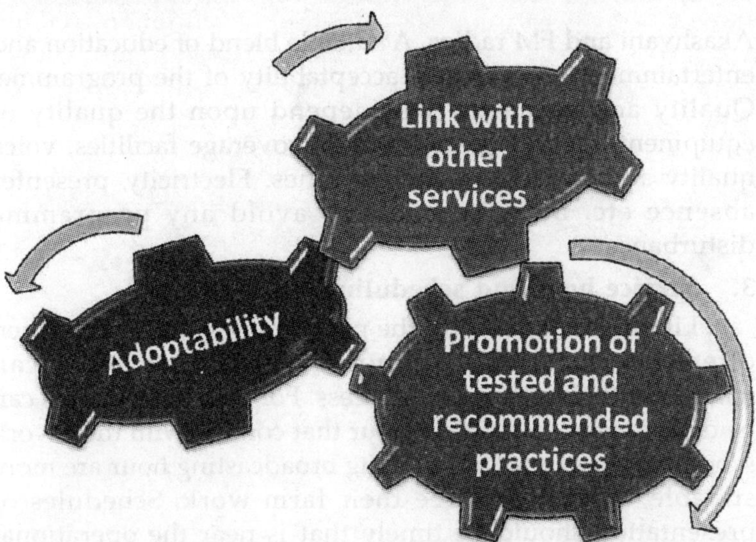

prevent then from doing the best they can. Resourceful mess means finding creative ways to solve problems with the resource at hand.

1. Practicability

Since community radio is managed by a non government organization. It needs to be managed through a practical approach. Minimizing paper work and maximization information use are crucial to analyzing programmes, solving problems, identifying trends, setting goals and using resources wisely. Collecting required and correct information is essential for planning. Providing feedback and receiving feedback also enhance the quality of the contents and presentation. To provide and receive constructive feedback, directors should determine whether information is being received on all key indicators all gaps in information management have been identified, information is accurate and reliable and decision or actions are based on the feedback.

2. Broadcasting quality and efficiency

Broadcasting quality and efficiency are of utmost importance in this competitive age. Competition is with

Akashvani and FM radios. A suitable blend of education and entertainment can enhance acceptability of the programme. Quality and efficiency will depend upon the quality of equipment, recording studio, field coverage facilities, voice quality and training of the machines. Electricity, presenter absence etc. must be made tp avoid any programme disturbance.

3. Service hour and scheduling

Listeners can listen to the programme more easily when offered at continents hour. Broadcasting hour can inadvertently limit listener's access. For instance, farmers can be discouraged by daytime hour that conflict with their work schedule. Noon and late evening broadcasting hour are more suitable; as they are free their farm work. Schedules of presentation should be timely that is near the operational time. It must also be ensured that required inputs are easily available in the area.

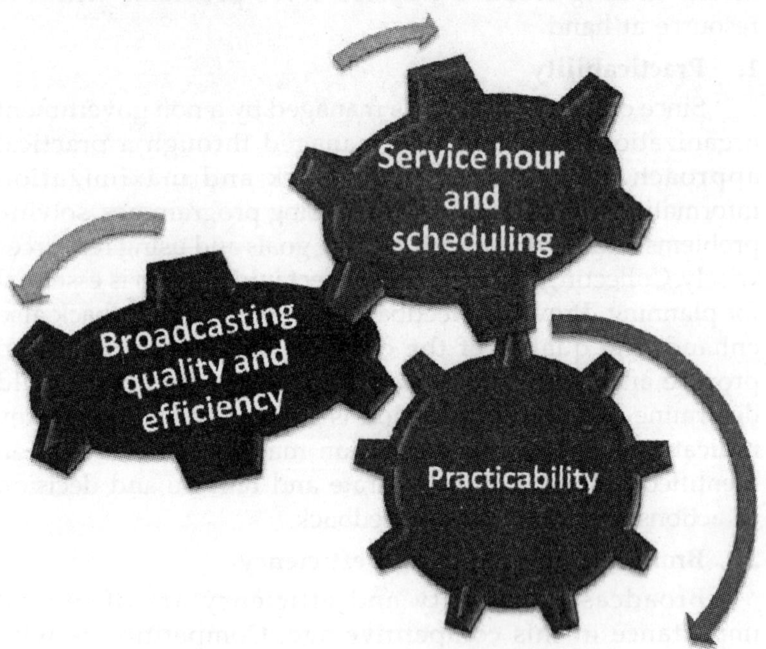

Participation

Community radio is for specific group of a selected area with predetermined objectives. Participation of the target group is essential to achieve the objectives of the radio. Participation can be enhanced by providing relevant and timely technical information, active involvement of the farmers, promoting debates and discussion.

1. Popularity

It can be enhanced through providing relevant, new and timely technical information. Entertainment and cultural promotion through the diffusion of various models of personal and collective recreation and enjoyment will also increase the number of listeners. Listeners; reactions can also help in improving the programme. Regular monitoring and evaluation is essential to win the confidence of the listeners. Giving to help farmers to solve their problems will also add to the popularity score. Credibility and trust are the other factors responsible for promoting better relations between communicators and listeners.

2. Active involvement

Community radios are for a specific community. Without the active involvemenbt of that community radio can not be called a community radio. Infact, Community radio must be by the community and for the community, farmers must be activity involved at every stage of the progrmme that is planning, execution and monitoring. Farmers should treat the radio station as an information and help centre. Community radio must ensure a two way communication. Infact, farmers of the area should treat the radio as their own.

3. Listeners self help groups

Leadership is vital for effective functioning of the radio. Active participation can be ensured through local leaders. Leaders inspire people through their own positive behaviour, ethics and values and serve as role models. Their shared vision provides fellow farmers with purpose and direction in their work. Radio listeners' self help groups are required to be organized for effective adoption of the information being communicative by Community radio. Farmers have to organized themselves keeping Community radio as a central link. Collective decision making, helping each other, collective purchase of inputs, marketing and processing of the producer is essential for agricultural development in future. Community radio must become the force to organize the farmers for self development.

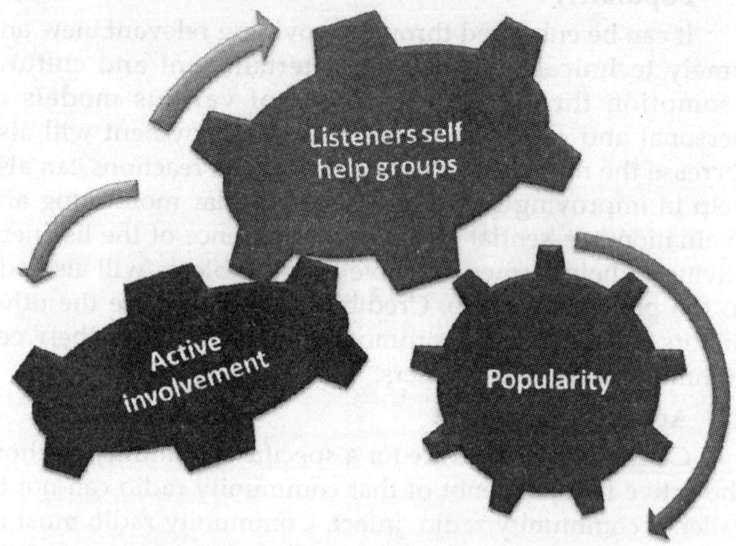

Status of Community Radio in India

This graph (*See graph on next page*) shows the status of community radio in India. Presently more than 100 community radio stations are working in India.

Community Radio Stations in India

With the notification of policy and procedure for establishing community radio by the Government of India in 2002, resourceful universities in a few selected cities established community radio and achieved the objective to some an extent as is evident from the following:

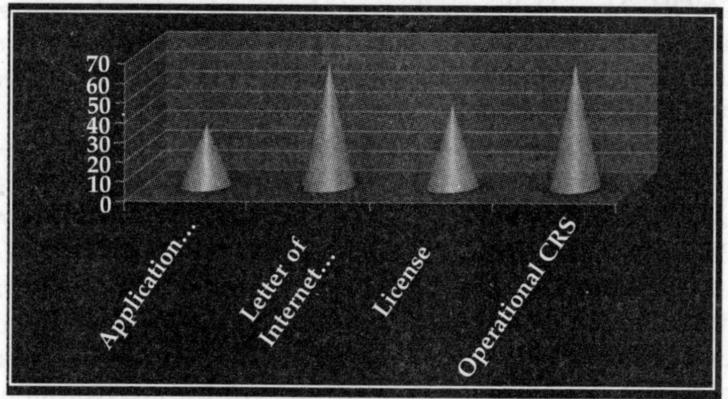

1. *Gyan Vani CR*: The Human Resources Development Ministry and the Indira Gandhi National Open University [IGNOU] with the help of Prasar Bharati launched Gyan Vani CR in 2001 operating initially through Allahabad, Banglore, and Coimbatore FM stations of India on test transmission mode, with the network expected to expand to a total of 40 stations. It operates as 'Media Cooperative' with the day-to-day programmes being contributed by various educational institutions, NGOs, Government and semi-Government organizations, UN agencies, Ministries [Agriculture, Environment, Health, Women and Child Welfare, Science & Technology], besides National level Institutions [NCERT, NOIS and State Open Universities]. It has target audience of students of open and conventional universities within a radius of 60 km covering entire city. Programmes relayed during 0600 AM to 1000AM focus to enhance teaching-learning process in Hindi or English; and cover a wide range of subjects, namely creating awareness about Panchayati Raj Institutions and their functionaries; Women Empowerment; Consumer Rights; Human Rights, the Rights of the Child; Health Education; Science Education; Extension Education; Vocational Education; Teacher Education; Non-formal Education; Adult Education; Education for the handicapped; Education for the down trodden; education for the tribal community. The Gyan Darshan Educational TV Channel of

IGNOU, New Delhi on its completion of a decade started catering to, through four channels, different cross section of audiences in Agra, Chandigarh, Jalandhar, Srinagar, Trichy and Thiruvanathapuram.

2. ***Our Voice*** **(Namma Dhwani)**, India was inaugurated in September 2001 in Budikote village of Kolar district in Kartanaka, in partnership among VOICES, MYRADA, UNESCO, and Groups of poor farmers in the Boodkote region in Kolar district. Its target audience comprises Farmers, Rural entrepreneurs, Youth and Children and programmes focus development issues related to agriculture, health, education, economic development, children, youth, environment, entrepreneurship and cultural affairs of immediate concern.

3. ***Anna University*** in Chennai,Tamil Nadu established CR in 2004 covering students and dense urban population of Kannigapuram, Kotturpuramm, Balajinagar, Saidapet, Little Mount, Kobalitittam, Chitra Nagar, Ventakapuram, all within a 10 km radius. Target audience comprised Students, day laborers and housewives [70% female audience]. Women listen and also participate in the programmes for 11 hours [7 am to 6 pm]. Programmes focus on Women empowerment; Entrepreneurship management; Vazhkaiyin Vannangal (life style programme); English Language Programme; Samudaya Nerkaanal (Face-to-Face with the Community Live Phone-in Interactive Talk Show); Music Programme; Science awareness; Consumer awareness; Careers guidance; Management aspects; Natchathira Nerkaanal (Interviews with lesser known stars from the community); Community matter; Programmes for Visually Challenged; Arokiya Vazhvu (Health is wealth); The CR arranges invite experts, celebrities and academia to participate in events or participate in phone-in programmes. Students from the Department of Media science volunteered to anchor *Samudhaya Neerkaanal*, a live phone-in community programmes.

4. ***Holy Cross CR*** was established in the campus of Holy Cross College, Tiruchirappalli, Tamil Nadu in December 2006. Its target audience comprises students, home makers, youth

and farmers and broad cast between 6.00 to 10.00 AM and 3.00 to 8.00 PM programmes with focus on creating awareness about critical areas of agriculture, social welfare, education, health and environment; preserving and promoting the traditional wisdom, knowledge and skills, thereby facilitating promotion of arts, crafts, culture and traditions of the rural population, besides enhancing participation of the local rural community in development; building capacity through education; providing opportunities to upgrade skills in the field of their interest. Its preferred formats integrate wide range of issues creatively in different formats like skit, magazine, folk songs, quiz, talk shows, discussions, phone in, interviews. Its qualified staff and volunteers helped the station to increase their broadcast hours from two hours to a nine hours a day.

5. ***Delhi University CR*** was launched at its School of Open Learning located in the North Campus of the varsity on October 2, 2007 and commenced broadcasting between 8.00 and 10.00 AM in the morning and 5.00 and 7.00 PM within a radius of 10 km a wide range of programmes with focus on creating awareness on Health, Hygiene; Anti smoking; Gender sensitization; Environment and other issues related to local communities; Phone-in Programmes with the experts on Health, Education, stress management, Environment, interpersonal relationship between parent and children, examination stress etc Spreading awareness among the students about various careers, career counseling and broadcasting other socially relevant programmes. Broadcasting the programmes of campus and colleges such as seminars, workshops, lectures, discussions, debates, cultural functions etc. for the student communities. Conducting (including academic counseling) interactive programmes for the students enrolled at School of Open Learning who could not get the opportunities for face-to-face teaching learning process. Broadcasting different community based programmes with the help of community members residing in the adopted slum areas and the community residing around Delhi

University.

7. ***Sangham CR*** was established on October 15, 2008 by the initiatives of the Deccan Development Society Community Media Trust in Village Machnoor of Jharasangam Mandal in Medak District, Andhra Pradesh. Target audience is rural women from the marginalized groups in particular and rural people in general. Programmes include Seed sovereignty and women; Food sovereignty and women; Women and biodiversity; Women and land; Ownership; Women and ecological agriculture; Ecological enterprises for rural women; Healthcare and plant medicines; Herbal care for animal diseases; Making children's education relevant to rural milieu; violence against women; legal education for women. Programmes also embody local issues in the light of global vision and are designed at the community level; Women Speak to Women with complete focus on women's issues. Programmes are being broadcast daily between 08 pm and 09.30 pm and has a plan to increase duration of broadcast upto four hours daily.

8. ***Kumoun Vani***: Ministry of Information and Broadcasting, Government of India had signed a Grant of Permission Agreement for establishing, maintaining and operating a Community Radio Station at "The Energy Resources Institute", Distt. Mukteshwar, Uttarakhand in 11 March 2000. The Community Radio Station named "*Kumoun Vani*" provides the opportunities to the local communities on a common platform and enables better communication and flow of resources between them. The main objectives of *Kumoun Vani* are: (1) To uplift the socio-economic status of rural poor. (2) To solve the problems of the community. Presently Shri Mohan Singh Karki is the head of this CRS. Its transmission time is 8-10am, 12-2 pm, 3-5pm. The programmes related to Agriculture, Health, tourism, Children's programmes, education, art and culture Telephony programmes are broadcast daily. Supporting Organizations are: (1) Vivakanand Krishi Anusandhan Kosi Almora; (2) Chetioshna Vaagvani Kendra Mukteshwar; (3) IVRI

Mukteshwar; (4) Private Organization. Kumoun Vani has some distinct features such as: *(i)* It allows true participatory communication, which is essential for sustainable development; *(ii)* It serves a specific community, which is recognizable for development as regards its characteristics and needs *(iii)* Its programmes are relevant to the community; *(iv)* It is an ideal communication tool for the illiterate population, which is still predominant in many countries; *(v)* It is cost efficient in terms of investments, which will make it financially and socially sustainable.

Table 16.1: Community radio stations in India

NAMMA DHAWANI COMMUNITY RADIO	
Launch in	September, 2001
Location on	Chitradugra in Budhikote village of Kolar district of Kartanaka
Programmes:	Agricultural, medical, educational, and cultural programmes, Watershed management, "Our health is in our hand"
Target group	Men, Farmers, Rural entrepreneurs, Children and Youth
Operated	A partnership between VOICES, MYRADA, UNESCO, and poor farmer groups in the Budhikote sector in Kolar.
Development Issues	Agriculture, Children, Youth, Environment, Health, Economic Development.
ANNA FM COMMUNITY RADIO STATION	
Launch in	1 February 2004
Place	Anna University, Chennai
Run by	Education and Multimedia Research Centre (EM^2RC)
Area covered	Kannigapuram, Kotturpuramm, Balajinagar, Saidapet, Little Mount, Kobalitittam, Chitra Nagar, Ventakapuram, all within a 10 km radius.

(Contd...)

Target audience	70 per cent female audience. Women listen and also participate in the programmes.
Transmission time	11 hours. 7 am to 6 pm
Frequency	90.4 MHz
HOLY CROSS COMMUNITY RADIO STATION	
On air since	December 2006.
Location	Holy Cross College, Tiruchirappalli (Tiruchi/ Trichi), a city in Tamil Nadu, South India.
Focus	❖ Enhancing participation of the local rural community in development ❖ Building capacity through education ❖ Providing creative opportunities to upgrade skills in the field of their interest
Frequency	90.4 Mhz
Target Audience	Students, home makers, youth and farmers
Preferred Formats	Integrating wide range of issues creatively in different formats like skit, magazine, folk songs, quiz, talk shows, discussions, phone in, interviews, characterization helps to seize the attention of the listeners.
DELHI COMMUNITY RADIO STATION	
Launch in	2 October 2007
Started by	Delhi University at School of Open Learning located in the North Campus
Target Audience	Women, youth
Frequency	90.4 Mhz
Range	10 KM
Broadcasting Hour	8 a.m. to 10 a.m. in the morning and 5 p.m. to 7 p.m. in the evening
Programmes	Awareness on health, Hygiene, Anti smoking, Gender sensitization, Environment and other issues related to local communities.
SANGHAM COMMUNITY RADIO STATION	
On-Air since	October 15, 2008

(Contd...)

Initiatives	Deccan Development Society Community Media Trust
Location	Village Machnoor, Jharasangam Mandal, Medak District, AP
Main Target Audience	Primary audience is rural women from the marginalized groups, also targets rural people in general.
Prime Themes	Seed sovereignty and women; Food sovereignty and women; Women and biodiversity; Women and land; Ownership; Women and ecological agriculture; Ecological enterprises for rural women; Healthcare and plant medicines; Herbal care for animal diseases; Making children's education relevant to rural milieu; violence against women; legal education for women.
Broadcast Timing	Daily between 8 pm to 9.30 pm (total 90 minutes). There is a plan to increase broadcast upto four hours daily in the next six months.
New Idea	Local issues, global vision - programme designing to be done at the community level; Women Speak to Women: Completely focused on women's issues.
KUMUAN VANI COMMUNITY RADIO STATION	
Launched in	11 March 2010
Area	Mukhteswar
Run by	TERI (The Energy Resource Institute)
Programmes	Environment, Agriculture, Culture, Weather
Radius	10 km
Coverage area	20 villages

Successful Women Empowerment Community Radio Programmes in India

1. Women Speak to Women

The Deccan Development Society (DDS) works in Zaheerabad of Medak district in Andhrta Pradesh.

Zaheerabad, which falls in the backward Telangana region, is contiguous with other least developed districts of North Karnataka. A semi-arid region sans industrilisation, people migrate during summers in large numbers since development schemes hardly reach the targeted population. It is in this geo-political and developmental context that the Deccan Development Society's efforts are centreed. The society works with about 100 Dalit women's groups (Sangams) consisting of nearly 4,000 members in 75 villages. Having working on areas like sustainable Agriculture and empowerment of Women, DDS established a media centre and its Women Speak to Women project is carried out through community radio and a community video project.

The DDS community radio station was set up with part funding from UNESCO.A total of Rs. 22 lakhs has been spent on the building and equipment including acoustics treatment, recorders, mixers, microphones, cables and installation. The FM station is designed to work on the audiocassette technology. It has two FM transmitters and a 100- metre transmission tower, which has a capacity to broadcast to a radius of 30 km roughly, the coverage area of DDS. With this installation and the nominal amounts paid to community members who the programme costs currently amount to about Rs. 500 per hour. It is estimated that if and when the station goes on air, it may be able to operate at Rs. 1000 - Rs. 1500 per hour. A five members technically trained team visits villages in the NGO's constituency and records programmes on a simple cassette recorder and edits it again on a cassette editor. The team has already prepared 200 hours of programmes and is awaiting a nod from the Government to switch on the transmitter that has a radius of about 30 Km covering some 70-oddd villages.

2. *Kunjal Panjee Kutch Ji* (Sarus Carne of Our Kutch)

The arid Kutch district of Gujrat has seen a silent revolution in the area of community radio. The Kutch Mahila Vikash Sanghatan and Drishti Collective decided to harness the potential of community radio to create awareness among women on Panchayat functions. All India Radio, has leased weekly air time to the NGO working with rural women. The all-women team produces a 30 minute serial every Thursday at 8 pm called *Kunjal Panjee Kutch Ji.* it began with 20 minutes but was increased to 30 minutes after the first three months after AIR loweresd its royalty rates. It completed a year of broadcast and then recently, in the post-air. Programmes scripted rehearsed and performed by the rural women with help of Drishti Collective are recorded and given to AIR in digital format for broadcast. The United Nations Development Programme funded this project for two years and its costs come over the period of broadcasting. The programmes are recorded and edited of broadcasting. The programmes are recorded and edited on digital audio format. Says one of the directors of the programme, "Just because it is for a rural audience, it should not be lacking in quality.

3. *Chala Ho Gaon Mein*

Palmau district of the newly formed state of Jharkhand, carved out of Bihar, is one of the most backward areas of northern India. Tribal and non tribal groups constitute majority of the population. They earn their livelihood out of minor forest produces and grow basic crops like paddy, Wheat and lentils. Ecological affected both the natural wealth of the region and the poverty with a sizable number of men dependent on more than 70 per cent of women illiterate. Poverty, however, has not hampered their natural aptitude for song-writing, musical compositions, folk theatre and non formal information dissemination.

Alternative for India (AID) and National Foundation for India (NFI) the two NGOs working in this area decided to dovetail the creative potential of the people with that of community radio to create awareness among prople in Palamau Trained in the basics of audio production, volunteers chosen from various villages of Paamau recorded quite a few field based programmes, including the signature tune being composed by the villagers themselves. The recorded programmes were then "narrowcast" in various villages.

Enthused by the response, the team then bargained for by the Palamau team focus on empowerment of the tribal communities with women as the focus. A few other significant initiatives by civil society groups in other parts of the country have given a fillip to the movement demanding space for communities in the FM spectrum.

Successful Case of Kumaun Vani CRS in Hill Area

The condition of hill women is even worse than rest of the world. Women in hills are actively engaged in all the activities right from the house to the fields. Women wake up early in the morning and go to the field or forest for the fuel wood and fodder collection. Fuel wood collection is the major time taking job of the hill women. On an average woman spent 3-4 hours in the kitchen and 4-5 hours a day in fuel wood collection and its management. Women as a weaker section of society in hill area are suffering from various health hazards as Anaemia, Back pain, Reproductive Tract Infection. Thus maternal mortality rate is higher in Uttarakhand rather than other states. Viewing the critical conditions of hill people Government of India had given permission to TERI for starting the Kumoun Vani Radio station in 2000. *Kumoun Vanni* community radio station is amidst of hill community who are the prime target audience. The main objective is to provide the information regarding best health Practices, Sanitation, Child rearing, family planning, better nutrition aspects etc.

A rural women belonging to one village nearer area of Mukteshwar claims that maternal mortality and problems among the hill women were less after applying all health practices which was broadcast on Kumoun Vanni. This community radio covers 25 villages around Mukteshwar. Another hill women adapted and implemented the advice given on Kumoun Vanni, which gave her better results and then the fellow hill women stared practicing it, which now almost all the nearer villages follows it. Similarly even in the vegetable field, one hill women used the pancakaavia as per the guideline of the programme and this improved the yield giving vegetables which helped them to gain profit. Ms. Renu from the same place after listening to the programme through radio used neem oil based preparation to control pests in her field. This gave better results in controlling pest gave a good yield, resulting in good profit. She expressed that the information provided through the radio programmes were very much useful for illiterate. Ms. Anchal started Bakery Business [Biscuit making through *Mandua- a hill crop]* after listening information on the radio. She earned the money from this enterprise and support to their family income. She was able to persuade nearly 30-35 women in the vicinity of nearby area to adopt Bakery enterprise as a support to their family income. Due to her less efforts she became successful and Bakery became the main profession of the women of most of the households. Mr. Mohan Singh Karki, Head of the Kumoun Vani said that we are trying our best to disseminate the information among the hill women. Presently 14 members team are working to design, develop and test the radio programme based on need assessment of the hill women. Our CR team is engaging in designing and developing the message regarding the various aspects as youth employment, human right, farming, entrepreneurship, health hazards etc. Our main aim is to empower the hill people on various areas. Thus many successful cases are created nearer area of Mukteswar after establishing the Kumaoun Vani community radio station.

Future Strategies for Community Radio Programme

On the basis of the past studies and experiences, it can be concluded that to produce any programme we have following strategies:

1. To establish a true community radio, it needs to bring community into the centre stage.
2. To produce any programme related to community radio, need assessment of the respondents is necessary.
3. The demand for community radio should be raised among the public a wide and stronger manner through networking and collaborating between NGOs and community radio lobbyists.

4. A community radio station would provide the permanent base for programme production with the involvement of local people.
5. To build up a viable community radio, due funding and a clear mandate from the communities are necessary to change their prevailing social, political and economic status.
6. Society is highly polarized, class and caste system and political rivalry exists across the rural area, where poor people can hardly raise their voice in front of local elites.
7. Give information which is both useful and usable.
8. Programme becomes more useful if it is based on edutertainment. (Education +entertainment).
9. Talk to audience as a friend in a conversational style.
10. Cultural compatibility is also a pre-requisite for effective communication.
11. Be brief. It is difficult to sustain the interest for more than 10-15 minut.

Challenges to Community Radio

Community Radio plays a central role in community development. To play this role they need to provide quality programmes to ensure continued audience, and support from the community. It has been a great success in developed nations but has lacked in developing countries because of illiteracy and lack of awareness among people. Community radio faces the challenges in effective and quality programme production in terms of content, production quality and community involvement:

1. A high turnover of staff that causes a lack of journalistic and technical skills and thus a consistent demand for training. Training on offer in most countries does not address the specific needs of Community Radio.
2. Community Radio derives its strength and popularity from community participation. In practise participation is harder than it seems, because it is labour intensive, requires the right attitude, skills and mobile equipment.

3. Without proper management skills, as well as some knowledge of financial management and income generation, it is very hard for Community Radio to survive without donor funding, which will always, eventually, dry up.
4. Community Radio is by definition relatively small and often situated in locations where basic services, like a constant supply of electricity, are lacking. Due to these conditions equipment suffers and needs to be vigorously maintained and/or regularly replaced.
5. In many countries there is still a lack of a clear regulatory framework in which Community Radio operates.

Among the various challenges faced by the community radio, the participation from the people is the major one and no community radio can survive without participation of people as it demands 70 per cent participation of the community people.

To ensure people participation essentially the leaders of the community: which include the elected and the religious authorities as well as the informal but also influential opinion leaders must be part of consultation process. But equally important is a consultation process that involves the community at large. Group discussions with various sectors in the community like farmers, fisherman, shop-owners, teachers, artisans, etc. are essential. It is also crucial to consult women and youth, who are traditionally marginalized in many rural societies. FGDs could be conducted to know about the prevailing situation and their opinion regarding it. Nor should any minority, cultural and linguistic group be left out. The points to be ascertained are to know about the listener's need, listener's preference and their listening habit. The staff should provide people with technical support and facilities to produce the programme. With the programmes of entertainment and local culture, they should also provide a platform to discuss relevant issues and village concerns in public, with local leaders called on to make respond and make their opinions and position clear. The programme recorded should be broadcasted next day if possible or as soon as possible this motivates the people to participate more and more. Also when the programmes are evaluated opinion of the community should be taken regarding their likings and disliking of the programmes and programme format, further their suggestions regarding programme implemented should be considered and implemented.

Conclusion

In summing up, community radio can play a very important role in development of country through empowerment of women in various ways. People listen community radio for information as well as entertainment. Community Radio is truly a people's Radio that perceives listeners not only as receivers and consumers, but also as active participants and creative producers of content. Community Radio covers all developmental and rights based issues and updates listeners on the latest developments in environmental, policy related and other issues. Community Radio has the responsibility to help sustain the diversity of the local cultures and languages and thus should be supported through legislative, administrative, and financial measures. Community radio is one cheapest medium which was listened by each and every people in the village even below poverty line. There were various aspects on which community radio had produced the programme. These programme had greater impact on the social aspects as well as health aspects. There is a need to produce various programme on the various aspect of social issues in which women are leg behind. Community radio is participatory medium through which information is communicated and creates a change in rural people as research studies confirms. It is popular because people seek out entertainment and pay attention to it. Anyhow, to be successful radio programme must be systematically designed, interactive, motivational and suitable to the needs, current knowledge and learning style to the listener. If the programmes have above characteristics, this will create a good impact on the development of women. Community radio is fastest growing media for change. The emergence of community radio goes back to 1947 with the first experience in Bolivia and Colombia known as Miner's Radio and Radio Sutatenza respectively. Although for India and other developing countries it's rather a new concept with its roots back in 1990's. It caters to the need and interest of certain area, broadcasting content that is popular to a local audience but which may often be overlooked by commercial or mass media broadcast. Community radio is also referred as rural radio, cooperative radio, participatory radio, free radio, alternative radio, popular radio, educational radio, community FM, association radio and bush radio in different parts of the world. The basic characteristic of Community Radio is that it is owned by the community, to serve the needs of the people. Most significantly, it is participatory in nature. People actively take part in formulating the station's policy, strategy and programme content. Community radio has been used in various fields for development in many countries of the world like health, nutrition, sanitation, women empowerment and also agriculture. Although there are few cases of using community radio for agriculture extension but by looking at the experience of community radio in different fields for development and learning from the challenges faced by them it can be applied in agriculture extension and help in betterment of agriculture and rural people.

Nutrition Policy and Strategy Status of Malnutrition in India

"Undernutrition is both a consequence of poverty as well as a cause of perpetuating poverty, eroding human capital through irreversible and intergenerational effects on cognitive and physical development."

Under-nutrition is a complex and multi-dimensional issue, affected mainly by a number of generic factors including poverty, inadequate food consumption due to access and availability issues, inequitable food distribution, improper maternal infant and child feeding and care practices, inequity and gender imbalances, poor sanitary and environmental conditions; and restricted access to quality health, education and social care services. A number of other factors including economic, environmental, geographical, agricultural, cultural, health and governance issues complement these general factors in causing under-nutrition of children. At different stages of child hood there are commonly identified factors those contribute to the under-nutrition. Hence intervention focused to those specific factors has to be designed to prevent and overcome under-nutrition.

The intergenerational cycle, manifests as low birth weight and is compounded further by gender discrimination and exclusion. Under-nutrition in adolescents, pregnant women, infants and young children leads to growth failure, increased rates of morbidity, increased risks to survival, impaired cognitive development, reduced learning capacity, poor school performance in children, sub-optimal productivity in adults, and reduced economic growth for nations. It is critical to detect and prevent under-nutrition, as early as possible, across the life cycle, to avert irreversible cumulative growth and development deficits that compromise maternal and child health and survival, achievement of optimal learning outcomes in primary education and gender equality. The national plan of action on nutrition will be centred around the following critical facts related to malnutrition:

1. Every fifth child in the world lives in India.
2. 22 per cent babies are born with low birth weight.
3. 42.5 per cent of children 0-5 years are underweight.
4. 53 out of 1000 live births do not complete their first year of life.
5. 79 per cent children (6-35 months) are anemic.
6. Declining female/male ratio in children Under-6 years – from 945 to 927/1000.
7. 35.6 per cent women with low BMI.

Nutrition Challenges: Some Facts

Some nutritional challenges are giving as following:

1. Maternal and Child Under-nutrition is the underlying cause of more than one third of the mortality of children under five years.
2. One fifth of maternal mortality can be averted by addressing maternal stunting and iron deficiency anemia.
3. One fifth of neonatal mortality can be prevented by ensuring the universal practice of early initiation of exclusive breastfeeding (around 22 per cent of neonatal mortality can be averted by this).
4. One fifth of child mortality (under 5 years) in India can be prevented by ensuring universal exclusive breastfeeding for the first six months and appropriate

complementary feeding practices after 6 months (along with continued breastfeeding till 2 years and beyond).

5. Over one fourth of all child deaths would be reduced in the short term, by available nutrition interventions, implemented at scale.

Impact of Malnutrition on Health and Survival

The impact of malnutrition on health and survival has emerged from many studies and reviews on programmes and policies. Predictive studies show that more than one third of deaths amongst children under five years have maternal and child undernutrition as an underlying factor. The Registrar General of India (RGI has been bringing out data on child mortality on an annual basis and causes of mortality on a 3 years average basis. The under 5 mortality as per NFHS-3 (2005-06) was 74 per thousand, which came down to 69 per thousand in 2008 as per the Sample Registration System Report of 2008. Therefore, there is a decline in under 5 mortality and the rate of annual decline varies between 1 to 1.5. The problem of malnutrition is multi-dimensional and inter-generational in nature and the nutritional status of the population is outcome of complex and inter-related set of factors which cannot be addressed by a single sector/intervention alone. Further, the problem of malnutrition being multifaceted in nature needs well coordinated efforts from different sectors such as agriculture including horticulture, food, health, rural development, biotechnology, water & sanitation, education, information and broadcasting, among others. Both, the National Nutrition Policy and National Plan of Action on Nutrition, have highlighted specific roles and responsibilities of different government Ministries/Departments of the Government of India and State Governments for addressing the challenge of undernutrition in the country. These need to be reiterated and updated. Further, the plan of actions requires to be implemented in conceptual settings in the states and districts.

The Policy Framework and Key Interventions

Priorities, process indicators and need for convergent action: The Eleventh Five Year Plan positions the development of children at its centre and recognizes nutrition as critical for ensuring child survival and development. It accords high priority to addressing maternal and child undernutrition through multi sectoral interventions by different sectors. The objectives of the Strategy to Address India's Nutrition Challenges, as defined in the Eleventh Plan Monitorable Targets, are as follows:

1. Reduce malnutrition among children (underweight prevalence) in the age group 0-3 years to half its present level, by the end of the Eleventh Plan.
2. Reduce anemia among women and girls by 50 per cent by the end of the Eleventh Plan. The process indicators for achieving the above objectives would be:

Table 17.1: Process Indicators for Achieving the Above Objectives

Sl. No.	Process Indicators	Current Status as per the Last Surveys
1.	Initiation of breastfeeding	40.2% (DLHS*-3, 2007-08) 24.5% (NFHS**-3, 2005-06)
2.	Exclusive breastfeeding of children under 6 months	46.4% (DLHS-3 2007-08 & NFHS** 3, 2005-06)
3.	Introduction of complementary feeding upon completion of 6 months, along with continued breastfeeding for 2 years	In the age group of 6-9 months 23.9% (DLHS-3 2007-08) 56.7% (NFHS-3 2005-06)
4.	Appropriate infant and young child feeding	20.7% (NFHS 3, 2005-06)

The nutritional status of the population is the outcome of complex and inter-related set of factors and cannot be improved by the efforts of single sector or action alone. The National Plan of Action on Nutrition 1995 lays down a systematic framework for collaboration among national government agencies, State Governments, NGOs, the private sector and the international community. It is a multi-sectoral framework for implementation of the national nutrition goals to be reached by 2000 AD. The multi-sectoral plan states the objectives and tasks of 14 different sectors namely, Agriculture, Food, Civil Supplies & Public Distribution, Education, Forestry, Maternal & Child Health, Food Processing Industries, Health, Information & Broadcasting, Labour, Rural Development, Urban Development, Welfare, Women & Child Development.

1. **National Nutrition Policy (NNP):** The National Nutrition Policy (NNP) 1993 identified key areas of action in various areas like agriculture, food production, food supply, education, information, health care, social justice, tribal welfare, urban development, rural development, labour, women and child development, people with special needs and monitoring and surveillance. The core strategy envisaged under NNP is to tackle the problem of nutrition through direct nutrition interventions for vulnerable groups as well as through various development policy instruments which will improve access and create conditions for improved nutrition. The National Plan of Action on Nutrition (NPAN) 1995 laid down the framework for systematic collaboration among national government ministries/departments, State Governments, NGOs, the private sector and the international community. Specific implementation arrangements suggested by NPAN includes National Nutrition Council headed by the Prime Minister, Special working groups in concerned Ministries/Departments, constituting similar bodies like Coordination Committees, Nutrition Council etc. at the state and district levels by the State Governments, among others. The interventions to address nutrition challenges in India mainly stem from the National Nutrition Policy and the National Plan of Action on Nutrition and policies of

related sectors such as health, food and agriculture. The Government of India has over the past few years, expanded the coverage under a number of programmes, which have the potential to improve the current nutrition security situation of the country. These programmes include the National Rural Health Mission (NRHM), Integrated Child Development Services (ICDS) Scheme, Mid Day Meal Scheme, National Food Security Mission, Horticulture Mission, Mahatma Gandhi National Rural Employment Guarantee Scheme (MGNREGS), Jawaharlal Nehru National Urban Renewal Mission and the National Rural Drinking Water Programme. Table 17.2 discusses the existing government schemes/ interventions listed by life cycle focus area.

Table 17.2: Existing Government Interventions (Listed by Life Cycle Focus Area)

Beneficiaries	Schemes
1	2
Pregnant and Lactating Mothers	ICDS, RCH- II, NRHM, JSY, Indira Gandhi Matritva Sahyog Yojana (IGMSY) – The CMB Scheme
Children 0-3 years	ICDS, RCH-II, NRHM, Rajiv Gandhi National Creche Scheme
Children 3-6 years	ICDS, RCH-II, NRHM, Rajiv Gandhi National Creche Scheme, Total Sanitation Campaign (TSC), National Rural Drinking Water Programme (NRDWP)
School going children 6-14 years	Mid Day Meals, Sarva Shiksha Abhiyan
Adolescent Girls 11-18 years	Rajiv Gandhi Scheme for the Empowerment of Adolescent Girls (RGSEAG), Kishori Shakti Yojana, Total Sanitation Campaign (TSC), National Rural Drinking Water Programme (NRDWP)

(Contd...)

1	2
Adults	MGNREGS, Skill Development Mission, Women Welfare and Support, Programme, Adult Literacy Programme, TPDS, AAY, Old and Infirm Persons Annapurna, Rashtriya Krishi Vikas Yojana, Food Security Mission, Safe Drinking Water and Sanitation Programmes, National Horticulture Mission, National Iodine Deficiency Disorders Contol Programme (NIDDCP), Nutrition Education and Extension, Bharat Nirman, Rashtriya Swasthya Bima Yojana
Pregnant and Lactating Mothers	ICDS, RCH- II, NRHM, JSY, Indira Gandhi Matritva Sahyog Yojana (IGMSY) – The CMB Scheme
Children 0-3 years	ICDS, RCH-II, NRHM, Rajiv Gandhi National Creche Scheme
Children 3-6 years	ICDS, RCH-II, NRHM, Rajiv Gandhi National Creche Scheme, Total Sanitation Campaign (TSC), National Rural Drinking Water Programme (NRDWP)
School going children 6-14 years	Mid Day Meals, Sarva Shiksha Abhiyan
Adolescent Girls 11-18 years	Rajiv Gandhi Scheme for the Empowerment of Adolescent Girls (RGSEAG), Kishori Shakti Yojana, Total Sanitation Campaign (TSC), National Rural Drinking Water Programme (NRDWP)
Adults	MGNREGS, Skill Development Mission, Women Welfare and Support, Programme, Adult Literacy Programme, TPDS, AAY, Old and Infirm Persons

(Contd...)

1	2
	Annapurna, Rashtriya Krishi Vikas Yojana, Food Security Mission, Safe Drinking Water and Sanitation Programmes, National Horticulture Mission, National Iodine Deficiency Disorders Contol Programme (NIDDCP), Nutrition Education and Extension, Bharat Nirman, Rashtriya Swasthya Bima Yojana
Pregnant and Lactating Mothers	ICDS, RCH- II, NRHM, JSY, Indira Gandhi Matritva Sahyog Yojana (IGMSY) – The CMB Scheme
Children 0-3 years	ICDS, RCH- II, NRHM, Rajiv Gandhi National Creche Scheme

Adapted from Overcoming the Curse of Malnutrition in India: A Leadership Agenda for Action, First Edition: September 2008, The Coalition for Sustainable Nutrition Security in India.

Schemes like, National Rural Health Mission (2005 – 06), National Horticulture Mission (2005-06), Mahatma Gandhi National Rural Employment Guarantee Scheme (2005-06), Janani Suraksha Yojana (2006-07), Total Sanitation Campaign, Mid Day Meal (2008-09), Integrated Child Development Services (ICDS) Scheme (2008-09) and National Rural Livelihood Mission (2010-11) have been expanded/ universalized in the recent past, and hence better results could be awaited in the years to come. All these schemes address one or the other aspect of nutrition. While the ICDS scheme continues to cater to the supplementary nutritional needs of children below six years and pregnant and lactating mothers, and the Mid- day Meal scheme takes care of the school going children (6-14 years), the recently introduced Rajiv Gandhi Scheme for Empowerment of Adolescent Girls (RGSEAG), namely, SABLA would provide a package of services including health and nutrition to adolescent girls in the age group of 11-14 years for out of school girls and 15-18 years for all girls for nutrition in 200 districts as a pilot. Additionally, a new scheme, the Indira Gandhi Matritva Sahyog Yojana (IGMSY) – The CMB Scheme would provide a better enabling environment for improved health and nutrition to pregnant and lactating mothers and support for providing early & exclusive breastfeeding for the first six months of life on pilot basis in 52 districts initially. In order to address the India's nutrition challenges every State Government and UT Administration has a crucial role to play. The National Nutrition Policy 1993 and the National Plan of Action on Nutrition 1995 specify clear institutional structure from national to grassroots level. Although some States/UTs have taken a few initiatives in this regard, the implementation of provisions and structures laid down in the National Policy and Plan of Action have largely not been put in place or made effective. Most of these programmes are being implemented by the State Governments/UT Administrations. It is important for the State Government and UT Administrations to understand the importance of these initiatives and take necessary actions for not only putting these mechanisms in place but also making them proactive. Every State Government and UT Administrations must make an effort to put in place a mechanism for inter-sectoral planning and coordination at State level. In particular, the following steps need to be urgently taken by every State Government and UT Administration for preparing themselves for meeting the nutritional challenges in their respective States & UTs:

1. Setting up an apex State level Nutrition Council to be chaired by the Chief Minister.
2. Setting up an Inter-Departmental Coordinating Committee headed by the Chief Secretary.
3. Setting up Special working groups in departments of Agriculture, Rural Development, Health, Education, Food and Women & Child Development.
4. Constituting District Co-ordination Committees and District Nutrition Councils at the district levels.
5. Developing State Plan of Action on Nutrition.

6. Developing District Plan of Action especially for high burden districts.
7. Developing district level diet and nutrition profiles with a view to enable area specific programme and nutrition education interventions.

2. **Rajiv Gandhi Scheme for Empowerment of Adolescent Girls (SABLA):** The Rajiv Gandhi Scheme for Empowerment of Adolescent Girls (SABLA) was launched in November 2010. The objectives of the Scheme are to address nutritional problems and improving the health status of adolescent girls in the age group of 11-18 years, equipping them with knowledge on family welfare, health and hygiene, providing information and guidance on existing public services and mainstream out of school girls into formal or non-formal education. The major activities that would take place in the next five years from 2011 till 2016 would mainly be implementation in 200 districts to begin with, followed by evaluation and further expansion across the country. The deliverables envisaged for the Scheme, in line with major activities to be performed between 2011 till 2016, are to ensure that nutrition and non-nutrition components of the Scheme are delivered to adolescent girls, utilisation of funds takes place as per norms and evaluation of pilot is conducted. The results of the evaluation would lead to expansion of the Scheme from 200 districts to the entire country during the XII Plan. The number of beneficiaries covered under nutrition and other components of the scheme and increased enrolment of out of school girls are some of the expected outputs from implementation of the scheme. The ultimate aim is to see empowered adolescent girls with enhanced self esteem, improved nutritional health and the capacity to make informed choices. All this will, in turn, help to provide a better equipped and confident women work force. The scheme would be evaluated in the 200 districts through concurrent evaluation, based on which expansion across the country would be planned.

The constraints that may impede implementation of the scheme are:

- *(a)* Implementation of the scheme and utilisation of funds by States/UTs may not be along expected lines.
- *(b)* Lack of competent functionaries.
- *(c)* Lack of effective convergence with other line departments at implementation levels.
- *(d)* Right resource persons may not be selected.

3. **Indira Gandhi Matritva Sahyog Yojana (IGMSY)** Indira Gandhi Matritva Sahyog Yojana (IGMSY) has been approved by the Government of India in October 2010. The objectives of the Scheme are to improve the health and nutrition status of pregnant, lactating women and infants by the promotion of appropriate practices, care and service utilisation during pregnancy, safe delivery and lactation; encouragement of women to follow (optimal) Infant and Young Child Feeding (IYCF) practices including early and exclusive breast feeding for the first six months; and by contributing to better enabling environment by providing cash incentives for improved health and nutrition to pregnant and lactating mothers. There would be a cash transfer of Rs. 4000/- in three instalments from the end of the 2nd trimester until the child turns 6 months old. The baseline survey would be completed within 2010-11 and the implementation of the Scheme would start. 2011-12 would be the first full year of implementation when the pilot would be tested in the 52 selected districts.
4. **National Commission for Protection of Child Rights (NCPCR):** The National Commission for Protection of Child Rights (NCPCR) was set up in March 2007 under the Commissions for Protection of Child Rights Act, 2005. The Commission's mandate is to ensure better protection of the rights of the child through the monitoring of constitutional and legal rights of children, review of

safeguards, review of existing laws, looking into violations of the constitutional and legal rights of children, and monitoring programmes relating to the survival, protection, participation and development of children. The Commission also has to ensure that all National laws, policies, programmes, and administrative mechanisms are informed by a "rights-based" emphasis and are in consonance with the child-rights perspective as enshrined in the Constitution of India and the UN Convention on the Rights of the Child. The functions of the Commission include:

(a) inquiring and investigating into complaints of violations and deprivations of child rights;

(b) inspecting any juvenile homes or any other place of residence or institution meant for children;

(c) examining and reviewing the safeguards provided under law for the protection of child rights;

(d) examining factors inhibiting the enjoyment of rights of children affected by terrorism, torture, disaster and domestic violence and recommend appropriate measures;

(e) looking into the matters relating to children in distress, marginalized and disadvantaged children without family and the children of prisoners;

(f) studying treaties and other international instruments relating to children, including the UNCRC;

(g) spreading child rights literacy and promote awareness of the safeguards available for the protection of these rights;

(h) undertaking periodic review of existing laws, policies, programmes and other activities on child rights and implementation of treaties and other international instruments in the best interest of children;

(*i*) promoting children's participation in matters affecting them; and

(*j*) compiling and analyzing data on children.

Since inception, the Commission has dealt with many complaints/representations of violation/deprivation of child rights. It has issued guidelines and made recommendations on corporal punishment. It has recommended the total abolition of child labour, urged expansion of prohibited category of child labour and proposed amendments to the Child Labour (Prohibition and Regulation) Act, 1986. It has also reviewed the functioning of Juvenile homes and made recommendations and guidelines for key reforms in the Juvenile Justice System in the country. The Commission has also been assigned a major role in monitoring "The child's right to education" under Section 31 of the "Right of Children to Free and Compulsory Education Act, 2009". In the next five years, the Ministry will advocate for the following in the context of NCPCR:

1. Provide the NCPCR with adequate resources and functionaries to act as a "watch dog" organisation working to protect the rights of children.
2. Support the NCPCR in promoting decentralized functioning mechanisms and facilitate better convergence and coordination between NCPCR and SCPCRs.
3. Seek and enlist NGO involvement to act as pressure groups for the setting up of SCPCRs in all states and continue advocacy.
4. Encourage the NCPCR to commission studies and take follow-up actions on the stakeholder (especially civil society) recommendations received during the consultative processes of the Five Year Strategic Plan.
5. **National Institute of Public Cooperation and Child Development (NIPCCD):** National Institute of Public Cooperation and Child Development (NIPCCD), is an autonomous organisation under the Ministry of Women and Child Development. The objectives of the Institute

are to develop and promote voluntary action, research, training and documentation in the overall domain of women and child development. NIPCCD takes a comprehensive view of child development and promotes programmes in pursuance of the National Policy for Children and evolves a framework and perspective for organizing children s programmes through governmental and voluntary efforts. In order to cater to the region specific requirements of the country, the institute over a period of time has established four regional centres at Guwahati (1978), Bengaluru (1980), Lucknow (1982) and Indore (2001). The institute promotes voluntary action in social development focusing on need based programmes for children. Thematic focus is given on child development and awareness generation on women s empowerment and gender issues, especially women s political, social and economic rights. The current thrust areas of the institute relating to child development are maternal and child health, nutrition, early childhood education, positive mental health in children and child care support services. The institute conducts research and evaluation studies; organises training programmes, seminars, workshops and conferences; and provides documentation and information services in priority areas in public cooperation and child development. The Institute functions as an apex body for training of functionaries of the Integrated Child Development Services (ICDS) Programme. The Institute as a nodal resource agency has also been entrusted with the responsibility of training and capacity building of functionaries at the national and regional level, under the Integrated Child Protection Scheme (ICPS).

Strategies and Implementation Plan: In order to address the nutrition challenge in India, there is a need for a comprehensive approach that addresses the different sectors and dimensions of the nutrition challenge. There are two complementary approaches to reducing undernutrition – direct nutrition-specific interventions and multi-sectoral approach. Multi-sectoral approach can help reduce undernutrition in following ways:

1. *Accelerating action on detriments of undernutrition* including inadequate income, agricultural production, gender equality & girls education, improved water supply, quality of governance & institution and issues related to peace & security.
2. *Integrating nutrition by including specific pro-nutrition actions in programmes* in other sectors for example incorporating nutrition intervention into agriculture, rural livelihoods programme and school & medical curriculums. Encourage more emphasis on nutrition objectives in related sectors and hold the sectors accountable for nutrition results by including an indicator of undernutrition to judge overall progress in these sectors.
3. *Increasing policy coherence through government – wide attention to unintended negative consequences of policies in other sectors that affect nutrition.* Better and timely analysis and inclusion of nutritional consequences in all government systems/mechanisms for policy coordination is required.

National Rural Health Mission *Towards Comprehensive Health Care*

The NRHM has focused heavily on child birth and pre-natal care. It must however expand to a more comprehensive vision of health care, which includes service delivery for a much broader range of conditions, covering both preventive and curative services. The Twelfth Plan will prioritise convergence among all the existing National Health Programmes under the NRHM umbrella, namely those for Mental Health, AIDS control, Deafness control, Care of the Elderly, Information, Education and Communication, Cancer Control, Tobacco Control, Cardio Vascular Diseases, Oral health, Fluorosis, Human Rabies control and Leptospirosis. Physical fitness is a prime and basic requirement for insuring good health and there is a growing recognition of the importance of sports for health, physical fitness and nutrition. Other innovative management reforms within health delivery systems will be encouraged with a view to improve efficiency, effectiveness and accountability. The Tamil Nadu intervention of creating a separate public health care and maternal death audit will be promoted. Programmes/schemes will be evaluated on the basis of outcomes rather than outlays. An accountability matrix will be devised in order to improve the seven health related goals articulated in the current Plan. The matrix will define the responsibilities of functionaries of the Health, Women and Child Development, and Water and Sanitation departments at the Block and habitation levels. Definite roles and accountabilities will also be assigned to Civil Society Organisations processes like real time data collection, community-based validation and medical audits to ensure quality, cost-effectiveness and promptness of healthcare will be introduced. While preventive health care is much cheaper than curative care, it has so far not received the attention it deserved. Existing frontline health educators and counsellors should play a lead role in compiling and disseminating preventive health practices in every nook and corner of the country. The State should play a lead role in building a culture of familiarity and knowledge around public health by involving Panchayati Raj Institutions (PRIs), Rogi Kalyan Samitis, Village Health, Sanitation and Nutrition Committees, Urban Local Bodies (ULBs) and the available cadre of frontline health workers, through innovative use of folk and electronic media, mobile telephony, multimedia tools and Community Service Centres. But most importantly, families and communities must be empowered to create an environment for healthy living.

Effectiveness of a Healthcare System

The effectiveness of a healthcare system is also affected by the ability of the community itself to participate in designing and implementing delivery of services. The opportunity to design and manage such delivery provides empowerment to the community as well as better access, accountability and transparency. In essence, the healthcare delivery must be made more consultative and inclusive. This can be achieved through a three dimensional approach of:

1. strengthening PRIs/ULBs through improved devolution and capacity building for better designing and management;

2. increasing users' participation through institutionalised audits of health care service delivery for better accountability; and
3. bi-annual evaluation of this process by empowered agencies of civil society organisations for greater transparency.

Methodologies based on community based monitoring, which have proved successful in some parts of the country, will need to be introduced in other parts.

Twelfth plan and NRHM

The Twelfth Plan must break the vicious cycle of multiple deprivations faced by girls and women because of gender discrimination and under-nutrition. This cycle is epitomised by continued deterioration in the sex ratio in the 0-6 year age group, revealed by the Census 2011; by high maternal and child mortality and morbidity, and by the fact that every third woman in India is undernourished (35.6 per cent have low Body Mass Index) and every second woman is anaemic (55.3 per cent). Ending gender based inequities, discrimination and violence faced by girls and women must be accorded the highest priority and these needs to be done in several ways such as achievement of optimal learning outcomes in primary education, interventions for reducing under-nutrition and anaemia, and promoting menstrual hygiene Health 89 in adolescent girls and providing maternity support. Also certain essential interventions outside the commonly understood 'area of health' need to be made, such as provision of sanitation facilities, including construction of toilets with water facility in schools, higher education opportunities and subsequent linkages to skill development. The effort to promote women's health cannot be without participation of men; hence, imaginative programmes to draw men into taking part in their health seeking behaviour and practices must be devised.

The Twelfth Plan must make children an urgent priority. This will involve convergence of Health and Child Care services. At present, Health and Child Care services to 83

Crore Rural Indians residing across 14 lakh habitations, 6.4 lakh villages and 2.3 lakh Gram Panchayats are provided, rather independently, through a network of around 11 lakh Anganwadi Centres (AWCs) of the Women and Child Development Department and 1.47 lakh Sub-Centres of the Health Department. Often, women attending AWCs with their children have to travel long distances to avail primary health care. While there is a case for expanding the network of AWCs to all habitations, even more urgent is the need to create a direct reporting relationship between AWCs and Sub-Centres so that interventions are better synergized, resources are optimized, while women and children attending AWCs continue to get health and nutritional services under one roof. Here, it is also important to mention that there are groups within the SC and ST populations, like Primitive Tribal Groups and De-notified and Nomadic Tribes, as also internally displaced people, who continue to be under covered. We must consciously include them while making provisions for sub-centres and anganwadis. The Twelfth Plan should aim at locating a Health Sub-centre in every Panchayat and an AWC in every habitation, their formal inter-linkage being a must for integrating the delivery of health, nutrition and pre-school education services. Through this approach, at least one ASHA would get positioned in each AWC; and at least one Auxiliary Nurse Midwife (ANM) / Health Worker (Female) would be available for a cluster of AWCs within every panchayat. Both could be brought under the oversight of the panchayat level health, nutrition and sanitation committee recently notified by the Ministry of Health and Family Welfare.

The health policy must focus on the special requirements of different groups, e.g., integrated geriatric health care and other needs specific to the elderly, 'adolescent friendly' health support services (and counselling) for victims of sexual or substance abuse, those infected with HIV/AIDS, those who are differently-abled, and those who belong to the lesbian, gay, bisexual, and transgendered (LGBT) community. Regional disparities must be addressed especially with respect to maternal health and child under nutrition in the 264 high focus districts of the NRHM. The high rate of growth of the population, particularly in certain States, must also be addressed. Mental health services, including psycho-social care and counselling, should be prioritized, in settings of transition due to migration, areas of conflict and disturbances, especially in the NER and J&K and in areas of natural disasters/ calamities. 9.15 Available estimates of HIV/AIDS show that there were about 23.95 lakh people living with HIV/AIDS (PLHAs) in 2008-09 in India. Of these 38.7 per cent are women and 4.4 per cent children. Women who are not able to exercise control over their sexuality form a considerable proportion of those affected by HIV/AIDS. A positive feature is that the prevalence of the infection has stabilised and has marginally declined in some places. In keeping with the general focus on women in the Twelfth Plan, and the promise of making service delivery more community-centric, the Plan shall encourage the use of frontline workers - AWWs, ASHAs, ANMs, and also women of the community, to provide comprehensive 90 Approach to the Twelfth Five Year Plan care for affected women, men and children. Special attention will be accorded to the needs of vulnerable groups like female sex workers, men having sex with men, and injection drug users. Infrastructure needs of high prevalence regions, especially the North East will be reviewed.

Other infectious diseases such as tuberculosis, malaria, also need focussed attention and a continued commitment to prevention and control. India also faces an escalating threat of non-communicable diseases like cardiovascular diseases, diabetes, cancers and chronic respiratory diseases which are major killers, especially in middle age. We have to respond through a package of policy interventions including tobacco control, early detection and effective control of high blood pressure and diabetes and screening for common and treatable cancers. These strategies should be integrated into the NRHM and the NUHM (National Urban Health Mission). The Twelfth

Plan should also encourage States to enact a Public Health Act (PHA), which enables proactive measures to avert threats to public health before an emergency occurs.

The Twelfth Plan hopes to address this issue by providing dedicated funding for family planning services in high fertility states, bundled with RCH services under NRHM. Convergence must also be established with programmes that address the underlying factors of high fertility like child mortality, women's empowerment, early age of marriage etc.

Health Infrastructure

One of the major reasons for the poor quality of health services is the lack of capital investment in health for prolonged period of time. The National Rural Health Mission had sought to strengthen the necessary infrastructure in terms of Sub-centres, Primary Health Centres and Community Health Centres. While some of the gaps have been filled, much remains to be done. According to the Rural Health Statistics (RHS), 2010, there is shortage of 19,590 Sub-centres; 4,252 PHCs and 2,115 CHCs in the country. 9.19 It is essential to complete the basic infrastructure needed for good health services delivery in rural areas by the end of the Twelfth Plan. This will require substantial Plan assistance to the states for upgrading existing PHCs and CHCs to IPHS norms, building Labour rooms and Operation Theatres, which are critical to reducing Maternal mortality and also building new PHCs. Government diagnostic services will have to be strengthened at the block and district levels. This would require not only infrastructural upgrades but also adequate human resource support and well developed service delivery protocols. States also lack infrastructure for ancillary services like drug storage and warehousing, medical waste management, surveillance and cold chain management. Such facilities will have to be ensured at the District level. District Hospitals need to be greatly strengthened in terms of both equipment and staffing for a wide range of secondary care services and also some tertiary level services. They should actually be viewed as District Knowledge Centres for training a broad array of health workers including nurses, mid-level health workers (e.g. Bachelor of Rural Health Care or Bachelor of Primary Health Practice), Paramedics and other public health and health management professionals. New medical and nursing colleges should preferably be linked to district hospitals in under-served States and districts, ensuring that districts with a population of 25 lakhs and above are prioritized for establishment of such colleges if they presently lack them. Each medical college, allopathic as well as AYUSH should be given responsibility of monitoring the status of health of the population in a defined surrounding geographical area, and work for the realisation of Plan targets in coordination with health care institutions and facilities in that area. States without any medical college can work with adjoining states for a similar arrangement. Such an arrangement will improve medical practice and link medical education to the unique needs of health care in each region.

The network of expanded Sub-centres, and fully functional PHCs and CHCs would be effective as a system only if prompt services for transportation of referred cases are available. The existing 1084 Mobile Medical Units (MMUs) will be expanded to have a presence in each CHC. MMUs may also be dedicated to certain areas which have a marked presence of moving populations. It will have to be ensured that each MMUs has requisite emergency equipment, drugs, basic diagnostics and a trained paramedic assigned to it. The possibility of transferring the Mobile Medical Units to the Fire-Brigade department, as is the practice in many developed nations, will be explored. While the National Rural Health Mission has taken up the task of providing health infrastructure in rural areas, there is no such public health care infrastructure at the urban level available to the common person. A major challenge in the Twelfth Plan is to ensure that all urban slums and settlements are covered with Sub-centres, and ICDS centres and PHCs, through NUHM. This infrastructure cannot be based on mechanical application of population based norms since many people in urban areas have access to private medical care. However, after taking these factors into account, there is need for further expansion, especially in areas where lower income people reside. The Twelfth Plan will innovate by creating local, low-cost treatment centres around relevant disease groups rather than generic ones, thus using resources more efficiently.

The Twelfth Plan must also aim at computerizing and interlinking all health facilities (Sub-centres, Primary Health Centres, Community Health Centres, District hospitals, Referral Hospitals and Medical Colleges) and use IT/Mobile technology for creating new interfaces. IT can be used to create and sustain robust surveillance systems to remedy the present absence of accurate information on disease burdens as well as the frailty of early alert system for outbreak of infectious diseases. The Integrated Disease Surveillance System (ISDP) has not fully delivered and surveillance of non-communicable diseases has just started. The district health system must be strengthened and links established with non-governmental health care providers to develop a reliable and accurate reporting network for infectious diseases and risk factors of non-communicable diseases. Without such information, policy and programme planning will be enfeebled and impact evaluation will be difficult to undertake. Thus, there is a need to build a vibrant Health Information System for monitoring and evaluation. Ensuring delivery of safe drugs is a major challenge. The Tamil Nadu Medical Services Corporation (TNMSC) provides a tested model for procurement and distribution to achieve economies of scale and use of monopsony power for procuring drugs at substantially marked down prices. The following may be done:

(a) Emphasis on local production of drugs, especially those that are relevant to the local disease burden. Public Sector Units (PSUs), which have manufacturing capabilities, can play an important role in ensuring reasonably priced supply of essential drugs and they should be strengthened for this process.

(*b*) Making the prescription of unbranded generic medicines mandatory by State government and Central government institutional doctors and mechanism to ensure its compliance by appropriate audit processes.

(*c*) Availability of drugs to be ensured through expansion of the existing Jan Aushadhi Stores in all district, Sub-division and Block hospitals.

In the Twelfth Plan, we must fund research into finding locally appropriate solutions to health issues. This would include studies to understand the uniqueness of disease epidemiology in the Indian population, development of effective and locally acceptable health practices, and scientifically validating best practices of Indian Systems of Medicine and Homoeopathy. Teaching in Medical Colleges should also be oriented to the unique needs of primary healthcare in the Indian population.

Human Resources for Health

Lack of human resources is as responsible for inadequate provision of health services as lack of physical infrastructure, especially in rural areas. According to Rural Health Statistics (RHS) 2010, there is shortage of 2,433 doctors at PHCs (10.27 per cent of the required number); 11,361 specialists at CHCs (62.6 per cent of the required number); and 13,683 nurses at PHCs and CHCs combined (i.e., 24.69 per cent of the required number). In addition 7,655 Pharmacists and 14,225 Laboratory Technicians are needed at PHCs &CHCs (27.13 per cent and 50.42 per cent of the required number) in the country. The status of Human Resources for Health (HRH) has improved during the Eleventh Five year Plan period, however much more needs to be done. The density of doctors in India is 0.6 per 1,000 and that of nurses and midwives is 1.30 per 1,000, representing jointly 1.9 health workers per 1,000. While no norms for Health Human Resource have been set for the country, if one takes a threshold of 2.5 health workers (including midwives, nurses, and doctors) per 1,000 population, there is an acute shortage of health workers.

Furthermore, because of a skewed distribution of all cadres of health workers, the vulnerable populations in rural, tribal and hilly areas continue to be extremely under-served.

The Twelfth Plan must therefore, ensure a sizeable expansion in teaching institutions for doctors, nurses and paramedics. Only 193 districts of a total of 640 districts have medical colleges – the remaining 447 districts do not have any medical colleges. Further, the existing teaching capacity for creating paramedical professionals is grossly inadequate. Against 335 medical colleges, there are 319 ANM training schools, 49 Health and Family Welfare Training Schools and only 34 LHV training schools. To fill the gap in training needs of paramedical professionals, the Twelfth Plan proposes to develop each of the District Hospitals into knowledge centres, and CHCs (4535) into training institutions.

The ongoing initiatives for integrating AYUSH and capacity development of other traditional health care providers such as Registered Medical Practitioners (RMPs) and Traditional Birth Attendants (TBAs) must be strengthened. Positive traditional care practices and local remedies should be encouraged. Efforts will be made to improve the working conditions and remuneration of frontline workers- both contractual and regular- and build positive environment which will reduce their sense of isolation.

The shortage of personnel to serve in rural and remote areas has led to a tendency to fill vacancies through Plan schemes which allow appointments being made on a contractual basis. Contractual appointments account for almost half of the doctors in the public sector (RHS, 2010). However, this practice also leads to high rates of attrition of staff. CAG has pointed out that more than half of the contractual staff does not complete their entire tenure. Thus while the ability to appoint doctors on contractual basis gives much needed flexibility; it is not a substitute for developing sustainable health care capacities at the State level through regular personnel. Even with the proposed levels of human resource training in district hospitals and CHCs, issues of regional equity, rural-urban distribution and quality would need special attention. In this regard, women from marginalized communities should be trained and hired to participate in the healthcare workforce. The strategy to enhance capabilities of these women in health, skill development, and access to sustainable employment will lead to their empowerment. Accordingly, scholarship and outreach schemes should be formulated to encourage them to train as nurses and paramedics.

Public health education must be developed as a multi-disciplinary, health system- connected, problem solving professional course and be open to both physicians and non-physicians. Expanding capacity of examination, certification and accreditation bodies is imperative. A start was made in the Eleventh Plan, but increased resources and a more evolved strategy is required to continue the work. The Twelfth Plan will establish a Human Resource Health Management system for improved recruitment, retention and performance; rationalise pay, allowances and incentive structures; and create career tracks for competence-based professional advancement.

The Twelfth Plan provides an opportunity of bringing together the world's largest health and child care systems through flexible frameworks that ensure a continuum of care with normative standards, while responding to local needs at village and habitation levels. Convergent action over the next Plan period will translate this vision into programmes that will touch the lives of all citizens, meet their expectations and also fulfilling their rights – particularly the rights of women and children in the communities, where they live and grow.

Recent Trend in Education and Twelfth Five-Year Plan

India which had a bottom-heavy population is now graduating to an economy with middle- heavy population. To reap the benefits of this demographic dividend to the full, India has to provide education to its population and that too quality education. The Twelfth Plan Approaches focuses on teacher training and evaluation and measures to enforce accountability. It also stresses the need to build capacity in secondary schools to absorb the passouts from expanded primary enrolments. The GER in higher education must be targeted to increase from nearly 18 per cent at present to say 25 per cent by 2016-17.

Elementary and Secondary Education

The government has initiated many schemes for elementary and secondary education. Some are as follows:

1. **Sarva Shiksha Abhiyan (SSA)/Right to Education (RTE):** Free education for all children between the ages of 6 and 14 years has been made a fundamental right under the RTE Act 2009. While the RTE Act was notified on 27 August 2009 for general information, the notification for enforcing the provisions of the Act with

effect from 1 April 2010 was issued on 16 February 2010. It mandates that every child has a right to elementary education of satisfactory and equitable quality in a formal school which satisfies certain essential norms and standards. The reform processes initiated in 2010-11 continued during the year 2011-12. Some recent developments in this regard include: *(a)* notification of Central RTE Rules on 8 April 2010, followed by notification of State RTE Rules by the states; *(b)* revision of the SSA norms to correspond with the provisions of the RTE Act including norms for sanctioning additional teacher posts, classrooms, teaching-learning equipment to enable states to move to an eight-year elementary education cycle, enhancement of academic support for better school supervision, and expansion of Kasturba Gandhi Balika Vidyalayas (KGBVs); *(c)* revision of the fundsharing pattern between the central and state governments for implementation of RTE-SSA programme from the earlier pattern in the sliding scale to a 65:35 ratio between the centre and states for a five-year period from 2010-11 to 2014-15; *(d)* notification of the National Council for Teacher Education (NCTE) as the academic authority for laying down teacher qualifications; *(e)* launching of a country-wide campaign for raising public awareness about the RTE and mobilizing communities to ensure that all schools become RTE compliant; *(f)* cumulatively 334,149 new primary and upper primary schools have been opened, 267,209 school buildings and 1,410,937 additional classrooms constructed, 212,233 drinking water facilities, and 477,263 toilets have been provided, supply of free textbooks to 8.77 crore children on annual basis, and in-service training to 19.23 lakh teachers (The number of out-of-school children has come down from 134.6 lakh in 2005 to 81.5 lakh in 2009 as per an independent study conducted by the SRI-IMRB). There are 3367 KGBVs in 26 States, providing residential schooling facilities at upper primary stage for girls belonging predominantly to SC, ST, OBC, and minority communities with 458 KGBVs in blocks with substantial Muslim population, 663 KGBVs in blocks with high ST population, and 1035 in SC-dominated blocks. A total of 2.83 lakh girls was enrolled in KGBVs, of whom 30.32 per cent were SCs, 25.43 per cent STs, 26.36 per cent OBCs, 9.51 per cent Muslims, and 10 per cent from the BPL category.

2. **National Programme for Education of Girls at Elementary Level (NPEGEL)**: This is a focused intervention for reaching out to the hardest to reach girls. It provides additional support for enhancing girls' education over and above the investments for girls' education under the SSA, including gender sensitization of teachers, development of gendersensitive material, and provision of need-based incentives. The scheme is implemented in educationally backward blocks (EBB) where rural female literacy is low. The NPEGEL is operational in all EBBs covering 40,623 clusters.

3. **National Programme of Mid Day Meals in schools:** Under the National Programme of Mid Day Meals in schools, cooked midday meals are provided to all children attending Classes I-VIII in government, local body, government-aided, and National Child Labour Project schools. EGCs/alternate and innovative education centres including madarsas/ maqtabs supported under the SSA across the country are also covered under this programme. At present the cooked midday meal provides an energy content of 450 calories and protein content of 12 grams at primary stage and an energy content of 700 calories and protein content of 20 grams at upper primary stage. Adequate quantity of micro-nutrients like iron, folic acid, and vitamin A are also recommended for convergence with the NRHM. During 2010-11, the budget allocation under this programme was ' 9440 crore against which the total expenditure incurred was ' 9128.44 crore.

About 10.46 crore children (7.33 crore in primary and 3.13 crore in upper primary stages) have been benefitted under the programme during 2010-11.

4. **Rashtriya Madhyamik Shiksha Abhiyan (RMSA):** The RMSA was launched in March 2009 with the objective of enhancing access to secondary education and improving its quality. In addition to ensuring access, the quality interventions include ensuring all secondary schools conform to prescribed norms, removing gender, socio-economic and disability barriers, providing universal access to secondary level education by 2017, i.e. by the end of the Twelfth Five Year Plan, and achieving universal retention by 2020. The central and state governments bear 75 per cent and 25 per cent of the project expenditure respectively during the Eleventh Five Year Plan. The funding pattern is in the ratio of 90:10 for the north-eastern states. The RMSA Annual Plan 2011-12 proposals received from all 35 states/UTs were considered by the Project Approval Board (PAB) of the scheme and major interventions such as opening of 4032 new schools, strengthening of 15,567 existing schools, 832 residential quarters for teachers, and 52,352 additional teachers have been approved. During 2011-12, the budget allocation for this programme is ' 2423.90 crore against which, 1996.40 crore (as on 15 February 2012) has been released to state governments.
5. **Model Schools Scheme:** A scheme for setting up 6000 model schools as benchmarks of excellence at block level with one school per block was launched in November 2008 with a view to providing quality education to talented rural children. The scheme has two modes of implementation: *(a)* 3500 schools are to be set up in as many Educationally Backward Blocks(EBBs) through state/UT governments; and *(b)* the remaining 2500 schools are to be set up under PPP mode in blocks that are not educationally backward. At present, only the first component is being implemented. The implementation

of the PPP component will start from Twelfth Five Year Plan. Since the inception of the scheme, approval has been granted for setting up 1942 model schools in 22 states. Financial sanctions have been accorded for setting up 1538 schools in 20 States and 1697.95 crore has been released as central share to these states. During 2010-11, 140 schools had become functional in Punjab (21 schools), Karnataka (74 schools), Chhattisgarh (15 schools), Tamil Nadu (18 schools), and Gujarat (12 schools) and ' 9.55 crore as recurring grants was released to these states. In 2011-12, the number of functional schools has increased to 438 in seven states.

6. **Inclusive Education for the Disabled at Secondary Stage (IEDSS):** The IEDSS scheme was launched in 2009-10 replacing the earlier Integrated Education for Disabled Children (IEDC) scheme. While inclusive education for disabled children at elementary level is being provided under the SSA, this scheme provides 100 per cent central assistance for inclusive education of disabled children studying in Classes IX-XII in mainstream government, local body, and government-aided schools. The aim of the scheme is to facilitate continuation of education of children with special needs up to higher secondary level. The scheme provides for personal requirements of the children in the form of assistive devices, helpers, transport, hostel, learning material, and scholarship for the girl child up to ' 3000 per disabled child per annum. In addition, assistance is also provided for salary of special teachers, capacity building of teachers, making schools barrier free, establishment of resource rooms, and awareness and orientation. A budget of ' 100 crore was allocated for this scheme during 2011-12 and over 1.30 lakh disabled children are proposed to be covered in this year.

7. **Vocational Education:** The revised centrally sponsored Vocationalisation of Secondary Education scheme aims to address the weaknesses of the earlier scheme to

strengthen vocational education in Classes XI-XII. The components approved for implementation in the remaining period of the Eleventh Plan, i.e. 2011-12, include: *(a)* strengthening of 1000 existing vocational schools and establishment of 100 new ones through state governments; *(b)* assistance to 500 vocational schools under the PPP mode; *(c)* in-service training of seven days for 2000 existing vocational teachers and induction training of 30 days for 1000 new ones; *(d)* development of 250 competency based modules for each individual vocational course; *(e)* establishment of a vocational education cell within the Central Board of Secondary Education (CBSE); *(f)* assistance to 150 reputed NGOs to run shortduration innovative vocational education programmes; and *(g)* pilot programme under the National Vocational Education Qualifications Framework(NVEQF) in Class IX in Haryana and West Bengal.

8. **Saakshar Bharat (SB)/Adult Education:** The National Literacy Mission, recast as Saakshar Bharat (SB) launched by the Prime Minister on 8 September 2009, reflects the enhanced focus on female literacy. The literacy rate according to the 2001 census was 64.83 per cent, improving to 74.04 per cent in 2011. The literacy rate improved sharply among females as compared to males. While the literacy rate for males rose by 6.9 per cent from 75.26 per cent to 82.14 per cent, it increased by 11.8 per cent for females from 53.67 per cent to 65.46 per cent. The target of the Eleventh Five Year Plan is to achieve 80 per cent literacy. With just one year to go for the Twelfth Five Year Plan, 74 per cent literacy has been achieved. Literacy levels remain uneven across states, districts, social groups, and minorities. The government has taken positive measures to reduce the disparities by focusing on backward areas and target groups. By March 2010, the programme had reached 167 districts in 19 states covering over 81,000 gram panchayats. During 2010-11, the programme was to cover 29,000 additional gram

panchayats in 102 districts. The programme had thus reached 24 states and one UT by the end of 2010- 11. By the end of March 2011, about 2 lakh literacy classes enrolling about 20 lakh learners were functioning in Andhra Pradesh (135,634), Karnataka (35,647), Chhattisgarh (13,048), Tamil Nadu (2875), Gujarat (3875), Rajasthan (2354), Uttarakhand (2176), Jharkhand (516), West Bengal (962), and Sikkim (450). The process of implementation of the programnme in the 102 districts sanctioned during 2010-11 has started and preparatory activities are being undertaken. By the end of September 2011, 372 out of 410 eligible districts had been covered under the programme comprising of 4441 blocks and 161,993 gram panchayats. Since the Mission has been envisaged as a people's programme, stakeholders, especially at grassroots level, have due say and role in its planning and implementation. The decentralized model of the Mission provides PRIs a pivotal role in implementation of the programme at district level.

Despite the efforts of the government in providing primary and elementary education, there is a lot more to be done. The Annual Status of Education Report (ASER) by Pratham, an NGO, in its seventh annual survey of rural children since 2005 conducted in 558 districts, 16,017 villages, 327,372 households, and 633,465 children highlights many positives as well as negatives. It particularly indicates that more needs to be done in terms of quality of education. Higher and Technical Education 13.32 Higher education is of vital importance for the country, as it is a powerful tool for building a knowledge-based twenty-first-century society. The Indian higher education system is one of the largest in the world. At the time of Independence, there were only 20 universities and 500 colleges with 0.1 million students; these have increased to 611 universities and university-level institutions and 31,324 colleges as on August 2011. To prepare for the challenges of the twenty-first century, the government has taken a number of initiatives during the Eleventh Plan period focusing on improvement of access along with equity and excellence, adoption of state-specific strategies, enhancement of the relevance of higher education through curriculum reforms, vocationalization, networking, and use of information technology and distance education along with reforms in governance in higher education. A large-scale expansion in university education has been initiated during the Eleventh Five Year Plan by setting up new educational institutions comprising 30 central universities, 8 new Indian Institutes of Technology (IITs), 8 new Indian Institutes of Management (IIMs), 10 new National Institutes of Technology (NITs), 20 new Indian Institutes of information Technology (IIITs), 3 new Indian Institutes of Science education and Research (IISERs), 2 new Schools of Planning and Architecture (SPAs), 374 model colleges, and 1000 polytechnics. Other important initiatives include upgradation of state engineering institutions, expansion of research fellowships and provision of hostels for girls, reservation for SCs, STs and OBCs, focus on backward, hilly and remote locations including the north-east, facilitating greater participation of students belonging to minorities, girls, and persons with disabilities, scholarships, provision of education loans with interest free subsidies, setting up of polytechnics in unserved areas, and degree colleges in low GER districts. The National Mission in Education through ICT, which aims at providing high speed broadband connectivity to universities and colleges and development of e-content in various disciplines, is under implementation. Open and distance learning is encouraged for increasing access to and making quality education available at any time, any place. Internationalization and collaborative arrangements and setting up of UNESCO Category I institute are other initiatives for extending the global reach of education. A new Scheme of Interest Subsidy on Educational Loans to EWS students has been introduced from 2009-10. Under the scheme, full interest subsidy during the period of moratorium on loans taken by EWS students from scheduled banks under the Educational Loan Scheme of the Indian Banks' Association for pursuing technical and professional courses from recognized institutions in India, is paid by the central government. Education being an important component of economic development and a driving force for economic growth, governments in India and across the world are subsidizing higher education. However, over the years, the diverging trajectories of costs and revenues due to rapidly increasing perstudent costs and increasing tertiary level participation has created immense pressures on the exchequer. Moreover, subsidies are inequitable in the sense that irrespective of one's parents' wealth, all individuals in a state subsidized institution get the same level of subsidy. Therefore, there are views that argue for reducing government support for higher education and replacing it with better commercial student loan schemes.

Some of the major initiatives taken during 2011-12 for promoting higher and technical education are the following:

1. *National Mission in Education through ICT:* Content generation and connectivity along with provision for access devices for institutions and learners are the major components of the Mission. So far nearly 400 universities have been provided 1 Gbps connectivity or have been configured under the scheme and more than 14,000 colleges have also been provided VPN connectivity. A number of projects have been sanctioned for innovative use of ICT. Creation of e-content for 996 courses in Phase II in engineering, sciences, technology, humanities, and management has been undertaken by IIT Madras. The Consortium for Educational Communication (CEC) has been tasked with creation of e-content for 87 undergraduate subjects. For creation of e-content for 77 postgraduate subjects, a proposal by the University Grants Commission (UGC) has been approved. More than 2000 e-journals and 55,000e-books from 297 publishers have been made available online under this programme. A major development during the year has been the launch of Aakash, the low cost access-cum-computing device that was launched on 5 October 2011. IIT Rajasthan has been granted ' 47.72 crore for acquisition

and testing of Aakash devices under the National Mission on Education through Information and Communication Technology scheme.

2. To address the increasing skill challenges of the Indian IT industry, the government has approved setting up of twenty new IIITs on a PPP basis. The partners in setting up the IIITs would be the Human Resource Development (HRD) Ministry, respective states where each IIIT will be established, and industry. Completion of the project is targeted in nine years from 2011-12 to 2019-20. In this regard, the government has invited proposals from the states for setting up of 20 IIITs.
3. An Expert Group was set up by the Prime Minister for enhancing employment opportunities in Jammu & Kashmir and for formulating a job plan involving the public and private sectors. One key recommendation of the Expert Group was to offer 5000 scholarships per annum over the next five years, for encouraging the youth of Jammu & Kashmir to pursue higher studies outside the State of Jammu & Kashmir. The scheme provides tuition fees, hostel fees, cost of books, and other incidental charges to students belonging to Jammu & Kashmir who, after passing Class XII or equivalent examination, secure admission in government colleges/ institutions and other select institutions outside the State of Jammu & Kashmir. This scheme is being implemented since 2011-12.
4. Some institutions like the IITs have, in order to promote innovation, created technology business incubation facilities in their campuses. These are proving to be focal points amongst students and faculty for working towards taking some of their applied research to the market through the creation of business models for the same. These efforts need to be expanded greatly: *(a)* by scaling up the previously successful centres of such innovations; and *(b)* by creating many such centres across the higher technical institutions in the country.

MAIN FINDINGS OF ASER 2011

Some Positives or status quo maintained

Enrollment: In 2011, 96.7 per cent of all 6-14 year olds in rural India are enrolled in schools. This number has held steady since 2010. States that had a high proportion (over 10 per cent) of 11-14 year old girls out of school in 2006 have made significant progress. For example Bihar out of school numbers have dropped from 17.6 per cent in 2006 to 4.3 per cent in 2011. Rajasthan shows a decline from 18.9 per cent in 2006 to 8.9 per cent in 2011. Uttar Pradesh has shown the least progress with 11.1 per cent in 2006 and 9.7 per cent in 2011. Substantial numbers of five year old children are enrolled in schools. The All India figure stands at 57.8 per cent for 2011. This proportion varies across states, ranging from 87.1 per cent in Nagaland to 18.8 per cent in Karnataka.

Private school enrollment is rising in most states: Nationally, private school enrollment has risen year after year for the 6-14 age group, increasing from 18.7 per cent in 2006 to 25.6 per cent in 2011. These increases are visible in all states except Bihar. In states like Uttarakhand, Rajasthan, Uttar Pradesh, Maharashtra, Andhra Pradesh, Kerala, Manipur and Meghalaya there has been an increase of over 10 percentage points in private school enrollment in the last five years. According to ASER 2011 data, between 30 to 50 per cent of children in rural areas of Haryana, Uttar Pradesh, Nagaland, Meghalaya, Punjab, Jammu & Kashmir, Rajasthan, Uttarakhand, Maharashtra and Andhra Pradesh are enrolled in private schools.

Better provision of girls' toilets: The proportion of schools where there was no separate girls' toilet has declined from 31.2 per cent in 2010 to 22.6 per cent in 2011. Also, there has been a substantial improvement in the proportion of schools that have separate girls' toilets that are useable. This figure has risen nationally from 32.9 per cent in 2010 to 43.8 per cent in 2011.

More libraries in schools, and more children using them: The proportion of schools without libraries has declined from 37.5 per cent in 2010 to 28.6 per cent in 2011. Children were seen using the library in more schools as well - up from 37.9 per cent in 2010 to 42.3 per cent in 2011.

Schools get their grants, but not on time: Between FY 2008-9 and FY 2010-11 the flow of SSA grants to schools improved significantly. However, this improvement occurred largely between FY 2008-9 and 2009-10. In fact a marginal decrease in the proportion of schools receiving grants is observed between FY 2009-10 and 2010-11. The data suggest that schools tend to get their grants during the second half of the fiscal year.

Not much change in compliance on Pupil-teacher ratio and Classroom-teacher ratio: At the All India level, there has been a marginal improvement in the proportion of schools complying with RTE norms on pupil-teacher ratio, from 38.9 per cent in 2010 to 40.7 per cent in 2011. In 2011, Kerala stands out with 94.1 per cent of schools in compliance, and in Jammu & Kashmir, Nagaland and Manipur, more than 80 per cent schools are in compliance with these norms. At the All India level, there has been a marginal decline in the proportion of schools with at least one classroom per teacher, from 76.2 per cent in 2010 to 74.3 per cent in 2011. In Mizoram, 94.8 per cent of schools comply with the teacher-classroom norms and in Punjab, Uttarakhand, Rajasthan, Uttar Pradesh, Gujarat and Maharashtra more than 80 per cent of schools are in compliance.

No major changes in buildings, playgrounds, boundary walls or drinking water: All India figures for 2011 show no significant improvement in the proportion of schools with an office cum store. This figure remains at 74 per cent. Similarly, for the country as a whole, about 62 per cent of visited schools had a playground, both in

2010 and in 2011. However, there has been an increase in the proportion of all schools that have a boundary wall, from 50.9 per cent in 2010 to 54.1 per cent in 2011. Nationally, the proportion of schools with no provision for drinking water remained almost the same at 17 per cent in 2010 and 16.6 per cent in 2011. The proportion of schools with a useable drinking water facility has remained steady at about 73 per cent. Kerala has the best record with 93.8 per cent schools that have a useable drinking water facility.

Some Negatives

Basic reading levels showing decline in many states: Nationally, reading levels are estimated to have declined in many states across North India. The All India figure for the proportion of children in Std V able to read a Std 2 level text has dropped from 53.7 per cent in 2010 to 48.2 per cent in 2011. Such declines are not visible in the southern states. In a few states there is good news. In Gujarat, Punjab and Tamil Nadu the numbers for 2011 are better than for 2010. Several states in the north-eastern region of India also show positive change. Karnataka and Andhra Pradesh numbers remain unchanged from last year.

Arithmetic levels also show a decline across most states: Basic arithmetic levels estimated in ASER 2011 show a decline. For example, nationally, the proportion of Std III children able to solve a 2 digit subtraction problem with borrowing has dropped from 36.3 per cent in 2010 to 29.9 per cent in 2011. Among Std V children, the ability to do similar subtraction problems has dropped from 70.9 per cent in 2010 to 61.0 per cent in 2011. This decline is visible in almost every state; only Andhra Pradesh, Karnataka and Tamil Nadu show improvements from 2010 to 2011. Several states in the north-eastern region of India also show positive change. There is no change in arithmetic levels in Gujarat.

Children's attendance has declined: At all India level, children's attendance shows a decline from 73.4 per cent in 2007 to 70.9 per cent in 2011 in rural primary schools. In some states, children's attendance shows a sharp decline over time: for example in primary schools of Bihar, average attendance of children was 59 per cent in 2007 and 50 per cent in 2011. In Madhya Pradesh it has fallen from 67 per cent in 2007 to 54.5 per cent in 2011 and in Uttar Pradesh from 64.4 per cent (2007) to 57.3 per cent (2011).

More than half of all Std. 2 and Std. 4 classes sit together with another class: Nationally, for rural government primary schools, over half of all classes visited are multigrade. For example, at the all India level Std 2 children were sitting with one or more other classes in 58.3 per cent of Std. 2 classes in primary schools. This figure was 53 per cent for Std. 4.

Thus, twelfth five year plan includes budget for various educational schemes. These schemes would be effective for various children including disable, gifted children.

Index

O

P

R

Z